MAJORITY WORLD THEOLOGY SERIES

SERIES EDITORS

Gene L. Green, Stephen T. Pardue, and K. K. Yeo

The Majority World Theology series exists because of the seismic shifts in the makeup of world Christianity. At this moment in history, more Christians live in the Majority World than in Europe and North America. However, most theological literature does not reflect the rising tide of Christian reflection coming from these regions. The Majority World authors in this series seek to produce, collaboratively, biblical and theological textbooks that are about, from, and to the Majority World. By assembling scholars from around the globe who share a concern to do theology in light of Christian Scripture and in dialogue with Christian tradition coming from the Western church, this series offers readers the chance to listen in on insightful, productive, and unprecedented in-person conversations. Each volume pursues a specific theological topic and is designed to be accessible to students and scholars alike.

So Great a Salvation

Soteriology in the Majority World

Edited by

Gene L. Green, Stephen T. Pardue, and K. K. Yeo

WILLIAM B. EERDMANS PUBLISHING COMPANY
GRAND RAPIDS, MICHIGAN

Wm. B. Eerdmans Publishing Co.
2140 Oak Industrial Drive N.E., Grand Rapids, Michigan 49505
www.eerdmans.com

26 25 24 23 22 21 20 19 18 17   1 2 3 4 5 6 7 8 9 10

ISBN 978-0-8028-7274-6

Library of Congress Cataloging-in-Publication Data

Names: Green, Gene L., editor. | Pardue, Stephen T., editor. | Yeo, Khiok-Khng, editor.
Title: So great a salvation : soteriology in the majority world / edited by Gene L. Green,
    Stephen T. Pardue, and K. K. Yeo.
Description: Grand Rapids, Michigan : William B. Eerdmans Publishing Company,
    [2017] | Includes bibliographical references and index.
Identifiers: LCCN 2017005466 | ISBN 9780802872746 (pbk. : alk. paper)
Subjects: LCSH: Salvation—Christianity. | Theology—21st century.
Classification: LCC BT751.3 .S67 2017 | DDC 234.09—dc23
    LC record available at https://lccn.loc.gov/2017005466

Contents

Contents

So Great a Salvation: Soteriology in the Majority World

K. K. Yeo

As a young Chinese born and raised in Malaysia, I encountered the living Christ through reading the Bible for salvation in the middle of the flux and vicissitudes of life. In the nihilistic and secular worldview of my youth, I yearned for meaning in life amid despair and dissonance. I hoped for racial reconciliation and peaceful coexistence among all people in a multi-religious and racial country. I lamented that my relatives went through the Cultural Revolution (1966–76) and prayed often for the national salvation of China.[1] Although I knew the *need* of salvation for all, I was not clear about the meaning of "salvation" and how the biblical God had anything to do with actualizing salvation in our world. I was puzzled by sermons I heard that declared salvation was mainly about "saving one's soul from the eternal torment of hell."

The Traditional Landscape and Biblical Repertoire

Traditional Theories of Salvation

What is salvation? Is salvation the same as redemption, liberation, enlightenment, awakening, forgiveness, attaining nirvana, or going to heaven? Theories of salvation abound in world religions and Christian theologies.

---

1. See K. K. Yeo, "Hope for the Persecuted, Cooperation with the State, and Meaning for the Dissatisfied: Three Readings of *Revelation* from a Chinese Context," in *From Every People and Nation: The Book of Revelation in Intercultural Perspective*, ed. David Rhoads (Minneapolis: Fortress, 2005), 200–221.

Traditionally, and primarily in the North Atlantic West, soteriology (the doctrine of salvation) is construed as:

1. mystical theory, the orthodox understanding of salvation as divinization of the human being via communicability of the divine-human nature and, later in Christian history, Friedrich Schleiermacher's understanding of God-consciousness
2. ransom theory (Athanasius, Origen, Irenaeus, Martin Luther, and Karl Barth), which views salvation based on the vicarious atonement of Jesus (Isa. 53:10, "an offering for sin"; Rom. 3:22–25; Heb. 10:12, 14; Mark 10:45) and thus understands Jesus as the Victor (Johann Christoph Blumhardt; as in Gustaf Aulén's *Christus Victor*) over enemies such as chaos, darkness, the devil, or sin and death
3. satisfaction theory, or the juridical view (Cyprian, Gregory the Great, Ambrose, Augustine; then Anselm of Canterbury, *Cur Deus Homo?* [*Why the God Man?*]), which argues that the salvation of humanity can be attained only by Jesus Christ the God-human, who alone can make satisfactory reparation for the wounded honor of God (against the previous view that the debt is paid to the devil)
4. penal substitutionary theory of the Reformers (John Calvin, J. I. Packer, Donald G. Bloesch),[2] which interprets salvation as Christ's bearing human sins in their place, thus taking the punishment on the behalf of sinners because sinners violated the demands of God's law, which requires God's holiness and justice from humanity (against the view of satisfying God's honor)
5. moral example theory (Peter Abelard, Friedrich Schleiermacher, Horace Bushnell), which holds that salvation is the work of Jesus Christ, whose death on the cross sets an example for people to imitate Christ morally, so that they will become fully human
6. participatory soteriology (James F. McGrath, Mark M. Mattison, Marcus J. Borg, and John Dominic Crossan), which sees the ones "in Christ" as those who participate in Christ's atonement work as they follow the path of dying and rising so that they themselves may be internally transformed.[3]

---

2. Donald G. Bloesch, *Essentials of Evangelical Theology: Life, Ministry, and Hope*, vol. 1, *God, Authority, and Salvation* (San Francisco: Harper & Row, 1978), 148–222.

3. Marcus J. Borg and John Dominic Crossan, *The First Paul: Reclaiming the Radical Visionary behind the Church's Conservative Icon* (New York: HarperCollins, 2009), 137. See

Daniel Treier, in his lead chapter in this volume, has given us a more detailed exposition of the Western understandings of salvation, from the Orthodox, Catholic, Lutheran, Calvinist, Anabaptist, Arminian, Wesleyan, to the Pentecostal. I agree with Treier, who observes that the chief lacunae in traditional dogmatic soteriology are the sociopolitical and cosmic dimensions of salvation. However, I attribute the cause of such lacunae to the Western tendency to read Scripture and construct theology without paying much attention to Scripture's contexts and that of the readers. Thus, by reading abstractly and turning inward on themselves, Western soteriologies, according to Treier, focus too exclusively on the personal blessings of participation in the new covenant.

The Biblical Semantic of "God Saves" ("Jesus" in Hebrew)

The Bible offers us a rich semantic and expansive repertoire about salvation, all pointing to God as the Creator (Isa. 40:12–31) and Savior (Isa. 43:14–44:6). Genesis 1 affirms that God created by means of redeeming, so that God made or created (*bārā'*, appearing forty-seven times in the Old Testament to describe God's action) as God called or named (speech-act) creation into being by delivering or redeeming them from the primordial chaos.[4] The Old Testament calls God the Savior (Isa. 45:15, 21) who brings salvation (Isa. 49:6) and who raises up saviors to deliver Israel (Judg. 3:9, 15; 6:36).

Consistent with the Colossians passage that names Jesus as the divine agent of creating and redeeming all things (1:15–20), the Nicene-Constantinopolitan Creed (AD 381) refers to the Son's creating ("through whom all things were made") and saving (what Jesus did "for us and for our salvation") functions. The verb "save" (*sōzō*) in the Septuagint and New Testament (John 3:17) and the noun "salvation (*sōtēria*) describe the Lord or God in terms of "my Savior" (Luke 1:47) or the one who gives "salvation from our enemies" (Luke 1:71). The word "Lord" in some biblical texts can refer to either God or Jesus, such as Jude 5,

---

also Jarvis Williams, "Violent Atonement in Romans: The Foundation of Paul's Soteriology," *Journal of the Evangelical Theological Society* 53 (2010): 579–99.

4. Gerald O'Collins, *Jesus Our Redeemer: A Christian Approach to Salvation* (Oxford: Oxford University Press, 2007), 23.

which speaks of "Jesus [a textual variant: the Lord] who once for all saved a people out of the land of Egypt."[5] The Lord's Prayer uses a synonym, *ruomai* (deliver, rescue), of *sōzō*: "deliver us from the evil one" (Matt. 6:13). In Matthew 27:42–43, the two words are used in the same sentence, serving as a pleonasm to emphasize the meaning of salvation: "He saved [*sōsai*] others; he cannot save himself. . . . He trusted in God; let God now deliver [*rysasthō*] him." Likewise, in Romans 11:26 the use of a synonym is not redundant but highlights the thought: "All Israel will be saved [*sōthēsetai*], as is written, 'out of Zion will come the Deliverer [*ryomenos*].'" Pointing beyond personal salvation, the sociopolitical contexts of these texts are prominent, as is the wide array of cognate words below. Treier's chapter seeks to critique the overly personal emphasis of salvation in Western Christianity, and using biblical theology he works hard to retrieve robustly the new creation aspects of salvation, such as its sociopolitical and cosmic dimensions.

"Liberation" (*eleutheria*) is a cognate of "salvation." Liberation *from what* is often the debate. Three New Testament verses seem to indicate liberation is on the personal, sociopolitical, and even cosmic levels: "If the Son has liberated you, you will be liberated indeed" (John 8:36); "the law of the Spirit of life in Christ Jesus has set you free from the law of sin and death" (Rom. 8:2); "creation itself will be liberated from the bondage of decay and will enter upon the glorious liberty of the children of God" (Rom. 8:21). Both Latin American scholars in this volume, Jules Martínez-Olivieri and Milton Acosta, as well as First Nations Canadian scholar Ray Aldred, work with this aspect of salvation in their chapters. But their perspectives on the "materiality of salvation" have particular nuances because their contexts are not the same.

A similar question could be asked about the next cognate, "redemption" (*apolytrōsis*; Rom. 3:24): redemption *from what*? Romans 3:24 is silent, but it does mention redemption as God's gift. Other scriptural verses mention redemption from the wrath of God (Rom. 5:9); the power of sin (Eph. 1:7, 14; Romans 5) and the power of death (Rom. 6:23); the curse of the law (Gal. 3:13); and the devil (Heb. 2:14; 1 John

5. The Nestle-Aland Greek New Testament 27th edition renders Jude 5 as "the Lord once for all saved a people out of the land of Egypt," but the 28th edition renders it as "Jesus once for all saved." See Institute for New Testament Textual Research, *Novum Testamentum Graece: Nestle-Aland* (Peabody, MA: Hendrickson, 2013 [28th ed.]; Stuttgart: Deutsche Bibelgesellschaft, 2004 [27th ed.]).

3:8). It is interesting that in the Old Testament God is called the *gō'ēl* (Redeemer; Ps. 19:14), but never in the New Testament is God or Jesus called Redeemer (*lytrōtēs*). The redemption metaphor comes from the context of the slave market (such as Exod. 21:8, Egyptian slavery; Isa. 51:11; 59:20, Babylonian captivity; Rom. 6:13–14, first-century Roman society). But the point is always about the new status of freedom. Thus the Bible speaks of the redeemed people as God's own possession (Exod. 15:16; 1 Peter 2:9), ransomed with a price (Isa. 35:10; 51:11; 62:12; 1 Cor. 6:20; 7:23; 1 Tim. 2:6). Elaine Goh's chapter seems to use this category well as she examines how Ecclesiastes can be used to speak to the redemption needed for Chinese who possess the mentality of fearing death, overconfidence, and workaholic tendencies.

Another favorite biblical word for salvation is "reconciliation" (*katallagē*; Rom. 5:10–11; 2 Cor. 5:18–20), translated by William Tyndale as "atonement" and thus focusing on overcoming the enmity between God and humanity (at-one-ment) rather than the broken relationships among people. Paul here is probably not using the Old Testament or Hebraic idea of atonement sacrifice (Leviticus 16), but the Greco-Roman background of transforming hostility into friendship or love. Such a relational and interpersonal connotation appeals to Majority World Christians, such as Sung Wook Chung, who examines the painful tension between North Korea and South Korea.

The last two terms are controversial, depending on the interpretive frame one uses to understand the concepts. "Being set right" (*dikaioumenoi*; Rom. 3:24) is often used to mean "vindicating" in the context of justice where God stands with the weak or the oppressed, thus justifying them (Ps. 82:1–3). But the second meaning is also used in the Bible: reversing the lowly from shame to honor (Ps. 31:1–2);[6] thus the shameful cross in the New Testament *sets right* the distorted value system of glory (aesthetic) and obscenity (shame). Unfortunately, the second meaning has often been ignored, especially in legal Western societies, and is picked up by Elaine Goh, Ray Aldred, and Emily Choge Kerama in the Asian, Native North American, and African chapters, respectively, in this volume.

The most controversial cognate word for salvation is *hilastērion*, translated as either "propitiation" or "expiation." "Propitiation" refers

6. Robert Jewett, *Romans: A Commentary*, Hermeneia (Minneapolis: Fortress, 2006), 281.

to the salvific work of Christ in placating divine justice or appeasing the wrath of God (Rom. 3:25; Heb. 9:5; cf. *hilasmos*, 1 John 2:2; 4:10).[7] My preferred translation, "expiation," traces its theological roots to the Hebrew word *kappōret*, that is, "mercy seat" on the ark of covenant in the Holy of Holies,[8] thus indicating that "God loved us and sent his Son to be the expiation [*hilasmos*] of our sins" (1 John 4:10). Jesus Christ is "the expiation [*hilasmos*] not only for our sins but also for the sins of the whole world" (1 John 2:2). Gerald O'Collins writes of *hilastērion* in this regard as "wiping away":

> The LXX never introduces this verb or related words (e.g. *exilaskomai*) to speak of sinners appeasing or rendering favorable an offended God [propitiation]. It is rather God who expiates, purifies, and deals with sin (e.g., Ezek. 16:13). Likewise in the NT it is God who is the agent or subject of expiator activity, lovingly providing the *"hilastē-rion,"* his only Son, who is the means and the place for wiping away the stain of sin.[9]

Soteriology is not simply about atoning sacrifice but also about offering love. Salvation is not simply "saved from," but also "saved to"; not simply delivery from sin and death, but also restoration to fullness of life; not simply suffering servant but also reigning king; not simply death and crucifixion, but also resurrection and consummation; not simply forgiveness, but also regeneration; not simply wrong and sin overcome, but also love and life abundant.[10] In short, salvation in the biblical understanding means God's creative deliverance of people in their situation of need from that which threatens wholeness of life, impedes the order of creation, and disrupts God's redemption in the world.

God so loves the Majority World. God's expansive love is expressed

---

7. C. E. B. Cranfield, *A Critical and Exegetical Commentary on the Epistle to the Romans*, vol. 1 (Edinburgh: T&T Clark, 1975), 217.

8. J. D. G. Dunn, *The Theology of Paul the Apostle* (Grand Rapids: Eerdmans, 1998), 213; J. A. Fitzmyer, *Paul and His Theology: A Brief Sketch* (Englewood Cliffs, NJ: Prentice Hall, 1989), 64.

9. O'Collins, *Jesus Our Redeemer*, 17.

10. See K. K. Yeo, *The Spirit Intercedes: New Testament in Prayers and Images*, trans. (into Chinese) Joseph Wang and May Lin, ill. Claire S. Matheny (Taipei: Campus Evangelical Fellowship, 2011), 236–51.

indigenously in global contexts through the back-roads and alleys of African villages, the new trails of Latin American valleys, and the highways of Asian cities. From the perspective of "saved from" to "saved to," here the language of the contributors to this volume varies, reflecting the myriad soteriological expressions in the New Testament: from sin to God (Acts 3:19), from death to life (1 John 3:14), from bondage to freedom (Philemon), from brokenness to wholeness (2 Cor. 12:9), from enmity to reconciliation (Eph. 2:16), from evil to goodness (Rom. 12:21), from despair to hope (1 Thessalonians). Just as these metaphors are multiple throughout Scripture, then, so also are the interpretations of soteriology in church history and even today: from guilt to judicial justification (John Calvin), from chaos to order (Gregory of Nazianzus), and from obscenity to beauty (Hans Urs von Balthasar).

Sin and Salvation: Toward a Soteriology of Truth, Goodness, and Beauty

Soteriology presupposes hamartiology (the doctrine of sin), but "sin" (or the "*power* of sin") is understood as all that impedes God's creation of superabundant life.[11] Yet salvation is not simply sin being broken, evil overcome, wrong forgiven. Salvation is also the broken image of God restored, God's presence and love and justice fully realized, and paradise regained—encompassing the past and present to the end of time (eschaton). The problems of humanity and the world we live in are real: the morbid condition of the brokenness in human beings and in their well-being with their Creator and creation, the prevalence of sin that binds and curses life in the cosmos, and the sting of death that obliterates the *shalom* of earthly flourishing.

There are three hermeneutical frames of sin and salvation, which should be understood as complementing rather than competing with each other since the semantic domain of all three categories is found in the Bible. The first perspective is that of goodness and evil in a moral sense. This view holds that a moral universe of goodness is in essence the psychological health of human beings or

11. For more, see J. Richard Middleton and Michael J. Gorman, "Salvation," in *The New Interpreter's Dictionary of the Bible S–Z*, vol. 5, ed. Katharine Doob Sakenfeld et al. (Nashville: Abingdon, 2009), 45–61.

the well-being of humanity. The perversion of the order of the moral universe means a departure from its norm; thus, sin is sickness of the soul (Ps. 32:3–5). Salvation then involves finding a cure, a therapy, often resorting to "medications" for healing. Examples are the ritual laws (Leviticus 13–15) on what is clean and what is unclean, and illnesses such as leprosy (Matt. 8:2–4) and blindness (John 9), which are regarded as sins.

The second frame assumes a truthful and legal universe, for God is the Lawgiver, and the laws are divine imperatives for human beings to maintain the principles of all things. Sin is missing the mark (*hamartia*), doing wrong (*ḥāṭā'* or *'āwâ*), or rebelling (*pāša'*) against the rules. Sin is law-breaking (1 John 3:4), the result of which is guilt (Psalm 32), and thus salvation is "forensic" justification. The Reformers especially favored this juridical understanding of sin (penal) and judicial atonement.

The third view assumes a holy and beautiful universe, one that is covered with its Creator's presence and glory. God as the beautiful wisdom (Proverbs 8) is the true nature of creation's web of relationship and its worthiness. Sin means one has "fallen short of the glory of God" (Rom. 3:23), and salvation is to have God's image restored in humanity (2 Cor. 3:18) and being clothed in glory (Rom. 13:14; Gal. 3:27).

In sum, salvation is that which is good, true, and beautiful. As Paul writes, "Do not be conformed to this age [*aiōn*], but be transformed [a major aspect of salvation] by the renewing of your minds [*noos*], so that you may discern what is the will of God—what is good [virtuous/ morality] and acceptable [delightful/beauty] and perfect [whole/truth]" (Rom. 12:2). The interplay of goodness, truth, and beauty can suggest an understanding of salvation as a process in which the aesthetic brings truth and good to our authentic selves and that of the cosmos. Jesus is the image of God (cf. Col. 1:15; Heb. 1:3), and he offers and epitomizes the wholeness and worthiness of humanity as their salvation. Indeed, "the grace of God has appeared bringing salvation to *all* human beings" (Titus 2:11).

Soteriology of the Global Church in the Majority World

How should we understand soteriology in our pluralistic world, especially in the Majority World in which pre- or extra-biblical knowledge of God abounds in the context of religious diversity? I find it interesting that not even one contributor to this volume addresses this crucial issue. For if Christ is sui generis, would Cyprian's dictum—*extra ecclesiam nulla salus* (outside the church there is no salvation)—still hold true today?[12]

Traditionally, three views have emerged from the debate over this question:

1. All religions lead to God and to the salvation of all people (universalism, pluralism, e.g., Origen, Irenaeus, Ernst Troeltsch, John Hick; or annihilationism, the belief all nonbelievers will be destroyed after death).
2. Salvation is universally available through Christ, who is predestined to do so (inclusivism, e.g., Justin Martyr's "Logos among Greeks and Socrates," Clement of Alexandria's "philosophy brought salvation to the Greeks as the Laws did to the Hebrews," Thomas Aquinas's "baptism of desire," Karl Barth's "election of Christ").
3. Salvation is available only in Christ (exclusivism, restrictivism, or particularism: R. Douglas Geivett, W. Gary Phillips).[13]

From the discussion above, we know that the traditional debate regarding Acts 4:12 ("there is no salvation through any else except Jesus; for there is no other name under heaven given among human beings by which we must be saved"), especially in the Majority World, remains challenging. Among the qualified inclusivistic views is that of Lesslie Newbigin and Alister McGrath, who argue for the assurance of salvation in Christ but acknowledge that they themselves are agnostic regarding those who have not heard of the gospel. Thus, they believe in the prevenient grace of God at work through the Spirit. Alistair McGrath writes: "I have stressed that there is a specifically Christian understanding of salvation, which is grounded uniquely in the life, death,

---

12. The context in Cyprian's dictum is not about religious diversity, but about his emphasis on belonging to the church of Christ, against the schism within the church. See Olli-Pekka Vainio, "Salvation and Religious Diversity: Christian Perspectives," *Religion Compass* 10, no. 2 (2016): 28.

13. Dennis L. Okholm and Timothy R. Phillips, eds., *Four Views on Salvation in a Pluralistic World* (Grand Rapids: Zondervan, 1996); Vainio, "Salvation and Religious Diversity," 27–34.

and resurrection of Jesus Christ. To affirm that there is a distinctively Christian understanding of salvation is not to deny that other faiths offer salvation in their own terms."[14]

Maybe Majority World scholars are not shying away from the "whether there is salvation outside the church" question, but responding by living out the breadth of biblical salvation (see "The Biblical Semantic of 'God Saves' ['Jesus' in Hebrew]" section above), being both true and critical of their *Sitz im Leben* (life situation). Thus, besides the intellectual rigors of the presenters at the Evangelical Theological Society (ETS) (November 19, 2015) and the Institute of Biblical Research (IBR) (November 20, 2015) "Scripture and Theology in Global Context" sessions, I am most touched by their personal stories. Ray Aldred shared how the European settlers conquered his land and destroyed his identity, and thus how "God as liberator" to the European settlers was "God the conqueror" for Native Americans. Elaine Goh recounts what a burden it is for Asian Chinese to fear being losers, and thus what a gospel of salvific hope the book of Ecclesiastes has become to them. Emily Choge Kerama tells the story of being born with a congenital defect in a Kenyan family and how her Christian parents witnessed to the power of God despite all odds.

While Western scholarship is often either prejudiced by cultural blind spots or prideful in its assumption of its own "normative" culture-less theology, many Majority World scholars educated in the West are tempted to mimic their mentors and make a contextual-global hermeneutic an afterthought, or worse, to resist the project this series promotes. The chapters in this volume are by no means perfect, but the contributors are seeking to live out their faith dynamically, faithful to the Scriptures and critical of their cultural assumptions. Similar to the rich young ruler in Luke 18, who thought practicing the law meant keeping the commandments (vv. 20–21), our presenters aim to complement one another on that "still one thing lacking" (v. 22) in each of our lives. "Still one thing lacking" has something to do with us "entering the kingdom of God" (v. 17) or "inheriting eternal life" (v. 18) by living out *the spirit* of the law. Contextually, it is selling his possessions and helping the poor for the rich ruler; it may suggest other requirements depending on context—such as embracing one's cultural identity (for the First Nations of Canada)

14. Okholm and Phillips, eds., *Four Views on Salvation*, 176.

or continuing to yearn for reconciliation between North and South (for the South Korean)—the strengthening of one's character as one participates in the suffering of Christ.

Thus, soteriology is a self-theologizing and existential act that is well served by the deep imbrication of theology, Scripture, and readers' contexts. The indicative and imperative moods of salvation must be held in tension. This tension calls believers into not simply abstract imputed righteousness. This tension calls all to real participation in, and a sharing in the merit of, Christ's righteousness (Matt. 5:20; Rom. 2:5–13; Phil. 2:12–13), thus affirming the primacy of grace and the necessity of works, similar to "faith without works is dead" in James (2:17) and "obedience of faith" in Romans (1:5; 16:26).

Conclusion

The doctrine of salvation in the Majority World is not a theological construct or abstract idea, but a matter of life or death. Christians in the Majority World find the Philippian jailer's question, "What must I do to be saved?" (Acts 16:30), a significant and timely reflection in the twentieth-first century. However, in most developed countries, especially in Europe and North America, faith in science and material prosperity, as well as a preference in cosmopolitan culture for therapies, often condition people to reduce or even brush aside their problems of plight, sin, and "lostness"[15] and, subsequently, their need of salvation.

Many who live in the Latino/a contexts of conflict, oppression, and violence are desperate to find liberation, peace, and hope.[16] African Christians address their world, which is plagued with HIV/AIDS, poverty, and war, by looking for a soteriology of emancipation from such ills and evils.[17] Asian multi-religious, scriptural, linguistic, and

15. Lee E. Snook, *The Anonymous Christ: Jesus as Savior in Modern Theology* (Minneapolis: Augsburg, 1986).

16. For an extensive bibliography by Majority World scholars apropos the use of the Bible to address their situation of life that calls for salvation, see K. K. Yeo, "The Bible in the Majority World," in *Oxford History of Dissenting Protestant Traditions*, vol. 5, *The Twentieth Century: Themes in a Global Context*, ed. Mark Hutchinson (Oxford: Oxford University Press, forthcoming).

17. Charles Nyamiti, "Contemporary African Christologies: Assessment and Prac-

racial social realities inevitably cry out for a soteriology that address-es natural disasters, epidemics, child labor, human trafficking, and dissymmetry of wealth. Christians of indigenous groups in the Unit-ed States, Borneo, and Australia wrestle with a soteriology that will save their land and bring them an identity of nationhood, political freedom, and self-determination. Understanding soteriology in one's context is nothing new. In *Salvation in the New Testament*, Jan G. van der Watt is adamant that "the documents of the New Testament [cannot] be classed as abstract theological treatises. They should rather be seen as reflecting [in the ancient world] the integration of the message into particular situations of the people involved in the first and original communication process."[18]

The hope of the series editors is that you will read this volume in conjunction with other volumes in the same series. For soteri-ology is the mega-theme of Scripture, "the integrating center of Scripture [and] the coordinating center of theology."[19] The salvation motif is prevalent in the Bible and Christian theology because of the "many dimensions" of soteriology by which "most key theo-logical issues . . . converge."[20] Soteriology is symbiotically related to the nature and work of God the Savior (theology; the author of salvation), the person and deeds of Christ (Christology; the agent of salvation), the work of the Spirit (pneumatology; the agency of salvation), the need and being of humanity (anthropology; togeth-er with the creation, the recipient of salvation), the identity and function of the church (ecclesiology; the channel of salvation to the world), the process and goal of history (eschatology; salvation consummated).

I believe that soteriology is about God's pneumatology of univer-sality (God's working out his plan of salvation in the whole creation) that has a Christological inclusivity (of all who are saved). Therefore, the church lives out that eschatological hope proleptically (Søren Kierkegaard's "life can only be understood backwards; but it must be

---

tical Suggestions," in *Paths of African Theology*, ed. Rosino Gibellini (Maryknoll, NY: Or-bis, 1994), 66.

18. Jan G. van der Watt, ed., *Salvation in the New Testament: Perspective on Soteriology* (Leiden: Brill, 2005), 505.

19. Joel Green, *Salvation* (Atlanta: Chalice, 2003), 2.

20. David Ford, *Theology: A Very Short Introduction* (Oxford: Oxford University Press, 2014), 103.

lived forwards")[21] and prophetically (mercy and justice) to the ends of the earth. Majority World scholars in this volume come to us from among the nations, and they offer us the courage and the grace to care for the world redemptively without borders.

*   *   *

The series editors wish to give thanks to many of our friends who partner with us in this project, witnessing to the global church in action regarding soteriology in the global context of Scripture and theology. We are grateful to the authors in this volume for providing numerous drafts of their presentations at the 2015 Atlanta conference of ETS (Evangelical Theological Society) and IBR. We are indebted to Scholar-Leaders International (especially Evan Hunter), the Rivendell Steward's Trust, and the SEED Research Institute (John Shen, Moses Cui) for their generous financial and prayer support. The leadership of ETS, IBR, and the Society of Biblical Literature (SBL) has provided hotel space and efficient logistical support for our conferences. Michael Thomson of Eerdmans continues to believe in our work and guide us to navigate smoothly through publishing waters. Chris Wright, Pieter Kwant, and Mark Hunt of Langham Partnership International encourage us and partner with us in publishing our work, but also in caring for the future scholars of the Majority World.

I praise God for the global church living out the mission of God sacramentally (salvation in and through the body of Christ), every time we meet, "breaking bread" at academic conferences or online/iCloud. Oh, "so great a salvation!" (Heb. 2:3). I echo Paul's words as a prayer: "For we are the aroma of Christ to God among those who are being saved and among those who are perishing; to the one a fragrance from death to death, to the other a fragrance from life to life" (2 Cor. 2:15–16).

---

21. *The Essential Kierkegaard*, ed. Howard V. Hong and Edna H. Hong (Princeton: Princeton University Press, 2000), 20.

CHAPTER 1

The New Covenant and New Creation:
Western Soteriologies and the Fullness of the Gospel

DANIEL J. TREIER

ABSTRACT

The focus of this opening chapter is to provide an overview of Western soteriologies. This overview begins by complicating the term "Western" before sketching eight soteriological traditions: Orthodox, Catholic, Lutheran, Calvinist, Anabaptist, Arminian, Wesleyan/Holiness, and Pentecostal. Next the overview concludes with recent trends affecting Christ's accomplishment of atonement and justification as well as the Spirit's application of salvation in believers' sanctification and glorification. After this overview comes possible critique, both internal and external, regarding Western soteriological tendencies.

From liberationist and Majority World perspectives, the sociopolitical and cosmic dimensions of salvation are the chief lacunae in traditional dogmatic attempts to represent the gospel's fullness. Such incomplete soteriologies focus too exclusively on the personal blessings of participation in the new covenant. Hence I conclude by suggesting that "new creation," with which the Old Testament prophets surround the new covenant, might fill up what is lacking in the soteriologies surveyed here—without divorcing sociopolitical and cosmic concerns from the new covenant's personal elements.

My primary goal is to provide an overview of "Western" soteriologies (assuming the quotation marks around this label "Western" throughout). This overview indicates that sociopolitical and cosmic dimensions are the chief aspects of salvation neglected by traditional dogmatics.

Such incomplete soteriologies focus too exclusively on the personal blessings of participation in the new covenant, which the end of this chapter addresses particularly in terms of Jeremiah 31. I conclude by suggesting that "new creation," a theme of God's saving action with which the Old Testament prophets surround the new covenant, might fill up what is lacking in the soteriologies surveyed here—without divorcing sociopolitical and cosmic concerns from the new covenant's personal elements.

"Western" Tendencies

Western soteriological tendencies reflect both major historical traditions and influential recent trends. Of course, such an assignment requires a gargantuan level of generalization, beyond the usual oversimplification that all education requires.

Such generalization begins with the very label "Western": in one sense it really means Northern, as opposed to Majority World theologies located largely in the Global South. In another sense, soteriologically, "Western" references the Augustinian tradition, which has generated Catholic and Protestant socially embodied arguments over many centuries. Yet the contrast implied in the present context, concerning Majority World theologies, probably includes the Orthodox tradition as well, since its heritage of *theosis* (deification) overlaps considerably with the Catholic tradition and even some Protestant accounts. Finally, for all the differences between Augustinian and Eastern tendencies, together they present another complexity: Augustine and other classic figures were African or Middle Eastern, not European—however Latin or Greek their language and however Roman their context. Hence "Western" functions quite imprecisely, as an omnibus contrast term.

Likewise, the boundaries of "soteriology" are fuzzy—overlapping with Christology, especially for atonement; pneumatology, especially for sanctification; and eschatology, especially for glorification. Systematic theology as modernity knows it, seeking an *ordo salutis* (order of salvation) that logically arranges the Spirit's application of Christ's saving benefits, is a comparatively recent invention. Its meandering development exacerbates the challenge of accurately characterizing Western soteriologies. Should Orthodox soteriology focus on creedal consensus, later theologians' tendencies, or priestly and popular beliefs? Should

Catholic soteriology focus on official dogma, catechetical material, historical eras, or geographical regions, let alone variety among priests, theologians, and the laity? For Protestant soteriologies, similarly, if their welter of systematic theologies reduces formal, printed variety to a somewhat manageable set of traditions and tendencies, then various denominations and popular trends quickly make such moments of apparent consensus less manageable. The following overview attempts to address both the gospel that is formally proclaimed and on occasion, however complex, what is apparently implied or actually practiced.

Traditions

The preceding qualifications notwithstanding, this overview of Western soteriologies begins with the major traditions they encompass. For all their variety, each somehow prioritizes salvation from sin and its consequences. Plus all of them ultimately focus on salvation's personal dimensions.[1] Yet each helpfully contributes an animating principle from which to learn.

Orthodox: Theosis beyond Mortal Corruption The Orthodox tradition has its focus and limits tied to early creedal consensus. Neither the informal rule of faith nor its later creedal formulations canonized a particular atonement theory or soteriology.[2] The first article of the Nicene Creed ("one God . . . maker of heaven and earth . . .") implies that salvation involves the Creator's establishing full and final lordship over the entire cosmos. Its second article ("one Lord . . . who for us and for our salvation . . .") focuses on the Son's incarnation for us and our salvation, rehearsing his divine identity and earthly pilgrimage. The "descent into hell" from the Apostles' Creed only adds soteriolog-

---

1. At least their orthodox or traditional or conservative versions do so. Modernist or liberal versions, arising since the Enlightenment(s), share common tendencies that transcend the distinctiveness of the traditions profiled here. Thus these profiles sketch the originating, conservative and distinctive, tendencies—leaving aside older liberal emphases on human freedom and a moral kingdom of God. Liberationist influence on contemporary progressive theologies surfaces here when highlighting traditional blind spots.

2. Very emphatically, John McIntyre, *The Shape of Soteriology: Studies in the Doctrine of the Death of Christ* (Edinburgh: T&T Clark, 1992), 2.

ical implications depending on debated interpretations. The second article's closing reminder of divine judgment ("he will come again to judge the quick and the dead . . .") and an eternal kingdom highlights the respective ends that soteriology puts at stake. The third article on the Holy Spirit, then, insists on baptism as the key soteriological entry point ("one baptism for the remission of sins . . .") and implies a set of key end points: forgiveness of sins, the resurrection of the dead, and the life of the world to come.

Orthodox theologies emphasize this soteriological entry point of baptism, consistent with liturgical Tradition. They emphasize the end point of *theosis*, consistent with the focus on resurrection: such "deification," or "divinization," does not make a human into God himself, but it does involve the saved human "participating in the divine nature" in a creaturely way. Broadly speaking, this soteriology centrally addresses mortal corruption. Each human imitates Adam's sin after having inherited his fallen mortality, with fleshly desires misdirected and disproportionate due to fear of scarcity. Christians experience God's forgiveness through the sacrament of the Lord's Supper. Salvation remakes humanity in union with the resurrected Christ by the Holy Spirit. Ultimately people transcend mortal corruption and become full (albeit still human) "partakers of the divine nature" (2 Peter 1:4) in resurrected bodies. In the meantime, the church's liturgy mediates union with the incarnate Christ so that once again humans can grow in virtue. Ascetic figures and groups underscore Orthodoxy's emphasis on efforts to undergo such transformation of mortal desire.

Catholic: Sacramental Renewal unto the Beatific Vision The Catholic tradition shares the creedal outline of salvation reclaiming God's creation through the Son's incarnation and atonement, with the Holy Spirit mediating union with Christ through the church. People enter into new life ("regeneration") at baptism, appropriate renewing grace through the sacraments (especially the Eucharist), and will enjoy its completion in a form of *theosis*.

Although Orthodoxy rejects the Pelagian idea that humans can grow toward righteousness apart from redeeming grace, the Augustinian concept of original sin is different from the Eastern one. Classically, Catholic theology has Adam's sin being not just necessarily imitated by humans (through corrupted desire stemming from cursed mortality) but imputed to them through real biological connection or another form of representation. Medieval Catholicism also made humanity's soteriological end somewhat more specific, construing *theosis* in terms of the beatific vision ("Blessed are the pure in heart, for they will see God" [Matt. 5:8]). While transcending cognition, this beatific vision involves the mind's eye, as it were. In between original sin and the beatific vision, medieval Catholicism applied an intricate legal and ontological construal of soteriological merit, along with a sacramental system for receiving grace.

Medieval Catholic soteriology's more technical terms resulted in less communal and cosmic focus than earlier creedal consensus might have supported (and Orthodox liturgies might claim). Modern Catholic soteriology is more amenable to those broader soteriological aspects, consistent with the doctrines of creation and churchly catholicity. Meanwhile, both Catholicism and Orthodoxy emphasize human dignity and freedom to pursue renewal in the divine likeness, reflecting more positive anthropologies than many Protestant soteriologies.

Lutheran: Justification by Faith Alone

Protestant soteriologies initially were and often remain critical of perceived errors of Catholic belief and practice. Yet Martin Luther, remaining as Catholic as possible, retained baptismal regeneration, the real sacramental presence of Christ, and Augustinian tendencies regarding original sin and divine predestination. Reemphasizing gracious divine initiative and the bondage of the human will, Luther believed that justification by faith alone was a biblically necessary break with the Roman Church—the article by which the church stands or falls.[3] Justification is preeminently an initial declaration of God's forgiveness and the believer's imputed righteousness in Christ, not an ongoing process of infusing Christ's righteousness into the believer—who must always cling to Christ, rather than cooperate with sacramental grace, for assurance. A cluster of changes followed this one, including "affirmation of ordinary life" as spiritually equal to the monasticism that Luther eventually rejected.[4]

Accordingly, the Lutheran account of sanctification champions

3. For example, "The Smalcald Articles," in *The Book of Concord: The Confessions of the Evangelical Lutheran Church*, ed. Robert Kolb and Timothy J. Wengert (Minneapolis: Fortress, 2000), 301.

4. Charles Taylor, *Sources of the Self: The Making of the Modern Identity* (Cambridge, MA: Harvard University Press, 1992), 211–85.

freedom and gratitude. Freed from concern over personal righteousness, believers gratefully love God and serve their neighbors as they truly need. Works of love emerge from faith but are never the basis for justification or Christian assurance. Law and gospel do not really contrast the Old and New Testaments; instead, they are contrasting aspects involved in encountering any biblical Word. A first use of the law preserves earthly society by restraining human wickedness in the temporal kingdom; a second use confronts sinners with their need for God's grace in Christ. The gospel focuses on making this offer of forgiveness, inviting people to enter God's eternal kingdom.

Calvinist: Election unto Union with Christ

While John Calvin shared Luther's commitment to justification by faith alone, he was more inclined to think centrally from union with Christ. Luther certainly depended on that union: justification by faith alone is not a "legal fiction," as often alleged, because believers in covenantal union with Christ enjoy a glorious exchange—his benefits for their sin—as with joint marital property. Some recent scholarship also suggests that Luther's soteriology was more ontological than previously thought.[5] Yet Calvin, less inclined to start with Catholic commitments altered only when necessary, instead sought a wholesale, ordered biblical theology for catechesis. His soteriology placed union with Christ in the overarching position, within which justification and sanctification became double graces.

As Luther's and Calvin's successors battled Catholics, Radical Reformers, and each other, they developed confessions, catechisms, and elaborate scholastic systems. Such Calvinism became known for predestinarian and covenantal or federal emphases: eternally the Triune God predestined the salvation of the elect—the Father willing to send the Son, the Son agreeing to become incarnate and atone for their sin, and the Spirit agreeing to unite the elect with Christ. According to the five points of Calvinism under the acronym TULIP, all humans after the fall become (1) *totally* depraved (not absolutely depraved, but sinful in every aspect), which is addressed by (2) *unconditional* divine election (God does not merely foresee but rather determines who will be saved), (3) *limited* atonement (Christ dies specifically for the elect), (4) *ir-*

---

5. For example, Tuomo Mannermaa, *Christ Present in Faith: Luther's View of Justification* (Minneapolis: Fortress, 2005).

resistible grace (the Spirit regenerates the elect, effectually calling them to faith), and (5) *perseverance* of the saints (regeneration preserves the elect in faith throughout their pilgrimage). Salvation's blessings are for those elected to have Christ (rather than Adam, due to imputation of original sin) as their federal head—representing them before God.

Calvinism emphasizes God's redemptive rule over the entire cosmos more than other Protestant traditions.[6] Correspondingly, Calvinists often pursue more cultural transformation. Such implications of redemption, however, do not displace personal salvation from its classical centrality. Calvinism adds a third use of the law to direct believers' pursuit of sanctification. But God's present work of cultural transformation outside the church remains common, not specifically redemptive, grace.

Anabaptist: Radical, Communal Discipleship

The third Reformation-era Protestant tradition involves the more radical and "Anabaptist" Reformers. Because they rejected infant baptism and believed that only confessing believers' baptism was biblical, they were labeled "rebaptizers"—for requiring that believers once baptized as infants be baptized again to become church members.

Radical Reformers were less wedded to justification by faith alone than magisterial Protestants; in some cases they opposed it. Like Lutheran Pietists soon after the Reformation, Puritans later, and others since, they placed justification in a larger context with different emphases. They emphasized pursuit of personal discipleship in small Christian communities. These communities would be alternative societies, typically modeling the nonviolent practice of Jesus while waiting eagerly for God's kingdom to come in fullness. Radical soteriologies were more biblicist, less formal, and correspondingly less consistent. Yet, separatistic tendencies and periodic aberrations aside, their core commitments have become widely influential in recent decades.[7]

---

6. Famously, Abraham Kuyper: "No single piece of our mental world is to be hermetically sealed off from the rest, and there is not a square inch in the whole domain of our human existence over which Christ, who is Sovereign over all, does not cry: 'Mine!'" (*Abraham Kuyper: A Centennial Reader*, ed. James D. Bratt [Grand Rapids: Eerdmans, 1998], 488).

7. Particularly through John Howard Yoder regarding the politics of Jesus and Stanley Hauerwas regarding communal ethics of Christian virtue.

Arminian: Freedom for Faith

Within Reformed circles, seventeenth-century Dutch thinkers such as Jacobus Arminius retained broadly Protestant soteriology while rejecting Augustinian/Lutheran accounts of the will's bondage and Calvinist accounts of divine sovereignty. Classic Calvinism became formally defined by the Synod of Dort and its rejection of the Arminian alternative. Arminianism then appeared within various traditions, offering no sharply defined and comprehensive system. In general, Arminian soteriologies emphasize human freedom (often labeled "libertarian") to accept or reject the gospel, with divine election being conditional (God foreseeing who will fulfill the condition of believing) or corporate (God deciding to form a servant community in the world rather than deciding the eternal destiny of particular persons). In some Arminian accounts human freedom seems to be a natural function of creation, but in others it is a universal redemptive blessing of prevenient grace—grace that comes before the possibility of human faith, as a result of Christ's work on the cross or the Spirit's convicting work in the heart.

Wesleyan/Holiness: The Second Blessing unto Perfect Love

A distinctive Arminian family is the Wesleyan/Holiness tradition, in which the possibility of human freedom for faith clearly stems from prevenient grace. If Lutherans and Calvinists are stereotypically monergistic, emphasizing that salvation is due to God's grace alone, then Wesleyans are synergistic, emphasizing that salvation involves human cooperation in a sense—exploring how divine grace works.[8]

John Wesley embraced justification by faith alone; indeed his "conversion" involved the strange warming of his heart when hearing Luther's treatment of Romans.[9] But Wesley did not want this objective aspect of Christian assurance to prevent believers from vigorously pursuing perfect holiness or subjectively receiving assurance in light of their growth in grace. He insisted that biblical commands regarding holiness, even perfection, implied the possibility of graced obedience, enjoying this end of salvation here and now. Wesley's focus was the heart, so perfection would not involve loss of finite weakness or error, or legally blameless lack of inadvertent sin, but complete love of God

8. Thomas A. Langford, *Practical Divinity: Theology in the Wesleyan Tradition*, vol. 1, rev. ed. (Nashville: Abingdon, 1998), especially 249–51.

9. John Wesley, "The Aldersgate Experience," in *John Wesley*, ed. Albert C. Outler (New York: Oxford University Press, 1964), 51–69.

and neighbor. If Calvinists and Lutherans championed Romans, with the latter marginalizing James, then Wesleyans renewed interest in 1 John.

Realizing Christian perfection would involve ongoing growth in grace, putting sin to death and putting on Christ. But sanctification would involve more than slow, sometimes steady, progress. Christian perfection would involve seeking a special work of grace after conversion, generally labeled a "second blessing." Such holiness meant a primarily personal focus concerning salvation, yet Holiness groups were frequent pioneers in nineteenth-century evangelical social reform: they were more typically involved in abolitionist, temperance, and women's suffrage causes than others. Meanwhile, populist commitments enabled Wesleyans to transform the Anglo-American landscape of church life. Such alternative movements as the Keswick Convention reflect broad Holiness outlines despite altered details: pursuit of a higher plane of sanctification through repeated crises of post-conversion filling with the Holy Spirit that punctuate ordinary life. Such approaches have had widespread evangelical influence.

Pentecostal: The Baptism and Gifts of the Holy Spirit

Emerging from the Holiness tradition is the family of Pentecostal movements originating near the turn of the twentieth century. Just as an Arminian stance cuts across church traditions—with Baptists, for example, being either Arminian, Calvinist, or an amalgam—so Pentecostal beliefs and practices, or openness to them anyway, cuts across other ecclesiastical and soteriological traditions.

Classic Pentecostalism emphasized not merely holiness but empowerment for bold ministry and joyful living. The second, or post-conversion, blessing was baptism with the Holy Spirit, with its initial evidence being glossolalia, or speaking in tongues. Most classic Pentecostals did not say that a person is unsaved without such an experience, but such an experience was to be normatively sought. Various Pentecostal denominations promoted this experience and the distinctively supernatural gifts of the Spirit.

The charismatic movement arose in the middle of the twentieth century across a range of churches, celebrating charismata and promoting Spirit baptism, albeit with less emphasis on the "initial evidence" of tongues. The Vineyard movement arose in the late twentieth century to continue celebrating charismatic and missional empowerment, often adopting a more Reformed account of progressive (less episodic or crisis-oriented) sanctification. Today "Pentecostal" is a broad adjective globally, having lost theological specificity concerning the classic Spirit baptism evidenced by tongues-speaking. Pentecostal soteriologies generally see themselves remedying more classical—not just Protestant but also Catholic and even Orthodox—deficiencies, bringing the Holy Spirit's work out from under the shadow of excessive Christ-centeredness.

Trends

Accordingly, one of the significant soteriological trends across various traditions is greater emphasis on the Holy Spirit's work. Western Christians and churches are increasingly aware of God's empowering presence within Global South Christianity. Simultaneously, traditional atonement-oriented accounts of salvation, tending toward anthropological pessimism and soteriological exclusivism, are increasingly unpopular in the West. Yet these do not exhaust recent soteriological trends, the rest of which loosely correspond to a traditional dogmatic outline.

Christ's Accomplishment: Atonement and Justification

Christ's work of atonement has frequently been reinterpreted in nonviolent or victorious terms, while justification by faith has been subject to both ecumenical dialogue and extensive debate in Pauline scholarship.

Justification is not a significant feature of Orthodox soteriologies. Catholic soteriology adopted a broadly Augustinian account involving transformative righteousness, in which justification itself is not primary except in debate with Protestants. Catholic soteriology does not teach justification by meritorious works, but justification by faith as fulfilled in love. This love relates transformative righteousness to ontological renewal through infusion of sacramental grace. Believers do not merit salvation as an achievement but as a fitting divine response to human appropriation of grace. By contrast, Protestants typically define justification not as a process of infusion but as the initial imputation of Christ's righteousness—at minimum a declaration of forgiveness based on Christ bearing believers' sins.

23

Until recently atonement theology operated with a distinction between the person and the work of Christ. The former comprised the focus of Christology; the latter fell into an ambiguous space, partly Christological and partly soteriological. Magisterial Protestants developed complex accounts of the *ordo salutis* in which justification became a primary benefit, the initial application of Christ's atoning work.

Ever since the Socinians of the early Protestant era, penal substitutionary atonement—according to which Christ suffered the punishment deserved by human sinners—has had opponents. Early in the twentieth century Gustaf Aulén, a Swedish Lutheran, proposed a threefold typology of atonement theologies.[10] Aulén's widely used typology suggested that (1) objective views, orienting atonement around change on God's side, arose in the Middle Ages when Anselm treated atonement in terms of God's offended honor. Such objective views bear hallmarks of feudal or legal or other realities in their originating contexts. (2) Subjective views, orienting atonement around change on the sinner's side, also arose in the Middle Ages, thanks to Peter Abelard. Yet subjective views focus on Christ's moral example or influence to the exclusion of other scriptural concepts, so they became widespread only in the modern era and are viewed as liberal, captivated by contemporary concerns. Aulén suggested that this binary opposition between objective and subjective views was not original to the Christian tradition, which had previously been characterized by (3) classical views orienting atonement around *Christus Victor*—Christ triumphing over all hostile powers, including sin, death, and the devil.

Aulén's work appealed to many who recognized that no single atonement theory had been canonized in the early creeds, who reveled in patristic or subsequent diversity, and who rejected the penal substitution model. Modern thought finds blood sacrifice and pessimistic anthropologies distasteful. Aulén's work opened a door through which feminist and other critiques of penal substitution walked all the more forcefully. To some, penal atonement theories entail "divine child abuse," fostering male violence along with female victimization—glorifying Jesus's suffering at the hands of an angry divine Father. Catholic René Girard is representative of other recent antiviolence theories,

---

10. Gustaf Aulén, *Christus Victor: An Historical Study of the Three Main Types of the Idea of Atonement*, trans. A. G. Herbert (Reprint, Eugene, OR: Wipf & Stock, 2003 [1931]).

reinterpreting Christ's sacrifice sociologically as an exposure of societies' scapegoating mechanisms.[11]

Alternatives to penal substitution have arisen periodically among more conservative Protestants. For instance, some Wesleyans find penal substitution to be extrinsic to their tradition and appeal to governmental models, in which Christ's sacrifice reflects God's justice in overcoming sin without addressing divine wrath for specific sinners. Alternatives have also arisen among biblical scholars: some argue that Scripture does not contain the penal substitution model, while others argue more modestly that Scripture does not require it.[12] In such accounts, Scripture provides multiple metaphors from which theologians are free to choose as contextually appropriate. Unifying these objections to penal substitution is the general charge that it is Lutheran and Reformed, not broadly evangelical, reflecting an outdated and excessively Pauline theology to the exclusion of other biblical priorities.

Traditional Protestants have responded by defending the presence of penal substitution in Paul's letters and its coherence with the rest of Scripture:[13] substitution is not merely one metaphor among others but the reality underlying them,[14] and the cross is integral to establishing God's kingdom as the fulfillment of Israel's story.[15] The historical contexts of penal substitution are receiving their due.[16] Implications of divine child abuse and allegations of promoting violence or victimization are eliciting more intentionally Trinitarian accounts: the Father, Son, and Spirit together lovingly accomplish our salvation; the

11. René Girard, *Violence and the Sacred* (Baltimore: Johns Hopkins University Press, 1979).

12. For example, Joel B. Green and Mark D. Baker, *Recovering the Scandal of the Cross: Atonement in New Testament and Contemporary Contexts* (Downers Grove, IL: IVP, 2000), which generally claims the latter but sometimes seems to imply the former.

13. Simon Gathercole, *Defending Substitution: An Essay on Atonement in Paul*, Acadia Studies in Bible and Theology (Grand Rapids: Baker Academic, 2015).

14. John R. W. Stott, *The Cross of Christ* (Downers Grove, IL: IVP, 1986).

15. Jeremy R. Treat, *The Crucified King: Atonement and Kingdom in Biblical and Systematic Theology* (Grand Rapids: Zondervan, 2014). Further defending penal substitution are several essays by Henri Blocher, including "*Agnus Victor*: The Atonement as Victory and Vicarious Punishment," in *What Does It Mean to Be Saved? Broadening Evangelical Horizons of Salvation*, ed. John G. Stackhouse Jr. (Grand Rapids: Baker Academic, 2002), 67–91.

16. For example, Adonis Vidu, *Atonement, Law, and Justice: The Cross in Historical and Cultural Contexts* (Grand Rapids: Baker Academic, 2014).

Son lays down his life of his own accord, and the Father does not punish a mere human but mysteriously pours out judgment on the Son in the bond of the Spirit's love.[17] This Trinitarian emphasis has also elicited attempts to recover the patristic fullness on the subject, which includes victory alongside considerable mention of sacrifice—more than Aulén's followers have acknowledged. These Trinitarian accounts include efforts to integrate Christ's incarnation more fully with his atoning work: his identification with fallen humanity already begins its healing.[18]

Justification as the declaration of forgiveness tightly correlates with penal substitutionary atonement. Though earlier modern alternatives to penal substitution may have been moralistic in their visions of the divine kingdom and human transformation, current alternatives are typically more optimistic or even universalistic regarding human salvation.[19] Forgiveness seems to involve sheer divine fiat or radically incarnational divine identification with our plight, not a divine work of gracious justice involving the cross.

The most substantial contemporary development concerning justification is the so-called new perspective on Paul. In brief compass, this perspective rejects the Lutheran parallel between Paul's "Judaizing" opponents and medieval Catholicism. Such a parallel suggested that just as Paul's opponents based sanctification or assurance on law-keeping in response to covenantal grace, so later Catholic belief errantly based justification on transformative righteousness through sacramental grace. Rejecting this parallel, newer perspectives on Paul characterize Second Temple Judaism in terms of covenantal nomism, not legalism or works-righteousness: works of the law simply demarcated God's (Jewish) covenant people (from Gentile pagans), with circumcision expressing initial commitment to the covenantal obligation of keeping Torah.

In that case Paul's critique of his opponents chiefly opposed ethnocentric failure to recognize prophetic fulfillment of Gentile inclusion in Christ, not soteriological failure to champion the "faith alone" an-

17. For example, Hans Boersma, *Violence, Hospitality, and the Cross: Reappropriating the Atonement Tradition* (Grand Rapids: Baker Academic, 2004).

18. This enduring emphasis of T. F. Torrance (and family) now finds advocates under the heading "evangelical Calvinism."

19. See, for example, Robin A. Parry and Christopher H. Partridge, eds., *Universal Salvation: The Current Debate* (Grand Rapids: Eerdmans, 2003).

thropology of true grace. Key Pauline texts, accordingly, may have in view the faith(fulness) of Christ rather than faith in Christ as what decisively accomplishes our salvation.[20] Apocalyptic readings proceed on this basis to suggest that Paul's gospel is more radically gracious than the Protestant Reformation suggested: not even human faith functions as any kind of condition for participating in the new reality of union with Christ, which has invaded and upended our earthly history.[21]

However, neither apocalyptic nor any of the various new-perspective readings have vanquished more traditional accounts. Certainly the newer scholarship has led to more careful portrayals of first-century Judaism, with corresponding debates about how its nomism relates to Pauline arguments. But if "works" must be addressed more chastely, still the traditional Protestant approach has contemporary exegetical and theological defenses—including the identification of misunderstandings and excessively narrow presentations from which it too suffers.[22]

The Spirit's Application: Sanctification and Glorification

Trends concerning sanctification involve regeneration, spirituality, and glorification, or *theosis*. For some, regeneration is the initial event of being made new by the Spirit, either logically preceding faith (as for most Calvinists and those affirming baptismal regeneration) or proceeding from it (as for most Arminians). For others, "regeneration" is a virtual synonym of "sanctification," denoting a process of renewal rather than initial reception of a new nature. Apart from interest in conversion as more process- and less event-oriented, few current trends affect regeneration as such.[23] In some circles, though, the positional aspect of sanctification—associated with justification as an

20. One way of getting up to date on such issues in Pauline scholarship is to examine the most important recent contribution: John M. G. Barclay, *Paul and the Gift* (Grand Rapids: Eerdmans, 2015). Barclay appropriates aspects of the "new perspective," especially its thicker treatment of first-century Judaism, while retaining theological aspects of the earlier Protestant tradition.

21. Douglas A. Campbell, *The Deliverance of God: An Apocalyptic Rereading of Justification in Paul* (Grand Rapids: Eerdmans, 2009).

22. Theologically, R. Michael Allen, *Justification and the Gospel: Understanding the Contexts and Controversies* (Grand Rapids: Baker Academic, 2013); more historically, D. A. Carson et al., eds., *Justification and Variegated Nomism*, 2 vols. (Grand Rapids: Baker Academic, 2001–4).

23. For example, Richard V. Peace, *Conversion in the New Testament: Paul and the Twelve* (Grand Rapids: Eerdmans, 1999).

initial event—is gaining renewed emphasis. "Sanctification" terminology in the Bible usually addresses being set apart positionally as God's people, a status that contains a continual calling toward holiness—yet not itself a process involving human initiative. When (instead) that process of sanctification (in more systematic-theological terms) is in view, the biblical-theological terminology focuses on being renewed, being transformed, growing in grace. From this perspective sanctification needs more emphasis on divine initiative than many views of the Christian life provide.[24]

Spirituality has certainly received contemporary theological attention. Classic theologians' spiritual priorities are being recovered, with particular attention to Christian virtues and practices.[25] Interest in spirituality without religion has elicited theological pursuit of authentic Christian responses to that cultural trend. Protestant openness to *theosis*, with attention to the contemplative end of our earthly pilgrimage, stems partly from trends in Pauline studies and connections with other New Testament corpora.[26] Perhaps it also stems from neglected aspects of Christ's work—broadening atonement beyond the cross to consider implications of his incarnation, earthly ministry, burial, resurrection, and ascension. Even on traditional Pauline terms, Western soteriologies need better accounts of Romans 4:25 ("He was delivered over to death for our sins and was raised to life for our justification"), especially in light of the encompassing Trinitarian vision of Romans 8.

Speaking of *theosis*, and/or glorification, completes our overview of the *ordo salutis*. Orthodox and Catholic accounts of salvation's final end have remained relatively stable, with the Orthodox rarely pursuing a technical *ordo* and the Catholic one being largely sacramental in nature. Yet their classic underpinnings challenge contemporary Protestants who have become more aware of patristic Christology. If early arguments for the Son's full divinity tie salvation tightly to the incarnation—God

24. David Peterson, *Possessed by God: A New Testament Theology of Sanctification and Holiness*, New Studies in Biblical Theology (Grand Rapids: Eerdmans, 1995).

25. For example, Ellen Charry's recovery of patristic and other pre-modern figures (*By the Renewing of Your Minds: The Pastoral Function of Christian Doctrine* [New York: Oxford University Press, 1997]); pastoral interest in Jonathan Edwards; Hauerwas's aforementioned influence; Simon Chan, *Spiritual Theology: A Systematic Study of the Christian Life* (Downers Grove, IL: IVP, 1998).

26. For example, Michael J. Gorman, *Inhabiting the Cruciform God: Kenosis, Justification, and Theosis in Paul's Narrative Soteriology* (Grand Rapids: Eerdmans, 2009).

taking on humanity in Christ so that believers might take on the divine nature in him—then salvation cannot solely consist in an atoning transaction accomplished by a human sacrifice (however flawless) on the cross. Such transactional myopia is actually not the classic Protestant view, but popular aberrations need correction: if Christ's full divinity is soteriologically essential, then evangelical theologies must more fully integrate incarnation and atonement, correspondingly relating salvation's end to the fullness of bearing the divine image.

As *theosis* rises in Protestant prominence, however, the communal embrace of humanity in the incarnation and the cosmic reach of its implications have elicited critique of limited notions of glorification. Sometimes it seems as if spiritual life and divine likeness do not involve the social, earthly dimensions of created humanity but instead transcend those tempting obstacles. Few theologies say as much, but many in Western traditions live as such. Again, popular aberrations need correction: *theosis*, the beatific vision, or glorification—by whatever name—is not individualistic, disembodied, passive, eternal gazing on the divine essence after the present universe has been annihilated. Against such assumptions based on texts like 2 Peter 3, there has been increasing biblical-theological emphasis on new creation and historical-theological emphasis on resurrection. In light of Christ's incarnation and his resurrection as the first fruits of ours, true Christian teaching resists an unhealthy dualism between the material and the spiritual.[27] Rather than escaping from the body, community, and the cosmos, Christians wait in hope for God to make all things new. Yet such an emphasis introduces further critique of Western soteriological blind spots.

Internal and External Critique

For all their variety, Western accounts of salvation strive for some comprehensiveness by encompassing past, present, and future. Regarding

27. Illustrating this emphasis are J. Richard Middleton and N. T. Wright, among others in biblical studies; historical works such as Carolyn Walker Bynum, *The Resurrection of the Body in Western Christianity, 200–1336* (New York: Columbia University Press, 1995); widespread Reformed worldview thinking in Christian higher education; and the account of the resurrection's ethical implications in Oliver O'Donovan, *Resurrection and Moral Order: An Outline for Evangelical Ethics*, 2nd ed. (Grand Rapids: Eerdmans, 1994).

the past, forgiveness of sin initiates new life; regarding the present, transforming grace works that new identity into patterns of living; regarding the future, the fullness of eternal life involves bodily resurrection and complete personal renewal in the joyful immediacy of God's presence. These soteriologies encompass the full history of human lives in this way, but particular persons are their focus. What therefore do they neglect?

The answer of some classically liberal and nearly all liberationist theologies, whether in the West or abroad—as well as other indigenous theologies from the Majority World—involves the gospel's sociopolitical and cosmic dimensions.[28] To mention a very concrete example, conservative Western soteriologies speak of "justification" and "righteousness" rather than "justice." What a difference such connotations make![29] Accordingly, traditional accounts narrowly construe salvation's future, overemphasizing personal destiny in disembodied, individualistic, and unearthly ways. Additionally, they ignore their own contextual character, applying adjectives only to other soteriologies—as if other indigenous accounts are syncretistic or at least situated whereas the West's are just fundamentally scriptural.

Traditional reactions to such critiques can be grudging or dismissive. Although evangelical Protestant theologians have begun to address the gospel's corollary matters of systemic evil and structural sin, those efforts have been sufficiently late and modest that the issues remain barely acknowledged at the popular level.[30] Corresponding soteriologies remain personally focused. Similarly, though professional or episcopal Orthodox theologies may have a slightly more cosmic focus, national and popular features of church life complicate any claim re-

28. In conference dialogue, Jules Martínez-Olivieri plausibly suggested that liberationist theology is a sufficiently established tradition, even in the West, to be included in the first section of this chapter—with its theme running along the lines of "salvation as historical experience." The reason for keeping the present arrangement is that each of the Western traditions sketched above has one or more church denominations distinctly named in association with its originating soteriology. By contrast, liberationist theologies suffuse various churches but have not claimed any particular, major denomination as their own.

29. An example mentioned by C. René Padilla in personal conversation.

30. For example, Michael O. Emerson and Christian Smith, *Divided by Faith: Evangelical Religion and the Problem of Race in America* (New York: Oxford University Press, 2001), profiling the "cultural toolkit" with which evangelicals contribute to racialization.

garding soteriological holism. Catholic soteriology, meanwhile, made liberation theology possible but also necessary.

The Catholic response to liberation theology has been complex. On occasion the Vatican has disciplined figures within that movement officially, while more often resisting aspects of its perspective. Yet the Vatican clearly adopted much liberationist critique of late modern global capitalism along with increased emphasis upon God's embrace of the poor, while most liberationist figures remain in good churchly standing. Much liberation theology appealed to the Bible for its broader account of sin and salvation, with the exodus as a starting point plus the prophets and Gospels as additional support.

Conservative critique addressed liberation theology's biblical priorities and proportions, often regarding what is not said more than what is. Official Vatican critique addressed Marxist theory and revolutionary practice as much as anything else. Still other critique came from seemingly more sympathetic quarters. Native Americans, among other indigenous or First Nations groups, faulted the exodus paradigm for failing to address its corollary, the conquest. This worry is not just conceptual but historical: the conquest of Canaan became a paradigm for European colonizers in America.[31] More broadly, postcolonial theorists critique liberation theologies for redeeming aspects of Scripture as if they were authoritative; the very notion of biblical authority is allegedly oppressive, if not most or all biblical content. By their own acknowledgment, though, such postcolonial thinkers frequently are not pursuing Christian theology but another enterprise that, despite its importance, must be seen in external rather than internal terms.[32]

Liberationist critique of traditional Western soteriologies originated among Majority World oppressed peoples, at priestly and popular levels. Soon liberationist models arose among marginalized groups within the West, as black theologies illustrate. Feminist theologies, with their womanist (emerging from black women) and *mujerista* (emerging from Latin American women) descendants, further illus-

---

31. As detailed, for example, in Sacvan Bercovitch, "The Typology of America's Mission," *American Quarterly* 30, no. 2 (1978): 135–55.

32. See especially the work of R. S. Sugirtharajah, surveyed by Daniel J. Treier, *Introducing Theological Interpretation of Scripture: Recovering a Christian Practice* (Grand Rapids: Baker Academic, 2008), chapter 6. But note the evangelical contribution of Kay Higuera Smith et al., eds., *Evangelical Postcolonial Conversations: Global Awakenings in Theology and Praxis* (Downers Grove, IL: IVP Academic, 2014).

trate the complexity of marginalization and oppression: they appropriate earlier liberationist elements while pursuing further liberation from aspects of those very movements. Various liberationist concerns now vie for influence in mainline Protestant and progressive Catholic circles. The complexity is illustrated in the interface with interreligious dialogue: should contextual theology in South Asia appropriate mainstream Hindu notions for the sake of dialogue, or side with Dalit persons for the sake of liberation?

Naming such complexities must not distract us from the central critique at issue. Traditionalist Western soteriologies apparently focus so much on the gospel's personal benefits, in particular concerning an individual's eternal destiny, that they neglect its communal and cosmic, perhaps even bodily, dimensions. Traditionalists find this personal focus emerging naturally from biblical texts. Hence we face this question: Are there lines of biblical teaching that widen soteriology's focus, while fitting alongside the personal aspects in the rest of the picture? Or do those other lines of biblical teaching generate a competing soteriological picture that minimizes or even lacks personal salvation?

Biblical Reform?

Such questions about traditional soteriologies and alternative possibilities probably inform the apocalyptic readings of Paul mentioned previously, and almost certainly elicit the aforementioned interest in biblical corpora beyond Pauline theology: Jesus in the Gospels bearing the healing kingdom of God in person; catholic epistles calling for moral transformation and addressing its cosmic context (which, incidentally, Paul addresses too!); the exodus and other Old Testament paradigms like the Jubilee fostering hope for liberation and justice; and the prophets denouncing the injustice, individualism, and idolatry of the covenant people's soteriological status quo. These biblical resources—and theological resources stemming from existing Majority World interest in such scriptural teaching—are deep and wide.

The remainder of this soteriological overview can only hint at one modest suggestion concerning the new covenant and its context of the new creation. The basis of this suggestion lies in the significance of the new covenant for the traditional focus on personal salvation. Jeremiah

31:31–34, not least in its use by Hebrews (8:7–13), presents a twofold focus: forgiveness of sins and transforming knowledge of God—loosely but dogmatically put, justification and sanctification. Even contemporary readings of Paul, with their communal focus, recognize the importance of these concepts for creating God's covenant people as a new humanity in Christ.

Simultaneously, given extensive recent concern over supersessionism,[33] the new covenant is important for keeping Christian soteriology anchored in the hopes of Israel's Scriptures—resisting appeals to Jesus Christ that would replace Old Testament faith with a merely human revolutionary program or a misguided churchly one. Far too often, Jews have needed liberation from oppressive Christianity's theological roots. So, however we construe the creation of a new humanity in Christ, Christians dare not lose the biblical and loving particularity of God's covenant history with Israel.

The new covenant is biblically important, moreover, for theologically integrating divine initiative and human transformation. Atonement—initially and vitally involving forgiveness of sin—depends on what God alone does in self-giving love. The resulting sanctification of God's people has both initial and ultimate dimensions that are divinely accomplished, plus an ongoing dimension that is divinely enabled. Yet that ongoing dimension, despite only being realized in the ultimate fullness of divine presence, is our very human calling: becoming holy as God is. These are not the only dimensions of new covenant saving hope, but they anchor such hope in loving divine initiative rather than human self-help—whether individual or communal or revolutionary or systemic. At the same time, the Old Testament prophets refuse to allow forgiven persons to wallow in idolatrous brokenness, as if continually calling on God with bloodstained hands. Judgment begins with the household of God, whose new covenant members must call on the

---

33. As defined by R. Kendall Soulen, "According to this teaching [supersessionism], God chose the Jewish people after the fall of Adam in order to prepare the world for the coming of Jesus Christ, the Savior. After Christ came, however, the special role of the Jewish people came to an end and its place was taken by the church, the new Israel" (*The God of Israel and Christian Theology* [Minneapolis: Fortress, 1996], 1–2). Racially anti-Semitic, and religiously anti-Judaic, forms of supersessionism leave Christians much to regret and repent for. New Testament claims about covenantal change are more complex, though, attempting to appeal in an internal sense to Israel's Old Testament hope.

Lord out of genuinely contrite hearts—not complacent appeals to a supposedly privileged position.

Admittedly, a comprehensive account of new covenant saving hope is impossible in this space. Yet, if the soteriological importance of that hope has been established, then we may turn briefly to its content. For that content the Isaianic new creation and new exodus passages, which shaped Jesus's self-understanding and prominent New Testament themes, would surely deserve substantial attention. They indicate that Jesus's presentation of the divine reign inaugurates the fulfillment of Jewish hopes regarding bodily healing, communal restoration, and creational *shalom*. The New Testament is replete with newness: Jesus called for new wineskins to hold the new covenant's new teaching, new commandment, new name, new song, and so forth.[34]

In suggesting the Old Testament prophetic context of new creation for scriptural reform of the new covenant's overly personal application, the remaining task is to highlight broader soteriological elements in Jeremiah 31. Verse 1 immediately sets the end of this saving hope in a communal context: God living with a restored, unified covenant people. As ensuing verses like verse 5 indicate, restoration will delight this people in the fruit of the land. In verse 6 they go to worship as a people, not just individuals. Verse 8 includes marginal persons in this joy: the blind, the lame, and pregnant women. No outdated social markers or ritual boundaries of cleanliness need keep anyone from joining in worship. In verse 9 the water of repentant tears gives way to physical streams and smooth paths. Radiant joy over creation's good things embraces not just the land's abundance but also animals in verse 12. The cosmic blessings of new covenant hope appear in the freedom with which the text uses physical imagery to convey holistic, even spiritual, flourishing. The restored joy in verse 13 and abundant provision in verse 14 affect every possible group in the community.

Verses 15–22 indicate that repentance is vital to the promised restoration and the new reality it brings. Colin Gunton helps to explain what is at stake: God's saving renewal of creation—as full-orbed as it will be—must begin by addressing sinful humanity because our misdirected and aggregated wills are the crux of the problem.[35] We are

---

34. Carl B. Hoch Jr., *All Things New: The Significance of Newness for Biblical Theology* (Grand Rapids: Baker, 1996).

35. Colin E. Gunton, *The Triune Creator: A Historical and Systematic Study*, Edinburgh Studies in Constructive Theology (Grand Rapids: Eerdmans, 1998), especially 168.

those who turn God's good creation into a source of idols, whose idolatry warps human cultures into systemic bearers of injustice and manifestations of broken relationships, and whose fearful and rapacious self-interest harms all that God lovingly made.

Back to Jeremiah 31, God shows particular interest in the disadvantaged according to verses 25–26, where weary laborers are promised refreshment. The fecundity and flourishing of people and animals in verses 27–28 are not inimical to the personal accountability in verses 29–30. For the new covenant in verses 31–34 makes people right with God and new on the inside, inaugurating the covenant community and creation's full healing. God appeals to creation in verses 35–37 as the reassuring basis of promised restoration: As surely as God lovingly made and sustains all things, so God promises to make the people new. Whatever the debated ecclesiological and eschatological implications, hope of new covenant restoration for the covenant people takes physical form in a remade, ever sacred city of Jerusalem.

Conclusion

Even this brief overview of Jeremiah 31 underscores that the new covenant context of new creation should be more prominent than Western soteriologies suggest. Many recent biblical debates and traditional dogmatic concerns over personal justification and sanctification still have a significant place in that framework. But then we can distinguish their initially prominent, even somewhat central, dogmatic place from their becoming so central that they exclude other soteriological concerns as rivals. The communal and cosmic dimensions of God's new covenant promises integrate Pauline theology and the rest of the New Testament more holistically. Attention to the new covenant further means reckoning with the Old Testament Scriptures, and thus Israel's identity and hope, more adequately.

One way of engaging the Majority World perspectives reflected elsewhere in this volume goes beyond framing them merely in terms of alternative concepts, differing contexts, and critique of or even opposition to dominant Western patterns. All of those elements may be prominent. Yet Majority World accounts often provide examples of the narrative theology for which Western intellectuals have been calling—but with rather modest results of their own. By contrast, other chapters in the present volume frequently provide narrative density to problematic Western readings of the Bible—both those that have been directly colonizing and others that have myopically produced unintended consequences. At minimum, Majority World theologies put problematic aspects of dominant traditions under a narrative searchlight that can also highlight alternative ways of engaging biblical soteriology. At maximum, Majority World theologies raise challenging questions about the very conceptual forms dominating Western traditions, given their systematic aspirations. And Majority World theologies help us to imagine more concretely what the fullness of salvation might look like in particular human lives, communities, and local contexts.[36]

The communal and cosmic dimensions of the biblical hope for a new creation underscore not only the context for salvation's personal dimensions and their complementary divine promises, but ultimately the fullness of Christian hope. They force us to reckon with the plight of so many people and other creatures in God's world—neither indulging in self-justifying escapism, nor despairing of change, nor arrogating to ourselves another gospel of human making. God has promised a new creation starting with a new humanity—and that renewal begins with my own heart. But it does not end there: God renews my heart not only to receive forgiveness, return loving worship, and bear grateful witness. This renewal also frees me from bondage—to my idolatrous self and other powers—so that I may learn to love all my neighbors and thereby participate in the healing of all creation.

Further Reading

Catechism of the Catholic Church. Washington, DC: U.S. Catholic Conference, 1997.

Demarest, Bruce. *The Cross and Salvation*. Foundations of Evangelical Theology. Wheaton, IL: Crossway, 1997.

Hill, Charles E., and Frank A. James III, eds. *The Glory of the Atonement: Biblical, Theological, and Practical Perspectives*. Downers Grove, IL: IVP, 2004.

Luther, Martin. *The Bondage of the Will*. Translated by J. I. Packer and O. R. Johnston. Old Tappan, NJ: Revell, 1957.

36. For a noteworthy North American example, see David H. Kelsey, *Imagining Redemption* (Louisville: Westminster John Knox, 2005).

McCormack, Bruce L., ed. *Justification in Perspective: Historical Developments and Contemporary Challenges*. Grand Rapids: Baker Academic, 2006.

McKnight, Scot. *The King Jesus Gospel: The Original Good News Revisited*. Grand Rapids: Zondervan, 2011.

Oden, Thomas C., ed. *The Justification Reader*. Grand Rapids: Eerdmans, 2002.

Stackhouse, John G., Jr., ed. *What Does It Mean to Be Saved? Broadening Evangelical Horizons of Salvation*. Grand Rapids: Baker Academic, 2002.

Stott, John R. W. *The Cross of Christ*. Downers Grove, IL: IVP, 1986.

Tidball, Derek, David Hilborn, and Justin Thacker, eds. *The Atonement Debate: Papers from the London Symposium on the Theology of Atonement*. Grand Rapids: Zondervan, 2008.

CHAPTER 2

Telling Our Stories: Salvation in the African Context

EMILY J. CHOGE KERAMA

ABSTRACT

Africa is ravaged by many ills—Ebola, HIV/AIDs, malaria, hunger, and extreme conditions of poverty—yet it is in Africa that the shift of gravity in the spread of the gospel has moved. This raises questions: What is the understanding of salvation in the African context? Why is there such a widespread response to the gospel? Is salvation seen to deal with these existential situations, or does it provide an escape from misfortune? What are the stories behind these two contrasting pictures of Africa? What are the stories behind the success, and what are those to the contrary? Are we able to imagine a future for salvation in the African context as it encounters powers and principalities? What type of salvation will grapple with these powers? This chapter seeks to bring out a holistic understanding of salvation in the African context. What does it mean to be saved in an African context?

I was born into an African Christian home. My father was a first-generation African Christian and my mother was a second-generation African Christian. The first missionaries had come to the coast of present-day Kenya in 1844. Dr. John Ludwig Krapf and Dr. John Rebmann landed at the Kenyan coast in 1844, and they did some work among the coastal people without much success. My maternal grandfather found himself at the Kenyan coast and was converted to Christianity by Church Missionary Society (CMS) missionaries in the early 1920s. When he went back to his homeland, he invited the CMS missionaries to come to his home area in Nandi in the western part of Kenya. My father was among the first to join the Christian school and church started in the 1940s through the influence of my grandfather. He did not go to school much since he was 20 years old at the time, but he became an evangelist and a teacher of the gospel from that time. He married my mother in the early 1950s, and I was born in November 1959, the third child of my parents.

I was a special child. I was born with a congenital defect that resulted in my left leg ending about 6 inches above the ground. I did have a right foot, though it was somewhat constricted. This was a challenge to my parents. I remember hearing my father exclaim, "What will become of this child?" In a traditional African setting, a child with disabilities was considered a misfortune, and her birth was interpreted as a curse or a punishment from God. However, because of his faith in Jesus Christ, my father believed in a good God, and he had the assurance that God would one day perform a miracle in my life. I remember he took me to some prayer rallies but nothing happened to my leg. Then he made the decision to take me to a school for girls that had been started by my grandfather. I was 6 years old at the time. The difficulty was that the boarding school started with standard five (grade five), and I needed to start from standard one. However, through the intervention of African hospitality, the matron and caretaker of the girls' boarding school offered to take me into her home and allowed me to attend the nearby mixed primary school until I could join the boarding school. I lived in her house for four years, and she treated me as one of her children until I was able to go to the boarding school. This changed my life because I was given the opportunity to go to school and also to hear the gospel.

When I was in high school (another school started by missionaries), doctors from the mission hospital in Kijabe came to my school. They examined my leg and recommended that the only way they could correct the problem was to do an amputation. I was 14 years old. The surgery was performed in December 1974, and I went back to school and walked with crutches for about six months. This did not interrupt my studies. Then I was fitted with a crude artificial leg—no foot, and just plain wood. I think I saw a character in *Pirates of the Caribbean* with one similar to it. It was not nice, but I was able to walk. Needless to say, I have had so many legs since then that I could display them in a museum to show the technological advancement of orthopedic work in Kenya.

The beauty of it all is that the helpless child who could not walk long distances was provided with basic education, and her father, who had had the courage to defy the African beliefs about curse and misfortune, was able to attend his daughter's graduation in 2004 in Pasadena, California, when he was 84 years old. He traveled all the way from Kenya, not knowing much English, so that he could witness the miracle of his daughter. He witnessed not only my graduation but also my running and completing a half marathon with a prosthetic leg. This, I think, is the power of salvation, the power of the gospel to transform the lives of people who are in dire situations like my own and bring them to be seated with princes. This is just amazing for me. I would like to see and hear stories that demonstrate the power of salvation to transform and confront the powers of physical deformity, mental malaise, and all other restrictions that have kept people enslaved in the continent of Africa and the world at large. So what is the existential situation for most people in Kenya? What are the powers and principalities from which they need deliverance and salvation?

Salvation in the African Context

In the area of systematic theology in Africa there has not been much reflection on the experience of salvation from an African perspective. The Catholic theologian Agbonkhianmeghe Orobator has written *Theology Brewed in an African Pot*, a work that uses most of the original sources in the African context such as stories, proverbs, myths, and prayers. Orobator writes:

> To the African religious worldview, stories and narratives are important elements of this worldview. Without pictures or paintings, narrative accounts were created and transmitted from one generation to the next, telling of the lives, times, and deeds of our forefathers and foremothers.[1]

The book is easy to read and since Orobator gives theology a narrative base it is also very interesting. The only drawback is that he does not

---

1. Agbonkhianmeghe E. Orobator, SJ, *Theology Brewed in an African Pot: An Introduction to Christian Doctrine from an African Perspective* (Nairobi: Paulines, 2008), 106.

include a chapter on salvation per se, but I look at what he says about Christology.[2] There is also a collection of essays, *Issues in African Christian Theology*, which covers a range of subjects in systematic theology, including salvation.[3] This collection is, like African Christian theology itself, a work in progress since, as the editors confess, "Christianity is being translated at high speed into modern African culture in almost every area except theology."[4] In the area of salvation, I would commend a classic from within the African context by Tokunboh Adeyemo, *Salvation in African Tradition*.[5] But there are not many recent works in the area of salvation. Nevertheless, with regard to deliverance and salvation from spirits and powers in the African context there is much lively activity.[6] I engage with these works with regard to salvation from the powers because this was an area that was neglected by European missionaries when they brought the gospel to Africa as confessed by a recent missionary:

> The issue of traditional African beliefs in the invisible world has been neglected in the past as if the gospel had nothing to say about it. . . . This was a serious failure in the effective discipling of new believers. Too often it left them with the impression that the gospel had nothing to say about the invisible world and the menace it represented—apart from the prohibition of all contact with it.[7]

An African theologian confirms the same:

> Unfortunately, many Western missionaries who came to Africa were unaware of the African worldview. Influenced by the philosophies of the age of Enlightenment these missionaries readily dismissed the spirit world as being nothing more than a figment of the imag-

2. The chapter bears the interesting and appropriate title "I Said 'God Had a Son,' But I Did Not Say 'He Had a Wife!'"

3. Samuel Ngewa, Mark Shaw, and Tite Tiénou, eds., *Issues in African Christian Theology* (Nairobi: EAPH, 1998).

4. Ngewa, Shaw, and Tiénou, eds., *Issues in African Christian Theology*, vii.

5. Tokunboh Adeyemo, *Salvation in African Tradition* (Nairobi: Evangel, 1979).

6. See Opoku Onyinah, *Pentecostal Exorcism: Witchcraft and Demonology in Ghana* (Dorchester: Deo, 2012); Kwabena Donkor, ed., *The Church, Culture and Spirits: Adventism in Africa* (Silver Springs, MD: Biblical Research Institute, 2011).

7. Keith Ferdinando, *The Battle Is God's: Reflecting on Spiritual Warfare for African Christians* (Bukuru, Plateau State, Nigeria: ACTS, 2012), 6.

ination. This left most African converts with no biblical teaching in relation to the spirit world, thereby leaving a huge gap in the faith of the African Christian.[8]

Another area where we see lively activity among scholars in Africa is Christology.[9] This shows that in the African context they take seriously the person who is the deliverer or the bearer of salvation. Most African authors show that Africans knew God but they did not know Jesus Christ. Orobator acknowledges that *"Jesu Kristi* has gained popularity on the lips of African Christians . . . songs have been written, liturgies composed, and humorous stories told about Jesus in local languages."[10] But he also notes that "Africans' quest for 'who Jesus is for us' cannot be satiated by simple formulas and models developed in foreign cultural contexts."[11] Therefore, there are many names, titles, models, and proposals for Jesus in the African context, "the ancestor, the diviner, the traditional healer, the chief, the guest, the life giver, family, friend, loved one, member, initiator, mediator . . . liberator, black messiah."[12] One of the most interesting titles recorded by Orobator is one coined by a prison inmate: "Jesus the bulldozer."[13] And now we look at an attempt to formulate a creed from the African context.

The Nicene Creed

There has not been much engagement with the Nicene Creed from an African perspective on a scholarly theological basis. I found one essay on the Apostles' Creed,[14] and it shows that Africans appropriate the creeds

8. Charles Salala, "The World of the Spirits: Basukuma Traditional Religion and Biblical Christianity," in *Issues in African Christian Theology*, ed. Samuel Ngewa, Mark Shaw, and Tite Tiénou (Nairobi: EAPH, 1998), 137.

9. Many books have been written on Christology in Africa, including the following: Kwame Bediako, *Jesus in Africa: The Christian Gospel in African History and Experience* (Akropong, Ghana: Regnum, 2000); J. N. K. Mugambi and Laurenti Magesa, eds., *Jesus in African Christianity: Experimentation and Diversity in African Christology* (Nairobi: Acton, 1998); Charles Nyamiti, *Christ Our Ancestor* (Harare: Mambo, 1986).

10. Orobator, *Theology Brewed in an African Pot*, 72.

11. Orobator, *Theology Brewed in an African Pot*, 72.

12. Orobator, *Theology Brewed in an African Pot*, 72–73.

13. Orobator, *Theology Brewed in an African Pot*, 76–77.

14. Eshetu Abate, "Confessing Christ in the Apostles' Creed," in *Issues in African*

as part of their worship. Since my father was an Anglican priest and I grew up most of my life in that church, I was exposed to the Nicene Creed in my mother tongue. The things I remember most in that prayer book were the prayer of Chrysostom and the Nicene Creed. When I read them in my mother tongue I had no idea that I was connecting with the historic faith of the church. Later, when I studied for my master's of divinity at a seminary in Nairobi, I realized that these were important people in the church and that the creed was historic, though there had been many challenges and controversies about the selection of its words.

What I can say about this creed and salvation is that it shows that we as the people of God are one people through the ages, and we should not be divided by schisms that have rocked the church across the years. The early church fathers formulated this creed so that they could be united in their profession of faith, and we can share in their struggles regarding what it meant to confess Christ as Savior in that Greek and Latin context. With regard to the Nicene Creed in the African context I have found one theological reflection. It is called the Maasai Creed, and the first two articles are as follows:

> We believe in the one High God, who out of love created the beautiful world and everything good in it. He created man and wanted man to be happy in the world. God loves the world and every nation and tribe on the earth. We have known this High God in darkness, and now we know him in the light. God promised in the book of his word, the Bible, that he would save the world and all the nations and tribes.

> We believe that God made good his promise by sending his Son, Jesus Christ, a man in the flesh, a Jew by tribe, born poor in a little village, who left his home and was always on safari doing good, curing people by the power of God, teaching about God and man, showing the meaning of religion is love. He was rejected by his people, tortured and nailed hands and feet to a cross, and died. He lay buried in the grave, but the hyenas did not touch him, and on the third day, he rose from the grave. He ascended to the skies. He is the Lord.[15]

Christian Theology, ed. Samuel Ngewa, Mark Shaw, and Tite Tiénou (Nairobi: EAPH, 1998), 175–85.

15. Vincent Donovan, *Christianity Rediscovered* (Maryknoll, NY: Orbis, 2003), 158.

This is the *Jesu Kristi* whom people have experienced as the Lord. And they turn to him in their troubles and in turn give him names such as "Jesus the bulldozer."

The Sad Stories of Africa's Existential Situation

In order to give Jesus the opportunity to "bulldoze" the problems of Africa, we need to examine some of the worrying trends in the continent. While there are stories of success like mine, it is important to hear other stories so that we can draft a story of salvation that will be able to speak to the true picture of the African situation.

Children with Disabilities

I was inspired to share my story in this chapter because on October 24, 2015, I went to visit a group of mothers whose children have spina bifida and hydrocephalus. October 25 is International Spina Bifida and Hydrocephalus Day, so these parents had come to spend the night together to encourage and support one another. I am chair of the advisory board of Bethany Kids, an organization that helps provide surgical interventions to children with these conditions in Africa, working mainly in Kenya. That day I needed to talk to these parents and children. Seeing them reminded me of my condition, and I could imagine where many of them lived: places with no running water, no paved roads, and very dire conditions of poverty. I shared my story with them. You could have heard a pin drop! They were so attentive and took in every word. At the end, they registered their appreciation for me sharing my life story with them. They were touched by the story and wondered how we could get a school for them so that their children could learn without stigma and discrimination. One of the challenges their children face is urinary and bowel incontinence.

I did not have an answer for them, but I told them that our organization had been trying to get money to expand the children's hospital in Kijabe so that it could take in more children and perform more surgeries. We had not even thought of schools for them. In Kenya, there are two such schools that have been started by the Salvation Army in Thika and Kisumu. Bethany Kids has been improving the restroom facilities in Thika. From this request, it is evident that there is a need for schools like this all over the country. How can the church preach the gospel of salvation to these parents and children with disabilities without addressing such pressing needs?

Growing Individualism

Conditions of children with disabilities are made worse by the growing individualism in the African culture. Africa in the past was known for its communal culture and worldview. One famous quote from a Kenyan philosopher, John Mbiti, sums it up this way: "I am because we are, and because we are therefore I am."[16] This strength of community is seen when people are in dire need and there is no cushioning from a social welfare system or social security system. Neighbors, friends, and relatives usually pay for funerals, doctor bills, and weddings. However, this system is slowly being strained, and we can see in urban areas a growing sense of individualism and a narrative of isolationism. We have these high walls that separate one house from another and people do not seem to know their neighbors anymore. In fact, there are cases where neighbors have been attacked and the closest neighbor does not even know it happened. Thieves and criminals have found this isolation easy to exploit. They come and confront homeowners at the gates of their yards and ask them to drive in. A passerby will not even notice what is happening, thinking that these are visitors accompanying the owner of the house. Now, the government is trying to introduce what is known as the *Nyumba Kumi* Initiative—that you have to know at least ten of your neighbors. Does the gospel of our salvation have something to say about this story of growing individualism? What should be done to change this narrative of despair?

Rampant Poverty

While there are growing individualism and violence in urban areas, rural areas have not been spared. Many move from rural areas into

16. John S. Mbiti, *African Religions and Philosophy* (London: Heinemann, 1969), 108.

urban areas and since they do not get jobs, they swell the population of informal settlements and slum areas. Nairobi is the home of one of the largest slum areas in the world. However, the population continues to grow in certain rural parts of the country (Kisii and Maragoli) and the land continues to dwindle. The land that supported a few people is forced to hold many more people, and the area where food crops used to grow is dwindling. Because of this pressure for land, we are hearing news stories about things that never used to happen in the country. Young people on the coast of Kenya are accusing their parents of witchcraft and hounding them out of their homes so that they can get the land from them. These elderly parents are forced to run to houses of refuge to escape from their children. In parts of the country where the pressure for land is acute, we have also heard of many accusations of witchcraft and gruesome executions without government intervention because the community does not know how to deal with these issues. Does the gospel have something to say to the poor and those who suffer because of false accusations? How does it help us understand the beliefs that misfortunes and deaths are caused by people?

The Double-Edged Sword of Young People

Africa is a young continent. Most of the population is under the age of 49, and this has great potential for the development and success of the country. Evangelists have said that the best time to introduce people to the gospel is when they are young. If you enter most of the churches in Kenya, the population of young people is really high. What can be done to reach and then keep these young people in the church? What is the gospel that will really get them to commit their lives to God so that they can avoid the ravages of HIV/AIDs, other sexually transmitted diseases, drugs, alcoholism, and crime due to unemployment? One-quarter of those who enter primary school manage to get into high school. The government has tried to introduce free primary education, but the retention is not very effective, and at the end of primary school many are not able to enter high school. So the question is, where do these young people go? The Kenyan media has exposed some ugly incidences of young people who have been found engaging in irresponsible sex, drugs, and alcohol abuse, which illustrates the temptations young people face. What is the gospel that will resonate with these young people? Is an African understanding of salvation able to confront the narratives of sexual immorality, drug abuse, and alcoholism?

The Prosperity Gospel

What is being preached in our churches? The health, wealth, and prosperity gospel continues to be taught. The leaders of the church demand that the parishioners "plant a seed" and say they will reap abundantly from God. What we see is the contrast of the wealth of the leaders of such churches and the poverty of the members who give everything they own to support these leaders. The leaders are very wealthy and they display all the trappings of such wealth: the latest model cars, expensive homes, and all sorts of luxury items. Most recently a renowned evangelist in Kenya came to my town. Traffic came to a standstill because of adherents who came from far and wide to give allegiance to this "Mighty Prophet of God." The cars that were part of the entourage were the latest and most expensive models and the display of wealth of this evangelist was absolutely immoral.

Political leaders are not exempt from this type of lifestyle. Once the population has elected them, they use their offices not to serve the electorate who put them there, but to accumulate wealth for themselves. The prophetic edge that religious leaders once provided to political leaders has been dulled because they are doing the same things, so the sheep are without a "shepherd" in the literal sense. How can the gospel of our salvation confront the challenges of wealth and prosperity?

The Threat of International Terrorism

In Kenya we not only face internal demons and powers; we also have to contend with the international terrorism that has wreaked havoc within our country. We have faced this since 1998, when the U.S. embassy was bombed, causing suffering and heartache in many lives. In 2013, one of the most gruesome attacks was the hostage-taking at the West Gate Mall in Nairobi where several people died. The most recent attack was the taking of Garissa University, where we saw innocent young university students being butchered. Kenya is a country of religious pluralism although the Christian population is the large majority. Christians and Muslims have lived in harmonious relationships in the past, but these attacks have brought suspicion and frustration as people of different faiths have attempted to relate to one another. What is the gospel of our salvation that will facilitate dialogue and not fuel violence in our country? How will we relate to people of other faiths, especially when they are hostile to us?

Reversing the Stories of Sadness: Factors Affecting Africa's Receptivity to the Gospel

Having listened to some of the sad stories and conditions within the African continent, we can turn now to the story behind Africa's receptivity to the gospel.

Dependence on God

Africans are notoriously religious. This is evident from the number of churches spread throughout Africa's villages and cities. Even in the primal religions of Africa, every community had a name for God, and when the Bible was translated into these languages the name for God was retained. Africa theologian Kwame Bediako used to say that the missionaries did not bring God to Africa, but God brought the missionaries to Africa. Orobator notes,

> Anyone coming to Africa for the first time cannot but notice the strong and profound sense of the divine that pervades the ordinary lives of many Africans. Often it has been misrepresented as superstition and fatalism. The awareness of the divine is so strong that you can see, hear, feel, and touch it in the way people talk, behave, even worship, sing and dance.[17]

No wonder there was a response to the gospel that has really been so overwhelming that Christianity has become a non-Western religion. Some of the beliefs and the practices in the Old Testament resonate

17. Orobator, *Theology Brewed in an African Pot*, 128.

with those of the African culture. For example, when there was misfortune or they needed to appear before God, the people of the Old Testament offered sacrifices of animals without blemish. O'Donovan mentions four or five categories of sacrifice in traditional practice, including propitiatory, substitutionary, mediatory, communion, and gift sacrifice.[18] There was opportunity for individual and also communal repentance when there had been a misfortune. This resonates in an African context. Sin and salvation are not just personal; they have a communal element. When we break relations with one another we need to mend those relationships. This means that the corporate aspect of sin and salvation touching the individual is well understood in the African context.

Dependence on Each Other: The Church as the Extended Family of God

The communal nature of African culture is also one that attracts Africans to the gospel. Salvation is not just individual; it also means bringing one into the community of faith that is known as the church. This relational aspect of the gospel means that people are not alone; they belong, as it were, to an "extended family." This is one of the strongest aspects of Christianity that has propelled the spread of the gospel in Africa. Now that the family system has broken up due to modernization and urbanization, the place that most people find a sense of belonging is the church. Whenever there are functions like funerals, weddings, and other social gatherings, what brings people together is the family of the church. Nowhere is this more strongly expressed than in the churches of the diaspora. Africans faced with the prospect of alienation and disorientation in a new culture that is strange and alien in every way find solace and comfort in the newly established churches among indigenous populations in various parts of the world. Even if members were not strong churchgoers in their home countries, they will go to these church gatherings in order to find support. There they find connection with their roots and culture, and with this, they are able to meet the needs of not only those who have come to the new country, but also to extend a hand to those back at home.

18. Wilbur O'Donovan, *Biblical Christianity in African Perspective* (Carlisle, UK: Paternoster, 1996), 104.

When my husband and I came for my sabbatical to Atlanta and my mother-in-law passed away in Kenya, we went to the Kenya American Community Church in Marietta and shared our situation. I know and I applaud the African sense of community, but even so the response amazed me. At the end of the service, the pastor called us to the front of the church and told the congregation about our situation—the fact that we had lost our mother and we needed to go back home to bury her. As always this was unexpected, and we did not have the finances, so he told them to come forward and greet us. As the church members came forward, they gave something small to help us return home to Kenya. Within about twenty minutes, the people of God had raised $1,300 for us, and this was enough in addition to what we already had to take us back home. We were so grateful for this family of God who supported us during this time of need. A strong sense of community is carried over into the new places where Africans go and settle.

Celebration and Music

Another conduit that brought African people to listen to the gospel is music and celebration within Christian worship. Africans celebrate with music and dance in all kinds of activities: birth, initiation, marriage, and death. One has to be sent home in style. The fact that the newfound faith had music in its worship enhanced this element of African culture. The traditional hymnbook and the songs in it cannot be recognized when they are sung in indigenous languages. The words have been translated into the languages, but they now have four or five tunes, depending on the community in which they are sung. One of the songs that I know, "My Hope Is Built on Nothing Less," has five or more tunes. In Kiswahili it has been translated as "Cha Kutumaini Sina." This shows that Kenyans have received these songs and made them their very own. Songs bring out the emotions and the feelings that cannot be expressed in any other way. In traditional African gatherings, some songs require a call and response so that all the people participate in the service. The African Mass within the Catholic Church that incorporates singing and the dancing is really an occasion to witness. One theologian notes:

In Africa, worship is never complete without singing and dancing, otherwise that worship would be considered cold and dead. Every aspect of the liturgical celebration is accompanied by joyful, vocal, and bodily expressions. . . . A shared belief of many Africans is that anything that is good must necessarily overflow. As one African proverb says, a good pot of okra sauce cannot be confined to the cooking pot with a lid. It must bubble up and overflow.[19]

The Translation of the Scriptures into African Languages

One thing that has allowed the gospel to make inroads into the African continent is the translation of the Scriptures into African languages. It has preserved the languages and the cultures of the people for whom it has been translated. These translations have been a resource for young people who have gone away to school, and therefore would not have been able to know their languages. Thus, the work of Bible Societies in translating the Bible into African languages is invaluable.[20] Students in the universities can study these African languages, and usually the literature that is most available for study is the Bible. One of the first translations was the Nandi Bible (1938). After twenty years another translation, the Kalenjin Bible, incorporated about ten dialects. A recent translation is the new Nandi Bible. Older people had complained that the combined translation did not quite capture the essence of the language as the original one had.

Provision of a Holistic Salvation

When missionaries came to Africa they did not divide the temporal and the sacred. They did not just emphasize preaching the gospel and saving souls. At the time the debate about whether the focus should be on the social justice or evangelism was yet to emerge. Evangelism came at the same time as the establishment of mission schools, hospitals, and farming stations. If that had been maintained, the scenario

19. O'Donovan, *Biblical Christianity*, 135.
20. See also Bediako, "Understanding African Theology," 65.

51

would have been different in Africa. Missionaries knew that they had to minister to the whole person, but today that holistic aspect is not seen. In fact, those who are supposed to minister to people who come to church exploit them instead. However, holistic ministry is something that originally helped Africans be receptive to the gospel.

Less Emphasized Stories of Salvation

I use the pilgrim motif that runs throughout the Scriptures, particularly in the book of Hebrews, as the metaphor that brings together the neglected aspects of salvation with the stories of success in the African context.

The Pilgrim Motif in Scripture

The people of God are enjoined to live as pilgrims and exiles in a foreign land. One who exemplifies this life is the father of faith, Abraham. Even in the Promised Land, he still lived in tents because he was looking for a "city with foundations" whose maker and founder was God (Heb. 11:10). The people of Israel were told to embody this attitude even as they showed hospitality to those who were aliens in their land. They needed to remember that they had been aliens and strangers in the land of Egypt and so they were to be kind to strangers. The stories and wise sayings of Africa have much to say about traveling and being a stranger, which exposes one to danger but at the same time opens one to the hospitality and generosity of hosts. One such saying is *safari ni taabu* (travel and you will encounter many challenges) but another one counters this: *safari uone mengi* (travel and you will see much). One proverb from Ghana notes: "One who has not traveled thinks that the mother's cooking is the best." All these sayings and proverbs give guidance, so that we know that we are not self-sufficient in our journey of salvation. Rather, we need God, we need one another, and we need courage so that we can overcome the challenges that we meet on the way.

So, as we look at aspects of salvation that we should pay attention to in the African context, the pilgrim motif helps to tie all these things together. The first aspect of this is that we need to emphasize the identity of Christ as the pilgrim par excellence, who for the joy that was set before him endured the cross (Heb. 12:2–3). Therefore, the church in Africa needs to proclaim the lordship of Jesus Christ over powers and principalities.

This Christ that is proclaimed in the book of Hebrews is higher than the angels, than Moses, and than the sacrificial system of the Old Testament. This means that Jesus Christ can deal with the world of powers and principalities that have been predominant in the African worldview. One author notes:

> The issue of traditional African beliefs in the world has been neglected in the past as if the gospel had nothing to say about it. Part of the reason for this is that in the nineteenth and twentieth centuries the good news of Jesus Christ was brought to Africa largely by western missionaries. In many cases their worldview no longer had much place for the notion of sorcerers and very little place for spirits either, despite abundant biblical testimony to their existence. Consequently, they had given little—if any—thought to these matters even though they are of central importance in the African conceptions of reality. They had no biblical responses to the pressing questions of their new converts, because they never had to face those questions in their own experience . . . failure to address the issue of witches and spirits from a solidly Christian perspective left a whole area of life unredeemed—excluded from the saving power of the gospel, so that new believers felt obliged to use the remedies they had trusted in before they knew Christ.[21]

The need for the proclamation of Christ over these powers is very evident in that recently there have been accusations of witchcraft against women, children, and older people. With the rapid social and economic changes and the breakdown of the family structure, it has been notable that even children have accused their parents of witchcraft so that they can inherit their lands. As I mentioned previously, this has been seen in the coastal part of Kenya. This aspect of the lordship of Christ cannot be overemphasized, as these practices are designed mainly to alleviate the sufferings of human beings harassed by spirits. Though Africans believe in a supreme being, they also have

21. Ferdinando, *The Battle Is God's*, 6–7.

myths to show that God has withdrawn from human affairs, so that people are constantly harassed by and threatened by all sorts of enemies, including spirits and sorcerers. Keith Ferdinando writes,

> They must defend themselves, or seek to appease or destroy their attackers. But the Biblical worldview while recognizing the existence of spirits and sorcerers as well as the harm they do to human beings, understands them in the context of a cosmos ruled by a sovereign God who is intimately involved in his creation and who is good and constantly accessible to his own people.[22]

But the proclamation of Christ over the powers should not be restricted to mystical powers or unseen powers; it also needs to confront political power that allows rampant corruption, nepotism, and various forms of social injustice. In the past the church has played a role in being the voice of the voiceless even as the powers of politics suppressed their voices. This was the case from the 1970s to the early 1990s in Kenya. There were leaders of great repute in the church like Bishop Henry Okullu, Bishop Alexander Muge, and Bishop David Gitari. In South Africa, the church played a role in bringing liberation from the apartheid system. It is not clear where these voices have gone or whether there are new leaders who can take the place of these fearless leaders and their prophetic proclamation.

The Church That Transcends Ethnic and National Barriers

Another aspect that needs to be emphasized in the proclamation of the gospel of salvation in the African context is the fact that the people of God transcend all national and ethnic barriers. This is also a strand that comes from the pilgrim motif. There are many "one another" exhortations in the book of Hebrews that show that Christians are not individualistic, lone-ranger people. The communal element is well emphasized, and it finds resonance within the African setting. However, what has worked against this is that when the gospel was brought into the African environment, various denominational bodies came to different parts of the country. For example, in Kenya, the Methodist

---

22. Ferdinando, *The Battle Is God's*, 45–46.

Church is predominant in the eastern part of the country, the Presbyterian Church is foremost in central Kenya, and the Anglican Church is in parts of western Kenya. This means that the church is divided according to various tribal and ethnic communities. It has meant that sometimes the church has been tied to political interests rather than being loyal to brothers and sisters of another community and Jesus Christ. In 2007 and 2008, there were tribal clashes in Kenya, and one church building was burned. This should have caused outrage, but instead one could see that loyalties to ethnic communities were stronger than loyalty to the body of Jesus Christ. Focusing on interdependence will counteract the negative narratives of individualism, the neglect of vulnerable children and youth, and even care for the stranger in the face of terrorist activities.

Hospitality as a Mark of Pilgrims

One of the strong aspects of African culture that needs to be incorporated into the church is hospitality. This was built into the African system from time immemorial. Africa supported the family of Jacob in Egypt, and they were hosted there until Israel became a great nation (Gen. 46:3; 47:13; Exod. 1:5–7). Jesus in his early years was hosted in Africa when his parents had to escape the wrath of the evil King Herod (Matt. 2:13–15). The word *mgeni* for "stranger" and "guest" in Africa is the same word. Thus, strangers are to be welcomed as guests. But in recent years some people have noted that such hospitality has become a "museum" relic. There have been incidences of xenophobic attacks in various parts of the continent, such as those recently in South Africa. One wonders how the practice of hospitality can be recovered. Since this is a central virtue in Scripture right from the beginning, we have to restore this as a key component in the African church. There are many resources within the African setting that give us guidance on how we can practice hospitality in the midst of modern challenges. One such saying is "mgeni siku ya kwanza, siku ya pili mpe Jembe" (a guest is only a guest for two days; on the third day give him a hoe). The wisdom in this saying is that the efforts of the stranger and the host are combined to make provision for the community. It is not just one-sided. All work together for the good of the community. It means that even as Christians live in their communities, they will make a difference like the early Christians made. A second-century Christian writer comments on the effectiveness of such a stance: "they lived in their homeland as a foreign land and in their foreign land as their homeland."[23]

Concrete Stories of Holistic Salvation That Africa Needs

The Ministry of Bethany Kids

I began this chapter with my story of the power of the gospel and how it transformed my father to transcend the prejudices and the fear of misfortune and curses until I experienced that power and became an agent of transformation. I have also shared the story of children with disabilities who are helped by Bethany Kids. This is a ministry that started in a mission hospital. A missionary doctor, Dr. Richard Bransford, was inspired to start this ministry because his daughter Bethany was born with spina bifida. The hospital treating these children at Kijabe was very small. Dr. Bransford started training surgeons from all over Africa so that they could also help such children. The work has now expanded to Sierra Leone, Uganda, and Madagascar. Mobile clinics doing follow-up work go to various parts of Kenya visiting children and giving them help. In these places, they are able to identify new cases and refer them to Kijabe. It is indeed a ministry that is giving hope to Africa's children. This is part of the healing ministry that Jesus gave his disciples to do, and this aspect of salvation is vital for the church in Africa.

The Ministry of the Africa Christian Initiation Program (ACIP)

The Africa Christian Initiation Program (ACIP) is a ministry that some university professors from Moi University started in 2004 to respond to the needs of young people in the community. I mentioned earlier the rich resource of youth in Africa. In traditional Africa, rites of passage were very important in the transition from one stage of life to another. With the coming of the gospel, however, most of these rites, especially

---

23. *The Epistle to Diognetus* 5.5.

female circumcision, were considered barbaric and condemned. No effort was made to learn what roles and functions these practices played in the community. One thing such rituals did was transmit values and teachings. Because of the rapid changes to which the community has been subjected, it was found that many young people were not prepared to face life's challenges. They were turning to drugs and alcohol, and many were at risk of being infected with HIV/AIDS. Adolescence is a crucial stage in the development of a person, and Africans have recognized this, which is why they had rites of passage.

A group of ladies came together and put together a program. They decided they would invite young people and their parents. The boys would be offered circumcision, and they would be operated on by a doctor. They rented a boarding school facility because this was done when students were on school holidays. The boys healed for a week while being taught the lessons of what it means to be a man as well as being mentored by model young and older people. The following week the girls were invited and they joined the boys in class. They were taught important things like health, how to take care of their bodies, appreciation for their physical bodies, how to avoid peer pressure related to drugs and alcohol, time management, and other important information for this stage of their life. The training manual that came out of this is entitled *My Life Starting Now: Knowledge and Skills for Young Adolescents* by Lucy Y. Steinitz and Eunice Karanja Kamaara. We have been doing this for the past ten years, and we are soon going to launch a study to evaluate how effective this program has been in transforming the lives of young people. This is part of the holistic salvation that Africa needs. It recognizes the values of the practices and traditions of African people and incorporates them into the modern system for the good of the people of God.

Conclusion

The gospel has the power to transform lives; as Paul notes in Romans 1:16, "it is the power of God for the salvation of everyone who believes; first for the Jew, then for the Gentile." I have highlighted such examples and I believe there are many more instances in the whole of the continent. However, there are powers in the African continent that, if not confronted and tamed for the good of the gospel, will be harmful and detrimental to the social, physical, spiritual, and economic welfare of the people of God. Among such powers are the traditions and practices that exclude those with disabilities, women, and children. There are great stories in this continent of how these powers and principalities have been overcome, and these stories need to be heard and celebrated. Armed with the resources of the pilgrim motif from the Bible and enriched by the practices of hospitality, we will be able to hear stories such as those of Bethany Kids, who have transcended the odds for those with disabilities. There are stories of how practices have been transformed into avenues of blessing rather than a curse for Africa's children. Such is the story of ACIP, which is transforming and giving hope, salvation, and life in abundance to Africa's children.

Further Reading

Donkor, Kwabena, ed. *The Church Culture and Spirits: Adventism in Africa*. Silver Spring, MD: Institute of Biblical Research, 2011.

Elolia, Samuel K. *Religion, Conflict and Democracy in Modern Africa: The Role of Civil Society in Political Engagement*. Eugene, OR: Wipf & Stock, 2012.

Ferdinando, Keith. *The Battle Is God's: Reflecting on Spiritual Warfare for African Believers*. Bukuru, Plateau State, Nigeria: ACTS, 2012.

Katongole, Emmanuel M. *A Future for Africa: Critical Essays in Christian Social Imagination*. Scranton, PA: University of Scranton Press, 2005.

Ngewa, Samuel, Mark Shaw, and Tite Tiénou, eds. *Issues in African Christian Theology*. Nairobi: East Africa Educational Publishers, 1998.

O'Donovan, Wilbur. *Biblical Christianity in African Perspective*. Carlisle, UK: Paternoster, 1996.

Onyinah, Opoku. *Pentecostal Exorcism: Witchcraft and Demonology in Ghana*. Dorset, UK: Deo, 2012.

Orobator, Agbonkhianmeghe E. *Theology Brewed in an African Pot: An Introduction to Christian Doctrine from an African Perspective*. Nairobi: Paulines, 2008.

CHAPTER 3

Luke 4:18–19 and Salvation: Marginalization of Women in the Pentecostal Church in Botswana

ROSINAH MMANNANA GABAITSE

ABSTRACT

Luke 4:18–19 has always been interpreted as Jesus's roadmap. In the Pentecostal context in Botswana, the text is taken seriously as it announces Jesus's mission, which was later to become the program of the church through the Holy Spirit. The interpretation of this text, however, has always been highly spiritualized, emphasizing spiritual blindness, spiritual poverty, and spiritual oppression and release with little or no focus on sociopolitical and physical blindness, poverty, and oppression. Spiritualizing texts is one of the characteristics of Pentecostal biblical interpretation. To a large extent this influences the way Pentecostals deal with the marginalization of women in its various manifestations. Oftentimes, the marginalization of women is minimized, ignored, or highly spiritualized. While the marginalization of women is ignored, women in Botswana and Africa in general experience dual patriarchies from indigenous cultures and the Pentecostal Church. Since patriarchy is oppressive, women are denied the right to experience the joy of holistic salvation on earth. In this chapter I seek to demonstrate that in Luke 4:18–19 Jesus was not only offering to release people from spiritual blindness, poverty, and oppression. He also offered people physical and social release from any system of oppression such as patriarchy. This chapter begins by offering a brief overview of Luke 4:18–19 in order to establish that salvation is holistic. I move on to discuss how patriarchy within Pentecostal hermeneutics and theology together with the patriarchy from indigenous cultures deny Pentecostal women the experience of holistic salvation.[1] I will further demonstrate that Luke 4:18–19 affirms that complete salvation is available and possible in the social world.

As a matter of interpretation and agenda, some interpreters of Luke 4:18–19 spiritualize the poor, the blind, and the oppressed and ignore the social aspect of the text, while others give the text both spiritual and social dimensions. A Pentecostal reading emphasizes spiritual aspects of salvation much more than the physical and the social.[2] This kind of interpretation emphasizes that salvation is eschatological and mainly concerned with the soul in preparation for the afterlife. It ignores and minimizes the experiences of social, economic, political, and cultural suffering in patriarchal societies like Botswana where the marginalization of women is very real.[3] Spiritualizing texts is problematic because the equality of men and women, which was inaugurated by Pentecost in Acts 2 and is alluded to in texts such as Galatians 3:28, is oftentimes spiritualized as well. When Marea Mpuse and I carried out research in 2011–12 among Pentecostal churches in Botswana on how they interpret Luke-Acts in general, some respondents stated that

1. Setswana (the culture of Botswana) is highly patriarchal, and therefore Setswana attitudes about women are reinscribed within Pentecostal hermeneutics. Further, Botswana in general is highly patriarchal. Patriarchy is found everywhere, in state policies, in laws, and in the seating arrangements for men and women during weddings and funerals.

2. When it comes to the marginalization of women, gender relations, gender inequality, and the position of women in the home, Pentecostals gravitate toward the spiritual. But when it comes to material things such as the acquisition of wealth and prosperity theology, Pentecostals emphasize that these must be enjoyed in the social world and in the present. This demonstrates that Pentecostals apply their hermeneutic selectively.

3. In this chapter, marginalization of women refers to any action, practice, teaching, or belief that disadvantages women and places them in an inferior status as compared to men. This may include but is not limited to stigmatizing women's leadership, using language of domination during biblical interpretation, pushing the ministry of women to the margins, committing violence against women, subordinating women to the authority of men through language and hermeneutic, and making women invisible in roles they play in church by minimizing their status as the weaker vessel. The worst form of marginalizing women is violence against women in any shape or form, be it physical, financial, or emotional.

Pentecost makes men and women equal on a spiritual level, women can preach both in the church and crusades, they can lead praise and worship, they preach on Sunday. But the Holy Spirit does not make men equal to women on a day to day basis. This means that in terms of authority, men have the authority over women at home and even in the church.[4]

Although writing within the Western context, Amos Yong argued that Pentecost, an event inaugurated by the Holy Spirit, should effect the empowerment of human beings in "concrete and political ways." That effect has not been translated into equalizing the status between men and women in Pentecostal churches. Yong argued that Pentecost should effect equality in male-female relations in home, church, and society.[5] However, through the selectiveness of the Pentecostal hermeneutic the Holy Spirit seems to give women recognition only in "things spiritual and ecclesial" while they are still located "in spheres under male domination."[6]

The Pentecostal Church in Botswana and surrounding countries such as Zimbabwe and South Africa teaches and enforces male supremacy with legislative force.[7] Spiritualizing texts and social problems

4. The analysis of this research can be found in Rosinah Mmannana Gabaitse, "Towards an African Pentecostal Feminist Biblical Hermeneutic of Liberation: A Case Study of Interpreting Luke-Acts with Botswana Women" (PhD thesis, University of KwaZulu-Natal, Pietermaritzburg, 2013).

5. Amos Yong, *The Spirit Poured Out on All Flesh: Pentecostalism and the Possibility of Global Theology* (Grand Rapids: Baker Academic, 2005), 45.

6. Yong, *The Spirit Poured Out on All Flesh*, 40.

7. It must be noted here that although African cultures and Pentecostal churches are patriarchal, not all women in Africa are abused and helpless and not all Pentecostal men in Africa are abusers just because the culture privileges the male over the female. That the Pentecostal churches preach the supremacy of a male and that all men reap the patriarchal dividends and benefits cannot be disputed. The literature cited below demonstrates that texts such as Ephesians 5 are interpreted literally to support male prestige and to call women to submission. In some churches, although the male is given a privileged position supported by the above texts, husbands are encouraged to also love their wives into submission, that is, husbands are encouraged to love their wives so that the wives will not have a problem submitting to their authority, thus demonstrating a softer, gentler side of patriarchy. Further, even though Pentecostal churches are patriarchal, they emphasize the belief that when a person is born again, his old being is transformed and he becomes "a new creation and a new man." The expectation from the Pentecostal Church is that the person will stop

has resulted in Pentecostal women experiencing marginalization that ranges from bad financial decisions by husbands that impact wives to different kinds of violence.[8] Yet, if Luke 4:18–19 can be read and interpreted to emphasize and elevate not only spiritual salvation but physical, sociopolitical, and economic salvation, the marginalization, exclusion, and subjugation of women could be critiqued easily. Using Luke 4:18–19 to critique the marginalization of women should not be a challenge to Pentecostals because Luke-Acts is prescriptive and normative for the development of most Pentecostal theologies. Furthermore, Luke-Acts in general emphasizes multidimensional salvation, justice, and egalitarian existence.[9] Therefore, Luke-Acts as a whole and Luke 4:18–19 in particular can provide the Pentecostal Church with frameworks that denounce the marginalization of women in its various manifestations. Because of its emphasis on the work of the Holy Spirit in directing Pentecostals' existence, the Pentecostal Church should be

---

drinking alcohol, using bad language, and having multiple sex partners. Stopping these can make a Pentecostal husband treat his wife better than husbands who are not "born again." However, the darker and harder side of patriarchy is that some men are more forceful with their wives as I demonstrate below because of the language of domination that characterizes the Pentecostal hermeneutic. Further, patriarchy becomes destructive when women are told by the people in authority (clergy) to stay in life-denying situations through the use of a few texts that seem to advance male supremacy. Interpretation has consequences. When both men and women are taught daily that a man is superior, that teaching can translate into how men and women live their lives in the home and church.

8. It is ironic that the Pentecostal Church, which claims to follow the experience of Pentecost as outlined in Acts 2, fails to live up to its name in terms of the gender injustice that it propagates. Elsewhere I have argued that Pentecostals "not only have a dependence on the Holy Spirit and trace this dependence back to the original Pentecost experience as recorded in Luke-Acts, they place the role of the Holy Spirit at the center of their hermeneutic. . . . The liberating power of the Holy Spirit is not just on issues of theology but the Holy Spirit is also experienced by men and women as a power that liberates. This goes to say that once the Holy Spirit is placed at the center of Pentecostal hermeneutic, the hermeneutic must necessarily be liberatory because the Holy Spirit is inherently liberatory. However, in spite of this, the liberatory role of the Holy Spirit is not necessarily emphasized and recognized, especially when it comes to elevating the status of women. This is the reality of Pentecostal frames of reading that need to be engaged." Gabaitse, "Towards an African Pentecostal Feminist Biblical Hermeneutic of Liberation," 6–7.

9. Ben Witherington III, *Women and the Genesis of Christianity* (Cambridge: Cambridge University Press, 1990); L. Swindler, *Biblical Affirmations of Women* (Philadelphia: Westminster, 1979).

inherently egalitarian. But it is not, as I demonstrate in the sections that follow.[10]

Salvation in Luke-Acts

Lukan scholars agree that the message of salvation is central to Luke-Acts.[11] Although Luke 4:18–19 does not use the usual "salvation" terminology such as *sōtēr* (savior), *sōtēria* and *sōtērion* (salvation), and *sōzō* (to save), what it describes and what Jesus sets out to do are acts that demonstrate salvation. David Bosch describes Luke's understanding of salvation as the "total transformation of human life, forgiveness of sin, healing infirmities and release from any kind of bondage." Further, salvation is the reversal of the consequences of sin committed against God and human beings.[12] Similarly, Mark Powell views salvation in Luke-Acts as "participation in the reign of God."[13] He further argues that salvation has both present and future dimensions so that it means "living life, even now as God intends it to be lived."[14] However, he argues that Luke puts more emphasis on salvation as a possibility in the present through his repeated use of the term "today." Further, according to Powell, Luke does not differentiate between what we might classify as "physical, spiritual and social aspects of salvation . . . God is concerned with all aspects of human life and relationships, and so,

10. The Holy Spirit should be able to subvert cultures of domination, including frames of reading and interpreting the Bible that subordinate women. But it is not happening in the Pentecostal Church in Botswana because of the belief that the authority of the man is ordained by God and therefore, there is nothing wrong with using the Bible to support the subordination of women to men. However, I strongly argue that the subordination of women is inconsistent with the work of the Holy Spirit, who levels inequalities between people as demonstrated throughout Luke-Acts. For example, it was through the Holy Spirit that Gentile-Jewish tensions were resolved. Acts 15:28 is especially profound, where Peter says, "It has seemed good to the Holy Spirit and to us to impose on you no further burden than these essentials." It was through the Holy Spirit that Mary, a woman, became a vessel for God's salvation in Luke 2.

11. J. B. Green, *The Gospel of Luke*, New International Commentary on the New Testament (Grand Rapids: Eerdmans, 1997).

12. D. Bosch, *Transforming Mission: Paradigm Shifts in Theology of Mission* (Maryknoll, NY: Orbis, 1991), 107, 117.

13. M. A. Powell, "Salvation in Luke-Acts," *Word and World* 12, no. 1 (1992): 5.

14. Powell, "Salvation in Luke-Acts," 6.

salvation may involve the putting right of any aspect that is not as it should be."[15] In this chapter, I adopt Powell's and Bosch's definitions of salvation as "participation in the reign of God" and "total transformation of human life and living life as God had intended." The poverty, blindness, and oppression mentioned in Luke 4:18–19 refer not just to spiritual aspects of being human. They involve all aspects of being human, including the social, political, and economic. John Nolland cautions that the poor in Luke 4:18–19 should not be spiritualized because Jesus was "deeply concerned with the literal, physical needs of men" as much as he was with their spiritual needs.[16] This kind of interpretation is helpful as it can serve as a yardstick for communities of faith to engage with the actual experiences of the marginalization of women in practical ways.

Luke 4:18–19: Jesus Sets the Captives Free

Luke 4:18–19 presents Jesus reading and quoting from Isaiah 61:1–2. Jesus proclaims that "the Spirit of the Lord is on me, because he has anointed me to proclaim good news to the poor. He has sent me to proclaim freedom for the prisoners and recovery of sight for the blind, to release the oppressed, to proclaim the year of the Lord's favor." Jesus uttered these words on the Sabbath, in a synagogue in Nazareth, his hometown. Therefore, he was aware of the challenges his listeners faced. Jesus came to perform five tasks: to proclaim good news to the poor, to proclaim freedom for the prisoners, to proclaim recovery of sight for the blind, to release the oppressed, and to proclaim the year of the Lord.

Throughout the Gospel of Luke, Jesus's claims in Luke 4:18–19 are accompanied by tangible acts of healing the blind and the sick, feeding the poor by multiplying loaves and fish, and forgiving sins. Jesus heals those who are spiritually blind (2:30; 7:39; 18:10) and physically blind (7:21; 18:35–43). Jesus provides for the economically poor (11:41; 12:33; 14:13; 18:22). People are healed from debilitating illness that has held them captive (6:9; 8:48), the lame walk (7:22), and the lepers are

---

15. Powell, "Salvation in Luke-Acts," 8.

16. J. Nolland, *Luke 1–9:20*, Word Biblical Commentary (Waco, TX: Word, 1989), 197.

cleansed (17:19). Jesus delivers people who are possessed or held captive by demons (4:35). All these demonstrate salvation in tangible ways. Throughout his mission, setting the captives and the oppressed free was at the center of his ministry. He tells people, "Go and tell John what you have seen and heard: the blind receive their sight, the lame walk, lepers are cleansed and the deaf hear, the dead are raised up, the poor have good news preached to them" (7:22).

Perhaps the oppression in Luke 4:19 refers to sociopolitical captivity. Jesus's listeners appreciated these words, considering that the Jews were under Roman rule at the time. Although the Jews exercised some freedom, it was limited because of the system of governance. Jesus did not fully explain the oppression he was referring to but we can infer that Jesus was aware that there were systems and circumstances that oppressed people and denied them life in abundance. He was aware that there were cultures and economic and sociopolitical systems that held people captive. After stating his intentions he executed his tasks by delivering people who were possessed by demons (4:31) and debilitated by sickness (4:39). Blindness, poverty, and oppression undeniably make human life and human existence uncomfortable and undesirable. Whichever way one interprets this text, it is clear that there are conditions and systems that bind people and keep them under oppression. These are conditions in which people find themselves that require salvation. Jesus was, therefore, intentional in dismantling these systems of oppression through providing tangible solutions to people inhabiting those systems. He was intentional about challenging oppression in its various manifestations, be it illness or poverty or evil spirits.

Further, Jesus stated that he had come to proclaim the year of the Lord's favor. He made reference to the Jubilee year mentioned in Leviticus 25, which was celebrated every fiftieth year. The Jubilee year required agricultural work to stop for the land to rest. The Israelites knew that the "the land shall not be sold in perpetuity, for the land is mine, with me you are but aliens and tenants" (v. 23). According to this text, the land belonged to God and it had to be distributed, perhaps equally to all Israelites so as to alleviate poverty and to give dignity to those who were landless. In the Jubilee year, debts were cancelled and slaves and servants were released and set free. To the first-century Palestinian, Jesus's words that he was under anointing to proclaim the year of the Lord were very profound given that the majority of the people were in debt and under a heavy tax burden imposed by the Romans.[17] They would immediately think of the economic relief the Jubilee year brought because of debt cancellation. They would experience an uplift in social status and dignity because of land redistribution and slaves would celebrate real freedom because they were released. The year of Jubilee, therefore, was the year of justice and jubilation, the year that reminded the Israelites about equality, dignity, and care of those less privileged. It was a year that eliminated economic and social inequities among the Israelites, when all people owned land and all were free.

Finally, in Luke 4:21 Jesus stresses that the salvation that he has described in verses 18 and 19 will be experienced *today*. His use of the adverb "today" indicates that salvation has a present dimension as much as it has a future dimension.[18] Further, Luke's Jesus demonstrated that salvation was meant for all people; it was physical, present, eschatological, spiritual, and social as well. Luke's Jesus was interested in the welfare of women. He empowered them; hence some women subsidized his ministry (8:1–3). Luke's Jesus was also interested in Gentiles and those who occupied a lower status and were underprivileged during the first century.[19]

Patriarchy in the Pentecostal Church and African Cultures

That Pentecostalism provides greater freedom for women cannot be denied.[20] Cheryl Johns writes, "In many ways Pentecostalism is not a culture that overtly suppresses women's abilities and gifts. From the early days of

17. R. Horsley, *A People's History of Christianity-Christian Origins* (Minneapolis: Fortress, 2010).

18. F. P. Viljoen, "Luke, the Gospel of the Saviour of the World," *Nederduits Gereformeerde Teologiese Tydskrif* 44, nos. 1–2 (2003): 199–209.

19. Witherington, *Women and the Genesis of Christianity*.

20. P. Mwaura, "Gendered Appropriation of Mass Media in Kenyan Christianities: A Comparison of Two Women-Led African Instituted Churches in Kenya," in *Interpreting Contemporary Christianity: Global Processes and Local Identities,* ed. O. U. Kalu and A. Low (Grand Rapids: Eerdmans, 2008); K. Asamoah-Gyadu, "'Fireballs in Our Midst': West Africa Burgeoning Charismatic Churches and the Pastoral Role of Women," *Mission Studies* 15–16, no. 296 (1998): 21; A. M. Boadi, "Engaging Patriarchy: Pentecostal Gender Ideology and Practices in Nigeria," in *Religion, History, and Politics in Nigeria: Essays in Honour of Ogbu U. Kalu,* ed. Chima J. Korieh and Ugo G. Nwokeji (New York: University Press of America, 2005), 182.

the movement women have been affirmed along with men as recipients of the same Spirit who distributes gifts and callings."[21] Pentecostalism has been hailed as gender friendly, opening up spaces for women[22] and providing greater freedom for women.[23] Pentecostal churches are perceived as spaces where men and women "relate to each other on the basis of equality."[24] Further, Pentecostalism is a space where the Holy Spirit is experienced by men and women as a power that liberates.[25]

However, the Pentecostal space is ambivalent toward women. Scholars note that Pentecostalism is full of tensions, contradictions, and ambiguities as women are still expected to preserve traditional expectations of male prestige while they are empowered by the Holy Spirit to preach, speak in tongues, and prophesy. Johns points out that in regards to women, "Pentecostalism is a culture of both exclusion and embrace," and it is a place where "biblical roles of men and women restrict the ministry of women."[26] It is a place where women's leadership is sometimes "stigmatised and demonized."[27] Sarojini Nadar, Isabel Phiri, and Masenya Madipoane writing in the South African context, Sidney Berman writing in Botswana, and Rekopantswe Mate writing in the Zimbabwean context, all argue that Pentecostal biblical interpretation can be life-denying to women and, further, that women are oftentimes pushed to the periphery.[28] Similarly, the Nigerian scholar Ogbu Kalu argues that in Pentecos-

---

21. C. Johns, "Spirited Vestments or Why the Anointing Is Not Enough," in *Philip's Daughters: Women in Pentecostal-Charismatic Leadership,* ed. E. Alexander and A. Yong (Eugene, OR: Pickwick, 2009), 170.

22. Mwaura, "Gendered Appropriation of Mass Media," 279.

23. Kalu, *African Pentecostalism,* 149.

24. Boadi, "Engaging Patriarchy," 182.

25. Gabaitse, "Towards an African Pentecostal Feminist Biblical Hermeneutic of Liberation," 6.

26. Johns, "Spirited Vestments," 170, 174.

27. Mwaura, "Gendered Appropriation of Mass Media," 279.

28. S. Nadar, "Journeying in Faith: The Stories of Two Ordained Indian Women in the Anglican and Full Gospel Churches in South Africa," in *Herstories: Hidden Histories of Women of Faith in Africa,* ed. I. Phiri, B. Govinden, and S. Nadar (Pietermaritzburg: Cluster, 2002), 144–58; M. Masenya, *How Worthy Is the Woman of Worth: Rereading Proverbs 31:10–31 in African-South Africa* (New York: Peter Lang, 2004); S. Berman, "Of God Image, Violence against Women and Feminist Reflections," *Studia Historiae Ecclesiasticae* 41, no. 1 (2015): 122–37; I. Phiri, "Why Does God Allow Our Husbands to Hurt Us? Overcoming Violence against Women," *Journal of Theology for Southern Africa* 114 (2002): 19–30; I. Phiri, "Domestic Violence in Christian Homes: A Durban Case Study," *Journal of Constructive Theology* 6, no. 2 (2000): 85–110. R. Mate, "Wombs as God's Laboratories:

tal churches "men tend to use the Bible to justify women's exclusion or relegation to the periphery."[29] What is discernible from the above scholars is that as much as Pentecostalism is a space of embrace it is also a space of exclusion. This exclusion and embrace cloaks women into invisibility even when they are supposed to be visible especially through the unction of the Holy Spirit who works among men and women equally and is no respecter of persons.[30] Further, the scholars cited above show that the marginalization of women is a reality within Pentecostal movements and this marginalization is structurally supported by biblical interpretation. Pentecostal biblical interpretation and theology are full of the gendered language of domination and subordination.

Men are given enormous power over women in home, in church, and in public and women still experience hierarchical exclusion due to patriarchal norms that are maintained through the use of the Bible.[31] This poses a challenge especially since most African theologians have consistently argued that indigenous cultures in Africa and the church are patriarchal. African theologians such as Mercy Oduyoye, Brigalia Bam, Masenya Madipoane, Sarojini Nadar, and Musa Dube have demonstrated that the patriarchal African culture and church mutually reinforce each other in marginalizing women. African attitudes about women are reinscribed within the church's theology so that the two mutually reinforce each other in allocating women to a marginal status.[32] Mercy Amba Oduyoye rightly captures this mutuality: "We see the visible manifestation of patriarchal structures and hierarchies

Pentecostal Discourses on Femininity in Zimbabwe," *Africa, Journal of the International African Institute* 72, no. 4 (2002): 566.

29. Kalu, *African Pentecostalism*, 150.

30. The Pentecostal Church must be a space of equality not just in the spiritual realm but in tangible physical, social, and political ways.

31. Nadar, "Journeying in Faith"; Berman, "Of God Image, Violence against Women and Feminist Reflections"; Phiri, "Why Does God Allow Our Husbands to Hurt Us?"; Phiri, "Domestic Violence in Christian Homes"; Mate, "Wombs as God's Laboratories."

32. M. A. Oduyoye, *Introducing African Women's Theology* (Maryknoll, NY: Orbis, 2001), 12, 28; B. Bam, "Women and the Church in (South) Africa: Women Are the Church in South Africa," in *On Being Church: African Women's Voices and Visions,* ed. Isabel A. Phiri and Sarojini Nadar (Geneva: World Council of Churches, 2005), 13; Masenya, *How Worthy Is the Woman of Worth*; D. Ramodibe, "Women and Men Building Together the Church in Africa," in *With Passion and Compassion: Third World Women Doing Theology,* ed. V. M. M. Fabella and M. A. Oduyoye (Maryknoll, NY: Orbis, 1996); M. W. Dube, *Postcolonial Feminist Interpretations of the Bible* (St. Louis: Chalice, 2000), 95, 108.

. . . in the church or in African cultures wherever we encounter the subordination of women's services or a refusal to listen to women's voices."[33] In Botswana, the dual patriarchies of Setswana and Pentecostal contexts are not static and isolated from the

> wider impacts of globalization and the hybrid cultural forms which global encounters produce. European and American cultural forms are highly influential within Botswana. This further complicates the position of a Motswana Pentecostal woman who must contend not only with the dual patriarchies of the Pentecostal church and Setswana culture but also with the import of aspects of wider global forms. This importation does not happen monolithically but selection frequently reflects pre-existent patterns of power and patriarchy, rendering new forms of oppression.[34]

Therefore, women within the Pentecostal Church are not only doubly marginalized. They have to contend with marginalization due to the importation of global cultures as well.

While female submission is reinforced through language and some cultural practices in the Setswana culture, Pentecostals advance hermeneutical approaches to the Bible that enslave and deny women an experience of salvation as described in Luke 4:18–19. A negative gender discourse lurks within Pentecostal hermeneutics, theology, and practice because a few texts are used to propagate gender inequality by reinforcing the idea of male supremacy. This is done through promoting male leadership, male power, and male control, and through advocating hierarchical relationships. Scholars of Pentecostalism have begun to pay attention to the oppressive nature of biblical interpretation toward women.[35]

For example, Mate condemns Pentecostal movements for advancing teachings found in most African cultures that perpetuate and maintain patriarchal ideologies such as female submission to the point of calling

33. M. A. Oduyoye, *Beads and Strands: Reflections of an African Woman on Christianity in Africa* (Accra, Ghana: Regnum Africa, 2002), 97.

34. Gabaitse, "Towards an African Pentecostal Feminist Biblical Hermeneutic of Liberation," 56.

35. S. Nadar, "The Bible Says! Feminism, Hermeneutics and Neo-Pentecostal Challenges," *Journal of Theology for Southern Africa* 134 (July 2009): 153; Mate, "Wombs as God's Laboratories," 566; R. M. Gabaitse, "Pentecostal Hermeneutics and the Marginalisation of Women," *Scriptura* 114, no. 1 (2015): 1–12.

women to blind obedience, that is, women must submit to their husbands even to the point of death.[36] African women theologians have consistently pointed out that violence against women in Africa is endemic and very serious. They have further maintained that patriarchy provides a breeding ground for all marginalization of women, especially forms of violence.[37] Isabel Phiri conducted research on violence against women among Pentecostal Indian women in Durban and her data reveal chilling details of the violence that happens within Christian homes perpetuated by born-again husbands using a few texts from the Bible that seemingly support the marginalization of women.[38] As a follow-up to this research, she published another essay in which she argued that Christian women are not immune to experiences of violence in their homes.[39]

Tinyiko Maluleke and Sarojini Nadar, also writing in a South African context, describe horrifying incidents of domestic violence in Christian Pentecostal homes. They tell the story of Khensani, a black South African Pentecostal woman who for years was subjected to severe beating and other kinds of violence by her husband. Numerous counseling sessions had taken place, and many times Khensani ran away from her marital home after which her senior aunts and uncles would return her home. Maluleke and Nadar write that

> in the last few years of their marriage they had both become born again Christians belonging to a Pentecostal church. Yet this reality did not change the situation of domestic violence to which Khensani was subjected to time and again. If anything, their new found faith and its theology appeared to reinforce the idea of male supremacy in marriage. Often Khensani appealed to the pastor for intervention, but he would only show her scripture verses that "proved" that she was wrong to complain and to question her husband's "right to violate her."[40]

What is discernible from Maluleke and Nadar's narration of the story of Khensani and Phiri's research on violence is that first,

36. Mate, "Wombs as God's Laboratories," 566.
37. N. Njoroge, "The Missing Voice: African Women Doing Theology," *Journal of Theology for Southern Africa* 99 (1997): 81.
38. Phiri, "Domestic Violence in Christian Homes," 95.
39. Phiri, "Domestic Violence in Christian Homes," 93, 99.
40. T. Maluleke and S. Nadar, "Breaking the Covenant of Violence against Women," *Journal of Theology for Southern Africa* 114 (November 2002): 11.

pastors are not actively denouncing the marginalization of women. Second, Pentecostal pastors are agents of patriarchy and they endorse a hermeneutic that fundamentally disagrees with Luke 4:18–19 because it oppresses women. Third, the accounts demonstrate how pastors use Scripture verses to maintain a hierarchical order between men and women. Biblical interpretation is used to keep women in life-denying situations, something Phiri classifies as spiritual violence:

> When a woman's faith is used to keep her from finding help and leaving an abusive situation, by telling her she must endure, submit, return . . . she is led to believe that the abuse is her fault, and that if she seeks to leave, she is un-Christian and will be condemned by God. The Bible is quoted to her literally and out of context, particularly passages that serve to "put her in her place," condemn divorce or glorify suffering.[41]

This is a demonstration of how patriarchy is not threatened or destabilized in the Pentecostal Church. Failure to overtly and intentionally destabilize patriarchy denies many African women like Khensani an opportunity to experience release from oppression while suffering is made normative through the selective use of the Bible.

One of the other aspects of Pentecostal theology that denies women an experience of salvation is the dualistic understanding of the world. The world is divided into the spiritual world and the physical/social world and the spiritual world is more important. When Christian women like Khensani and the women in Phiri's research experience violence, their experiences are "hyper spiritualized" and rationalized. They are told to "fast more," "seek God more," submit to their husbands more, or hold on to the hope that "God will not allow you to go through things, which you cannot manage to handle."[42] Stories of women being told to ignore actual experiences of pain and trauma are many. To these women, salvation is abstract as it does not translate into the social, political, and economic world that Khensani and the women in Phiri's research inhabit. Because of Pentecostals' tendency to spiritualize, they fail to overtly challenge

41. Phiri, "Domestic Violence in Christian Homes," 95.
42. Phiri, "Domestic Violence in Christian Homes," 105.

and deconstruct the marginalization of women with a clear, loud, and unambiguous voice. While spiritual experience and prayer are essential to Pentecostal living, both men and women must be taught that violence committed against women is not normal. In addition, they should be taught that the marginalization of women in any form and shape is not acceptable because it denies women an experience of salvation in the social world.

There is danger in emphasizing spiritual experience while down-playing social experience because political, social, and religious systems that support the oppression of women are not challenged. Further, when people suffer in the social world, they may despair and lose the joy of the salvation which, according to Pentecostal teaching, is the right of those who have accepted Jesus as their personal Savior and have accepted the full gospel. Johns argues that "Pentecostals have failed to clearly enunciate the ontological and soteriological implications of the liberating power of the full gospel. As a result, they have created an environment characterized by ambiguity and confusion."[43]

A thorough analysis of salvation in Luke-Acts and an analysis of Luke 4:18–19 in particular demonstrates that there is no need for spiritual and social salvation to exist in antagonism. Allen Anderson captures this: "The power of the Holy Spirit has more than just spiritual significance. It also has to do with dignity, authority and power over all types of oppression. God loves and desires the welfare of the whole person: and so needs his Spirit to bestow that divine, liberating ability and strength."[44]

Luke 4:18–19: A Critique of the Marginalization of Women and Violence against Women

What does proclaiming good news to the poor and setting the captives free look like in the contemporary world? What does Jesus's declaration mean for Pentecostal women who are faced with masculine interpretations of the Bible that do not take their experiences of suffering seriously? The existence of the unfavorable conditions described in Luke 4:18–19 is real and these conditions prevent human beings, both

43. Johns, "Spirited Vestments," 174.
44. A. Anderson, *Moya: The Holy Spirit in an African Context* (Pretoria: University of South Africa Press, 1991), 63.

men and women, from experiencing complete salvation. The oppression described in Luke 4:18–19 can be imposed on people by political, sociocultural, and economic systems. For example, suffering caused by violence against women is imposed on women through a patriarchal system of governance that thrives when certain groups of people are enslaved. Some women continue to be materially poor because patriarchy creates economic inequalities between men and women. Jesus was aware that as much as salvation was a present reality, and could be experienced and enjoyed by people regardless of ethnicity and gender, there were systems that prevented people from experiencing it (Luke 11:52). It was necessary for those systems to be dismantled. Therefore, Luke 4:18–19 is a relevant text because it points to the existence of systems that deny people an experience of salvation. Contemporary Pentecostals could use this passage as the basis on which to intercept and deconstruct patriarchal practices that prevent women from experiencing complete salvation. There is no reason for any woman who has given her life to Jesus and believes in Pentecost to be kept captive and oppressed by any system, theology, or frames of reading and interpreting the Bible.

An encounter with Jesus should be life-giving because the gospel in general and Luke 4:18–19 in particular liberates. Luke 4:18–19 is subversive as it exposes the oppressive lies of patriarchy that women experience violence because they fail to "submit enough" or "pray more" or they are untamed. The text demonstrates that people suffer because they are denied salvation in the social world through systems of domination. Luke 4:18–19 should unsettle and judge the church for not only failing to make it possible for women to experience fullness of life because they inhabit patriarchal oppressive spaces, but also for using the Bible to advance and support patriarchal norms that oppress women, thus colluding with the Setswana culture in oppressing women. Therefore, the Pentecostal Church has to reflect on the heart of the mission of Jesus, which was to set people free.

In fact, the Pentecostal Church sins against women through enforcing an oppressive system that maintains male domination and female subordination. The sin of the Pentecostal Church translates into individual men's sins like those of Khensani's husband, who violated his wife as a way of demonstrating power and control based on a false interpretation of the Bible. It is ironic that the language of subordination that results in the marginalization of women is found in a community that is led by the Holy Spirit and believes in the Pentecost narrative of Acts 2. The Holy Spirit, who directs Pentecostal living, is transformative and radical, hence the Spirit is often referred to as an "equal opportunity employer."[45] Elsewhere I have argued that "Pentecost is a rejection of exclusion and marginalization. The Pentecost narrative was communal, *all* are praying, *all* are assembled (2:1), *all* are filled with the Spirit (2:4), the Spirit is for *all* flesh (2:17), the Holy Spirit is given to 'each of you' (2:37)."[46] Through the Holy Spirit, Pentecost gives us a glimpse of an egalitarian transformed community of faith where discrimination on the basis of gender does not exist. It is in the construction and maintenance of gender inequalities through biblical interpretation that the marginalization of women is made normative. The existence of gender inequalities takes away from the Pentecostal Church the opportunity to be the real church of Pentecost, the church led by the Holy Spirit where exclusions were ignored for a while.[47]

Conclusion

In this chapter I have demonstrated the darker side of Pentecostal hermeneutics and theology much more than the positive side. The positive side of Pentecostal hermeneutics and theology includes but is not limited to women prophesying under the influence of the Holy Spirit and women not bound by traditional rules of dress and Levitical taboos. I pointed out the darker side of Pentecostalism because there is potential to make the Pentecostal space truly egalitarian, embrac-

45. E. S. Spencer, *The Gospel of Luke and Acts of the Apostles* (Nashville: Abingdon, 2008), 67.

46. Gabaitse, "Towards an African Pentecostal Feminist Biblical Hermeneutic of Liberation," 178.

47. As much as Pentecost was egalitarian, I am aware that as the story of the church progressed male leadership was sometimes preferred (Acts 6). However, the story of Acts is a story of how the Holy Spirit moves the church toward egalitarian existence. It is a story in which God will pour God's Spirit on the young men, the old men, and the young women, the free and the slaves. So that even if the church in Acts may gravitate toward male leadership, God has made a promise through the Holy Spirit for the equality of all people and that promise subverts even the culture of Luke-Acts. See Gabaitse, "Pentecostal Hermeneutics and the Marginalisation of Women," 11.

ing men and women equally, if texts such as Luke 4:18–19 are read to advance multidimensional salvation. Luke 4:18–19 is a powerful resource that the Pentecostal Church can use to transform social lives of women who are experiencing patriarchal oppression from indigenous and global cultures.

A saved Pentecostal community should advance hermeneutics and theology that affirm salvation for all people regardless of gender, ethnicity, or race. A Spirit-led and saved community continuously seeks ways of transforming unequal gender relations and affirming the lives of its members so that men and women experience jubilee and social salvation. For this to happen, the Pentecostal Church needs to acknowledge that its frames of reading and interpreting the Bible contradict the work of the Holy Spirit who through Jesus declared that "I have come to set the captives free." This can also happen if the church can take the experiences of women's marginalization seriously by acknowledging that it has caused women pain through its hermeneutics. In addition, the Pentecostal Church has to acknowledge that cultures of oppression need to be challenged because they cause women real problems such as trauma from violence inflicted on them. Therefore, Luke 4:18–19 could be a resource for the Pentecostal Church to acknowledge that patriarchal practices of subordinating women rob them of experiencing salvation and that Jesus came to set human beings free from oppression.

Biblical texts are living and have the potential to transform lives if they are allowed through the Holy Spirit to do so. Luke 4:18–19 is transformative enough to explode and challenge the patriarchal framework of Pentecostal theology and hermeneutics. Pentecostals could use this text to challenge the unjust and unfair cultural practices that rob women of an experience of social salvation. It is a text that could critique laws and practices that repress women and children, as much as they critique cultures that allow violence to happen and ways of uncritically reading texts such as Ephesians 5 to support the authority of the husband over the wife. Laws, practices, and cultures that oppress and uncritically read the Bible are not consistent with salvation described in Luke 4:18–19. Jesus's proclamation of holistic salvation must be the message adopted by the Pentecostal movements and the church in general because the church is the representative of Christ on earth. The kind of salvation Luke-Acts presents "knows no distinction between the physical, spiritual and social."[48] Salvation takes different forms and shapes, depending on circumstances and contexts. However, the end results of salvation are the same for all humanity, and God desires a healed whole humanity. Human beings are saved when their souls are saved and when their circumstances allow for sociopolitical, physical, and economic salvation as well.

Further Reading

Seim, T. K. *The Double Message: Patterns of Gender in Luke-Acts.* Edinburgh: T&T Clark, 1994.

Shillington, G. *An Introduction to the Study of Luke-Acts.* New York: T&T Clark, 2006.

Thomas, C. "Women Pentecostals and the Bible." *Journal of Pentecostal Theology* 5 (1994): 41–56.

West, G. "Reading the Bible Differently: Giving Shape to Discourses of the Dominated." *Semeia* 73 (1996): 21–38.

Williams, D. K. "'Upon All Flesh': Acts 2, African Americans and Intersectional Realities." In *They Were All Together in One Place: Toward Minority Biblical Criticism*, edited by B. Randal, Ben Tat-Siong, and F. Segovia, 289–310. Atlanta: Society of Biblical Literature, 2009.

48. J. B. Green, "Salvation to the End of the Earth: God as the Saviour in the Acts of the Apostles," in *Witness to the Gospel: The Theology of Acts*, ed. I. H. Marshall and D. Petersen (Grand Rapids: Eerdmans, 1998), 89.

CHAPTER 4

Con Las Venas Abiertas:
The Hope of Life and Salvation in Latin American Theologies

JULES A. MARTÍNEZ-OLIVIERI

ABSTRACT

The doctrine of salvation in Latin America is construed as a divinely enacted experience that begins in historical reality with the transformation of people freed from both personal and collective expressions of sin for life in communion with God and neighbor. The contextual realities of Latin American theologians in the late twentieth century provided a historical occasion to elaborate on the concept of sin and liberation that amounted to new emphases. Explorations of sin and salvation among Roman Catholics and Protestants share some overlap, but diverge in a few important ways. This chapter seeks to assess the differences, articulating their hermeneutical intuitions and the subsequent conclusions that were produced by their doctrinal formulations.

In 1971, Edwardo Galeano published a book entitled *Con las venas abiertas de America Latina*.[1] It was one of the most visceral accounts of the consequences of the power relations between Europe and the United States over Latin America, which resulted in economic exploitation. Armed with powerful, critical rhetoric, Galeano brought to the center of political discussion how international political policies had affected the people in Latin America, particularly the forgotten masses of the impoverished and those ravaged by violence. In hindsight, the

---

1. See Eduardo Galeano, *Open Veins of Latin America: Five Centuries of the Pillage of a Continent*, 25th anniversary ed. (New York: Monthly Review, 1997).

economic and political conditions were even more complex, and Galeano underestimated how corrupt local governments were equally responsible for the systemic evils that plagued many countries in the region. Still, the suffering of the masses in Latin America, and in many postcolonial regions of the world, is an undeniable and grotesque fact.

Christian theology in Latin America was born from this unacceptable reality of a multitude of peoples suffering in the absence of social justice, economic well-being, and the possibility of a livable life. The rise of Roman Catholic liberation theology and Protestant theology is in part the result of Christians thinking critically about the relevance of Christian salvation, the life of the church among the most vulnerable, and the witness required to proclaim that Jesus is the Lord of life and liberator of humanity.

My task in this chapter is to offer an exposition of the doctrine of salvation in Latin American theologies. As such it is necessarily a selective exercise, which can suffer for its brevity, but one that can nevertheless provide a map of the theological terrain. I do not pretend to speak for all of the voices, but simply aim to zero in on a few frameworks to see how their intuitions illustrate the broader trends in Latin America. And even so, within a single tradition there can be variety. For our purposes, this chapter broadly traces the soteriology of liberation theology in its Roman Catholic and Protestant depictions.

The Hope of Life and Salvation

Christian theology in Latin America[2] presents itself as an attempt to take on the question of how to discern God's presence in a situation of destitution and human turmoil. The challenge is connected to the political nature of Christological and soteriological discourse. The primary challenge is not tethered to philosophical naturalism or materialism of a secular Western society, but rather what is communicated by the actions and attributes of God, who is already assumed in Jesus Christ. This gospel emphasis takes a notable interest in speaking

2. "Latin America" is a geopolitical term used to refer to the territories comprising Mexico, Central America, the Caribbean, and South America. See Alan Barnard and Jonathan Spencer, *Encyclopedia of Social and Cultural Anthropology* (London: New York, 1996).

against and deconstructing the political and religious ideologies that diminish human life. This God is the God of life and liberation.[3]

According to the Christian faith, salvation is the central need of humanity. It is the experience of being saved by God from sin and its effects. Salvation is a gracious divine act whereby human beings are brought into right communion with God and neighbor, and as such, are saved from alienation from God and neighbor (personal sin), as well as sin in its communal expressions in political, economic, and social systems that perpetuate inhuman conditions (structural sin). This restored communion with God and neighbor activates an alternative human praxis that confronts these structural evils. Salvation, hence, is understood in part as a future eschatological reality free of evil that breaks into present human history. Salvation is in history; that is, it has a definitive historical referent, but is not limited to history. Consequently, the Christian experience of salvation can be seen in three dimensions: (1) as redemption, deliverance from sin; (2) as flourishing in grace toward wholeness (sanctification); and (3) as satisfaction of the deepest human longings for transcendence (eternal life). The concept of salvation is manifested in all three senses.[4]

Theological reflection in Latin America exemplifies this consciousness of the contextuality of human theologizing. Theology, as human discourse done in faith, takes the concerns of the historical moment that shaped the life experiences, cultures, and linguistic mediations of their producers. Theological proposals do not enjoy a de facto transcultural relevance.[5] In Latin American theology, doctrine finds validation in the public orthopraxis of the church. That is, the church community is a visible sign of the truth of Christian theology. Theology serves the people of God by plotting possibilities for expressing the faith and

3. Rolando Muñoz avers: "the problem is more so the 'idolatry' of the privileged groups and the 'cults,' those who more or less consciously use 'God' to legitimize their accumulated wealth, their excluding knowledge, their power of domination; is the 'atheism' of the dominant groups that believe that God 'does not see' the exploitation of the poor and the assassination of the innocent, that He 'does not hear' the clamor of the oppressed." Ronaldo Muñoz, *Dios de los cristianos* (Santiago: Ediciones Paulinas, 1986), 29.

4. See Olegario González de Cardedal, *Fundamentos de cristología: meta y misterio*, vol. 2 (Madrid: BAC, 2006), lx–lxii.

5. Gerardo A. Alfaro, "¿Cómo hacer teología evangelica? Preliminares de un método teológico evangélico," in *Teología evangélica para el contexto latinoamericano: Ensayos en honor al Dr. Emilio A. Nuñez*, ed. Oscar A. Campos (Buenos Aires: Kairos, 2004), 58–59.

judgments that correspond to the gospel and the testimony of God's communication in Jesus Christ.

Two Soteriological Traditions: Catholic Liberationist and Protestant

Approaches to soteriology can generally be divided between Roman Catholic liberation theology and Protestant theologies, although there are shared methodological, thematic, and practical convergences between them. For Protestantism, I make use of José Míguez Bonino's typology of the "faces" of Protestantism in Latin America.[6]

Liberation Theology on Salvation

Some scholars have labeled theologies of liberation as a type of retrieval theology. However, liberation theologians are quick to clarify that liberation theology is not another theology of the genitive. Or stated differently, it is not merely another theology with a new adjectival clarifier in the list of many others. It is not a mere attempt to retrieve one aspect of dogmatic reflection that was ignored or undervalued. Neither is it a theological application of a dogmatic locus to politics and sociology, although it is analytically interested in both. Instead, the adjective modifying theology is intended to categorically reconfigure Christian theology as a theology predicated on the confession that God in Christ is the liberator of humanity. Hence, as Ignacio Ellacuría argues, liberation theology should not be understood as a form of political theology, but as a theology of the reign of God focusing on how all dogmatic areas of theology should be framed in their liberating dimension.[7] Methodologically, the primary object is not politics in itself, but the church, as Christ's broker of embodied salvation. The church has a decided preference for theologizing in light of those who suffer, and on the centrality of Christian praxis as a verification of gospel commitment.

---

6. Míguez Bonino suggests several "faces" of Protestantism in Latin America: the ethnic, liberal, evangelical, and Pentecostal. See José Míguez Bonino, *Faces of Latin American Protestantism* (Grand Rapids: Eerdmans, 1997).

7. Ellacuría, *Historicidad de la salvación*, 325.

The concept of "liberation" in liberation theology has a biblical referent that points to the scriptural testimony of God rescuing and establishing justice among his people.[8] "Liberation" is a soteriological concept that attempts to capture the historical experience of divine redemptive acts. Gustavo Gutiérrez explained three fundamental soteriological levels: (1) the sociopolitical level: the liberation of those "exploited classes, marginalized races, despised cultures";[9] (2) the anthropological level: liberation for the attainment of a society of equals; (3) the theological level: liberation from sin, which is the origin of all evil and injustice, for a life of communion and participation.

Therefore, history is the realm of divine action in which human transformation is experienced. The cognitive content of salvation has a narrative shape. It begins with the acts of Jesus in his ministry. Jesus's own praxis is liberating; he is the messianic "liberator." Leonardo Boff argues that Jesus is the "liberator of the conscience oppressed by sin and by all kinds of alienations; liberator of the sad human condition in its relationships towards the world, each other and towards God."[10]

Jesus's designation as "liberator" enjoys more theological capital than Jesus as represented in the language of the ecumenical creeds. The status of creedal Christology (e.g., Councils of Nicaea, Chalcedon, Ephesus) in contemporary theology in Latin America is somewhat ambivalent. The creeds are considered a valuable (though not normative) dogmatic and hermeneutical framework in Latin American theologies among both Roman Catholics and Protestants. The confessional language provides grammatical rules (fitting concepts) that safeguard the identity of the agent of salvation in the gospel, in its own time and across generations. However, even as the identity of the Savior is ontologically specified, the work of the Savior in saving humanity and the shape of the praxis of his followers is not a concern reflected in the creeds. Hence, the creeds do not offer a sufficient foundation for the mission of the church. The creeds are not formulated in a way to give doctrinal preference to Jesus's example—namely, his message and actions. In a narrative conception of salvation, the praxis of Jesus is identified as the historical realization of the kingdom of God and the

8. Rosino Gibellini, *La Teología del siglo XX*, Coleccion Presencia Teológica (Santander: Sal Terrae, 1998), 378.

9. Gustavo Gutiérrez, *La fuerza histórica de los probres* (Salamanca: Sígueme, 1982), 243.

10. Leonardo Boff, *Jesucristo Liberador* (Santander: Sal Terrae, 1980), 253.

basis of the process of liberation. The ecumenical creeds, given their attention to metaphysical and theological issues regarding Jesus's divinity and Trinitarian ontology, do not assess the material content of the historical expression of salvation based on his praxis. The creeds, therefore, do not pay attention to the content of God's kingdom, which should be fundamental to soteriology. However, when the historical actions of Jesus genuinely shape a broader vision of salvation, then the expectations of God's reign described by the creeds become more meaningful.

Liberation Christology privileges Jesus's proclamation of the kingdom and its advancement. The Gospels skillfully highlight Jesus's actions on behalf of the impoverished. His actions on behalf of victims who suffered a plurality of maladies constitute the establishment of the rule of God in history. Jesus is depicted as the definitive mediator of the kingdom, summoning people to live under God's rule.[11]

Fundamental to the Christian view of salvation is the notion that God's acts in human history are open to human apprehension. Divine action not only sustains the faith of the church, but also shapes the embodiment of Christian praxis. In Latin American theologies there is a methodological, pastoral, and missional interest in the historicity of salvation as a public experience of the faith. Praxis, specifically Christian praxis, refers to actions characterized by the intent to transform situations that negate the kind of life that the gospel offers. It promotes holistic well-being for all human beings.

For liberation theologians, Christian praxis has a potential salvific role to play to the extent that it is the consistent testimony of Christians involved in the shaping of a just world—a praxis of salvation. That is, Christian social and political involvement should seek "maximal coincidence between what God wants from human beings and what human beings do."[12] Ellacuría goes further, proposing that human praxis has a soteriological capacity, a "formally salvific power" that shapes, even saves history, not apart from, but in collaboration with God.[13]

Both Roman Catholic and Protestant theologians agree that the modern theological scheme of two histories, a sacred history and a

11. Jon Sobrino, *Jesus the Liberator: A Historical-Theological Reading of Jesus of Nazareth*, trans. Paul Burns and Francis McDonagh (London: Burns & Oates, 1994), 108–9.

12. Ellacuría, *Historicidad de la salvación*, 327.

13. Ellacuría, *Historicidad de la salvación*, 341.

profane history, is not sustainable for theology given the Scriptures' rendering of human history as the single space of divine action and human participation. God's actions and human praxis are not logically dichotomous, but complementary. God's activity is always related to human beings' activity. In fact, God's activity is so intimately connected to human activity that it can be said that human actions bear the presence of God. The agency of God is principally human activity. "There is an omnipresence of God in history," Ellacuría says, that is not reducible to the natural or supernatural.[14]

The divine presence in history leads liberation theology to deal with the idea of transcendence. Transcendence is framed as the divine reality that sustains history in time and space, while extending beyond it, not against it or in contraposition to it. Transcendence is not over history or beyond it, but through history. The referents for this view of transcendence in history are the exodus event and the incarnation. In the exodus event, the paradigmatic salvific event of the Old Testament, the salvific gift of freedom from slavery comes as covenantal freedom for a people, so that they might worship the Lord and in doing so become an alternative society. Worship is dependent on the sociopolitical experience of liberation. In the incarnation, the eternal and transcendent God communicates himself in the Son's humiliation. This is where the eternal and contingent come together in unity but without confusion. Hence, human history is the "privileged field to show the irruption of the transcendent God as the unseen novelty that opens human contingency to divine hope."[15] For this reason, the nature of salvation is inextricably linked first to how God relates to history.

In terms of the Gospel narratives, liberation is what Jesus defined as integral to his reign. Jesus's messianic mission is displayed by his healings, exorcisms, and confrontations with those who religiously and politically oppressed the masses. It is acutely portrayed by his giving of food to the multitudes, and the formation of a new community of sacrificial service to neighbor. These are the signs of the kingdom. These are the historical conditions that both confirm Jesus's identity and provide the content of his liberating work. Salvation and liberation are, primordially, a material, sociopolitical, and verifiable experience. Salvation is not fully lived unless it reaches the temporalities of

---

14. Ellacuría, *Historicidad de la salvación*, 327–28.
15. Ellacuría, *Historicidad de la salvación*, 332.

human existence.[16] In light of the scriptural testimony of a God who intervenes to save, salvation refers to God's ultimate activity of bringing *shalom* (the Hebrew conception of wholeness and right relationship between Creator and creation) to humanity. Liberation refers to those conditions in history, personal and collective, that point to the presence of God's liberating actions.

One of the main contributions of liberation theology to Christian dogmatic theology is the conceptual expansion of sin as an alienating condition of relational brokenness. The expansion includes societal structures that threaten human flourishing and the very possibility of human life. To be saved is to experience God in Christ liberating people from personal sin and the "objectification of sin" in social and political life: the impoverishment of the masses; the marginalization of those on the periphery; the oppression and killing of women, children, and indigenous groups; and the sex trafficking of millions under the logic of supply and demand. Groups who are doubly oppressed by patriarchy, political subjugation, and racism are victims of what Xavier Zubiri calls "historical sin."[17] These conditions are structures that work against essential aspects of the God who offers abundant life in Christ. God is a God of life, justice, and love. The salvation enacted by God in Christ includes the hope of liberation from these maladies by creating a messianic people that through the inhabitation of the Spirit confront the oppressions of the world; whose sociopolitical praxis is a testimony to the God who calls human beings to just lives. God, in Christ, enacts redemption in them, and so contradicting the historical structures of sin with the emergence of new historical "structures of grace."[18] Structures of grace are established in the cross and the resurrection, as these events are interpreted in light of the arrival of God's kingdom. Those who have been impoverished and oppressed by sinful religious, secular, and political systems, now are understood as privileged recipients of the reign of God.[19]

16. Ellacuría, *Historicidad de la salvación*, 340.

17. X. Zubiri, *Naturaleza, historia, Dios* (Madrid: Alianza Editorial, 1963), 394.

18. Ellacuría avers: "The first question is to see what is there of grace and what is there of sin in men and in history, but a grace and sin not seen primarily from a moral point of view, and even less from the point of view of fulfilling laws and obligations, but seen primarily from that which makes the life of God present in the midst of men" (*Historicidad de la salvación*, 356–57).

19. Sobrino, *Jesus the Liberator*, 67.

How do people and ecclesial communities maintain preference toward the impoverished and oppressed? Jesus's example and his own resistance to oppression prevent the Christian faith from the temptation to decontextualize (and overspiritualize) his mission—which is also their mission. Where the social, political, and religious aspects of the cross are neglected, the most vulnerable and preferential beneficiaries of the gospel become obscure.[20] Significantly, the death of Jesus is the consequence of this proclamation. It is the death of a human being whose life is identified with the transcendent God.[21]

Consider briefly feminist liberation theologies as one particular expression. Feminist theology in Latin America is critical reflection on the experience of God by women. Women not only suffer oppression like men, but are doubly oppressed for their gender by the prevailing logic of patriarchalism and its patterns of domination. Feminist theology seeks "to transform the causes that produce the impoverishment and violence against women as a social group, with the goal of advancing towards new social relations based on justice and the integrity of life for women and all organisms of the Earth."[22] For some feminist theologians, ignoring the historical causes of the cross is dangerous, as it makes the meaning of salvation susceptible to ideological uses. Sadly, in some religious communities the idea of atonement has been used to perpetuate the suffering of women, proposing that suffering is inherent to a life that emulates Jesus's own suffering.[23]

Nevertheless, Roman Catholic feminist theologians and liberation theologians are hesitant to elaborate on the metaphysical effectiveness of the atonement. They feel more comfortable viewing the death of Jesus primarily in light of its theological symbolic power. For Jon Sobrino, the effectiveness of the cross lies in the capacity to evoke a pattern of life in light of the kingdom of God. The power of the cross lies "in the form of an exemplary cause more than of an efficient cause."[24] However, to be saved is to come to new subjective and objective realities. Subjectively, the experience of liberation is constituted by faith

---

20. Nancy E. Bedford, *La porfía de la resurrección: ensayos desde el feminismo teológico latinoamericano*, Colección FTL (Buenos Aires: Kairós, 2008).

21. Sobrino, *Jesus the Liberator*, 220.

22. Maria Pilar-Aquino and Elsa Tamez, *Teología feminista latinoamericana*, Pluriminor (Quito: Ediciones Abya-Yala, 1998), 16.

23. Pilar-Aquino and Tamez, *Teología feminista latinoamericana*, 158.

24. Sobrino, *Jesus the Liberator*, 230.

and love for God and neighbor. Objectively, to be saved is to be liberated for the production of a new praxis and an alternative social order. Humans are both saved and made free through the Spirit of Jesus who brings freedom and makes Christians co-participants in God's redemptive history.

Protestants on Salvation: Evangelical, Pentecostal, and Ecumenical

Soteriology in the Protestant tradition has historically been a central concern for both theology and the mission of the church. Protestants emphasize the theme of Christian salvation and liberation from sin for a life of communion with God and love of neighbor. This God saves people and transforms societies beset by personal and structural evil.[25] As I have argued elsewhere:

> Protestants have also used the nomenclature of salvation as liberation. . . . The concept of liberation/salvation is informed via Christology: Jesus Christ paradigmatically fulfills the OT trajectories of the exodus freedom and the prophetic visions of God's actions to free the people of Israel from internal oppression and the oppression exerted by foreign political powers. In Jesus the messianic vocation is redefined in terms of liberation of the captives—the sinners, the sick, the maltreated, the afflicted, the poor, and the victims. Hence, since salvation entails liberations from sinful captivities, personal and societal, it is not a meta-historical concept or experience but "a reality indissolubly tied to the history of human beings."[26]

For Protestants, the kingdom also serves as an interpretive lens for soteriology.[27] Jesus's salvific praxis is understood in light of God's kingdom establishing actions. The consequence of people being saved

25. José Míguez Bonino, "Las iglesias protestantes y evangélicas en América Latina y el Caribe: un ensayo interpretativo," *Cuadernos de teología* 14, no. 2 (1995): 31.

26. See my "¿Quién Vive? ¡Cristo!: Christology in Latin American Perspectives," in *Jesus without Borders: Christology in the Majority World*, ed. Gene L. Green, Stephen T. Pardue, and K. K. Yeo, Majority World Theology Series (Grand Rapids: Eerdmans, 2014), 80–100.

27. José D. Rodriguez, *Introducción a la teología*, 2nd ed. (Mexico, D.F.: Publicaciones El Faro, 2002), 17.

from fundamental sin (and the praxis of sin) is the formation of an alternative society, a people under the lordship of Christ. The community of the liberated is constituted by God's grace extended to the most vulnerable: women, children, the impoverished, and victims who dream for justice.[28] These are the primary recipients of the kingdom. Samuel Escobar argues: "'To preach the gospel to the poor, To heal the broken hearted, To preach deliverance to the captives and recovery of sight to the blind, To set at liberty them that are bruised.' These are words that cannot be spiritualized in a world like ours, where there are millions of persons who are poor, brokenhearted, captive, blind and bruised."[29] Through his death, Jesus redeems from personal and collective slavery. He is the one true innocent who brings redemption. He is the liberator of humanity, the mediator of the life of God beyond any human or state mediation.[30] Orlando Costas says:

> Jesus unequivocally shifted the whole concept of salvation—from benefit and privilege to commitment and service. To be saved by faith in Christ is thus to come to Jesus where he died for the world and gave his life for its salvation; it is to commit oneself to those for whom he suffered. Salvation lies outside the gates of the cultural, ideological, political, and socio-economic walls that surround our religious compound and shape the structures of Christendom. It is not a ticket to a privileged spot in God's universe but, rather, freedom for service.[31]

That salvation lies outside the "structures of Christendom"—that is, the shared moral vocabulary, sociopolitical organization, and ecclesial practices associated with cultures under the influence of Christianity—is a de facto intuition in the Pentecostal face of Protestantism.

---

28. Cf. Justo L. González, *Jesucristo es el Señor*, 2nd ed. (Lima: Ediciones Puma, 2011).

29. As cited by Sharon E. Heaney, *Contextual Theology for Latin America: Liberation Themes in Evangelical Perspective*, Paternoster Theological Monographs (Colorado Springs: Paternoster, 2008), 142.

30. C. René Padilla, "Christology and Mission in the Two Thirds World," in *Sharing Jesus in the Two Thirds World: Evangelical Christologies from Contexts of Poverty, Powerlessness and Religious Pluralism.*, ed. Vinay Samuel and Chris Sugnen (Grand Rapids: Eerdmans, 1983), 28.

31. Orlando E. Costas, *Christ outside the Gate: Mission beyond Christendom* (Maryknoll, NY: Orbis, 1982), 191.

Pentecostalism is the fastest growing tradition of Christianity in Latin America and in the Majority World.[32] Pentecostals share theological commitments with *evangélicos*, particularly with the paradigmatic Reformation *solas*, a pietistic ethos of personal devotion, and emphasis on evangelistic mission. At the same time, great emphasis is placed on conversion as a moment of crisis when the old life subjected to the slavery of sin is liberated to a new holy life (morally and liturgically) dedicated to serving God through the empowerment of the Holy Spirit.[33] In Pentecostal theology, to be saved from sin is not only to be freed from fundamental sin, but also to be liberated from the "infra-human conditions"—not metaphorically, but concretely—that keep human beings in spiritual chains to the enemy of the souls, Satan.[34] The cross of Christ has an intensely personal effect on those who come to faith in Jesus and are united to him by the Spirit: it makes them fully human. The Holy Spirit's fullness in individual lives has the power to change those impoverished and marginalized so that they become proclaimers of a new and just life.[35] The victims of personal and collective sin are given the resources necessary to be considered actors in the work of love and justice, and by the empowerment of the Spirit, the church becomes a center of social liberation.[36] Samuel Solivan argues that "orthodoxy, narrowly defined as propositional truth, dehumanizes revelation and elevates the cognitive . . . we are not saved by what we know but by whom we know, and how God informs and transforms our lives and our neighbors' lives."[37] For Pentecostals, the application or experience of salvation extends beyond the intellectual apprehension of the gospel or the knowledge of doctrinal truths. Salvation stems from a personal encounter with the Lord of life, Jesus. Christians are not

32. Cf. Ondina E. González and Justo L. González, *Christianity in Latin America: A History* (New York: Cambridge University Press, 2008), 270–96.

33. José Míguez Bonino, *Rostros del protestantismo latinoamericano* (Grand Rapids: Eerdmans, 1995), 64.

34. Dario Lopez R., *Pentecostalismo y misión integral. Teologia del Espíritu, teología de la vida* (Lima: Ediciones Puma, 2008), 103.

35. See Eldin Villafañe, *El Espíritu liberador: hacia una ética social pentecostal hispanoamericana* (Grand Rapids: Eerdmans, 1996).

36. R. Dario Lopez, *Pentecostalismo y misión integral. Teologia del Espíritu, teología de la vida* (Lima: Ediciones Puma, 2008), 103–4.

37. Samuel Solivan, *The Spirit, Pathos and Liberation: Toward an Hispanic Pentecostal Theology*, Journal of Pentecostal Theology Supplement (Sheffield: Sheffield Academic, 1998), 62–63.

people who respond to propositions, but to a divine narrative of cosmic rescue. The individual's encounter with the Spirit that testifies to Christ is verified in the new habits of individual piety in the church, which validates the reality that Christ is a Savior.

Pentecostals articulate a view of salvation as liberation for a full and blessed life that enjoys divine acts of liberation. To this extent, there is a parallel interest in the materiality of salvation that is a feature of liberation theologies.[38] At the same time, there is a strong apocalyptic impulse that views salvation in terms of the ultimate eradication of evil in the world by Jesus in the *parousia*. This is a conviction that finds little elaboration in liberation theology.

Recently there have been attempts at renewing soteriology in a way that accommodates the liberal face of Protestantism and its concern for social transformation. Some theologians have found theological capital in a move toward a panentheistic view of salvation.[39] Panentheism construes God's relation to the world as ontologically necessary. It suggests that the world is part of God's being and that the divinity of God is part of the world, although the divine being transcends the world.[40] Jorge Pixley adopts process theology to make such a case.[41] He argues that this is the most fitting theological framework for the biblical testimony regarding God's liberating actions in the history of Israel, in the person of Jesus, and the demand for human participation. Pixley argues: "If human beings, like God, are creators at any moment of history, this means that God cannot, or does not desire, to impose his will against the will of the creators. The creative action of God is manifested in his will for all and each of the creatures. But that will does not impose

38. Cf. Miroslav Volf, "Materiality of Salvation: An Investigation in the Soteriologies of Liberation and Pentecostal Theologies," *Journal of Ecumenical Studies* 26, no. 3 (1989): 447–67.

39. Roman Catholic theologians like Ivone Gebara and Leonardo Boff began to move to a process view of God in the 1990s. But their attention was primarily directed to the doctrine of God, not to soteriology per se. See Ivone Gebara, *Longing for Running Water: Ecofeminism and Liberation* (Minneapolis: Augsburg Fortress, 1999); Leonardo Boff, *Ecología: grito de la tierra, grito de los probres* (Madrid: Trotta, 1996).

40. Cf. John W. Cooper, *Panentheism: The Other God of the Philosophers—From Plato to the Present* (Grand Rapids: Baker Academic, 2006).

41. In process theology, the God-world relationship not only is construed as metaphysically interdependent, but also God is seen as sharing in the metaphysical categories of process, such as temporality, relatedness, and change.

itself, but through *persuasion*. . . . Therefore the future is always open."[42]

Even though the cross and the resurrection are the center of the drama of redemption, Jesus's proclamation of the arrival of the kingdom to his generation was simply wrong. Even God, Pixley argues, is subject to his relations. God cannot simply circumvent the creative actions of creatures who resist his rule. For Pixley, the metaphysics of process theology help explain why the kingdom of God did not immediately arrive. The arrival of a new reality to the world is a collaborative, even co-dependent effort of divine and human will. Nothing in human reality objectively changes in the atonement of Jesus. For process theologians, divine agency and action are inextricably and necessarily entangled in temporal processes. God's relations with the world are internal to the divine being, hence, they effect and compel divine action. God's will to save, then, can be interpreted as God's will to call humans to experience the Spirit who operates in Christ so that they might in turn imitate the praxis of Jesus, even in his suffering. This proposal is consistent with the basic intuition in liberation theology that God is a God of salvation in history.

Liberation: Is There Life before Death?

Human beings, due to their fallen nature, create cultures of violence, impoverishment, and dehumanization. Xavier Zubiri calls this social consolidation of sin *pecado de los tiempos* (sin of the times), or *pecado histórico* (historical sin).[43] The gospel's liberating announcement confronts this anti-kingdom reality, for it posits that salvation is accomplished through the life, death, and resurrection of Jesus Christ. "God was reconciling the world to himself in Christ, not counting people's sins against them" (2 Cor. 5:19).

Certain formulations of salvation, or liberation, come across as reductionistic. For instance, when the theologian conceives and describes the significance of Jesus's death only in terms of a superb exem-

42. Jorge V. Pixley, *La Biblia, teología de la liberación y filosofía procesual. El Dios liberador en la Biblia*, Tiempo Axial (Quito: Abya-Yala/UPS, 2009), 56.

43. Antonio González, *Trinidad y liberación: la teología trinitaria considerada desde la perspectiva de la teología de la liberación*, Colección Teología latinomericana (San Salvador: UCA, 1994), 77.

plary action, its transcendent consequences will be left undervalued. The cross is treated as an epic event. For example, the death of Jesus is sometimes described as the result of the political and religious persecution of a messianic leader and his group of revolutionaries who were crushed under the weight of history. Jesus identified with people in the margins of society and died in solidarity with them. The execution of Jesus reveals that God identifies with the victims. Solidarity and work in favor of those who need it most is a Christian calling, obligation, and virtue.

But this rendering of salvation, though affirming the historical acts and the character of God, tends to minimize the metaphysical aspects of Christ's actions. First, God is in solidarity with the victims of sin as the one who liberates them for a future of cosmic reconciliation and justice. This liberation is overwhelmingly portrayed in Scripture as God's irruption in history in speech and acts, especially in the person of Jesus, the crucified messiah for the sins of the world. Divine action is primarily effectual, not merely exemplary. God's liberating actions are experienced both historically (already) and eschatologically (not yet) for those in union with Christ. Second, salvation entails the shaping of an embodied existence according to the *telos* of God in Christ through faith. It is the experience of the restoration project of creation. God in Christ through the Spirit is the one who reigns, and human beings are called to participate in this reigning activity.

Therefore, a more fully realized (and even embodied) definition of salvation promotes disciples who participate in the exaltation of the crucified, resurrected Son who is the true human being. To the extent that the experience of salvation is in the "already" of temporal existence, it is conceived as liberation. Salvation points to the union with and participation in the reign of the Lord Jesus through the Spirit for the creation of a world of perpetual *shalom*.

The *ecclesia* is commissioned to embody this renovation of human life, particularly in the face of suffering. It does so by rehearsing a drama of another possible world in a social space (i.e., local church); it taps into the collective imagination of another possible humanity. Life *before* death is an imminent concern. Latin American theology has influenced contemporary literature with the exploration of this new human praxis that longs for a different future. Isabel Allende in her novel *Eva Luna* draws a vivid portrait of such a person, Huberto Naranjo, as he changes/transforms into a new human:

Outwardly, [he] was made of stone, but as the months passed by, something primal softened and broke on the inside, and from within, a new fruit came forth. The first symptom was compassion, unknown to him, since he had never received it from anybody nor had he ever had the occasion to practice it. Something warm was growing behind his hardness and silence, something like an unlimited affection for others, something that surprised them more than any of the other changes he had suffered thus far. He started to love his comrades, wanting to give his life for them; he felt a powerful desire to hug them and tell them: I love you, brother. Then that feeling extended itself until it encompassed the entire anonymous multitude of the town, and he understood that the rage had turned around.[44]

Beginning with the most vulnerable of humanity, men and women are not only united to Jesus the liberator but are empowered to live as a gathering of a new people, becoming both witnesses to and actors in the reign of the Triune God.

Further Reading

González, Antonio. *The Gospel of Faith and Justice*. Maryknoll, NY: Orbis, 2005.

Gonzalez, Justo, and Ondina E. Gonzalez. *Christianity in Latin America: A History*. New York: Cambridge University Press, 2008.

Martínez-Olivieri, Jules A. *A Visible Witness: Christology, Liberation and Participation*. Emerging Scholars. Minneapolis: Fortress, 2016.

Sobrino, Jon. *Christ the Liberator: A View from the Victims*. Maryknoll, NY: Orbis, 2001.

---

44. Isabel Allende, *Eva Luna* (Mexico D.F.: Edivisión, 1989), 170.

CHAPTER 5

From What Do We Need to Be Saved?
Reflections on God's Justice and Material Salvation

MILTON ACOSTA

ABSTRACT

This chapter explores the general understanding of salvation in some prayers in the book of Psalms, in the New Testament, and in Latin American theologies (liberation theology and the Latin American Theological Fellowship) in order to highlight the materiality of salvation as an expression of God's justice. The continuity of the materiality of salvation from the Old to the New Testament is more evident than it seems at first, perhaps because the apostle Paul's theology of salvation and suffering has been so dominant. Latin American theologies are in many ways a return to the importance of the continuity between the Old Testament and the New Testament on the importance of God's justice and the materiality of salvation.

A significant portion of the Psalms are prayers of individuals who see themselves as poor and oppressed, and ask God to deliver them from these social evils (Ps. 35:10). This understanding of soteriology occupies a prominent place in Latin American theologies. By Latin American theologies I mean documents produced by both liberation theologians and by theologians affiliated with the Latin American Theological Fellowship (Fraternidad Teológica Latinoamericana, or FTL). Given the multiplicity of voices, emphases, and theological methods, it is not possible to speak of "one" theology. For liberation theologians salvation has been articulated as liberation and for the FTL as integral redemption. Perhaps the two main questions that drive these theologies are, "What do human beings need to be saved from?" and "How are they going to be saved?" For the most part Latin American theologians coincide in stating that the people of Latin America need to be saved from poverty and oppression. Contrary to popular belief, most theologians have envisioned a salvation from these evils through peaceful means while only a few have endorsed violent ones.

A large portion of the Latin American soteriological discourse has to do with material salvation.[1] On this, these theologies are in agreement with the Old Testament, where God is committed to save humanity and particularly his people from any form of threat to their well-being. Thus, when believers of the Old Testament ask God to save them, they are usually referring to an enemy of flesh and blood or to a situation of social injustice, and not so much to sin.

In Latin American evangelical piety, however, salvation has been understood mainly as salvation from sin and eternal damnation. That is, God saves us from condemnation in order to give us eternal life. This may be the reason why in the face of social injustice evangelicals in Latin America have a tendency to favor a response along the lines of Christian maturity, sanctification, and sharing in Christ's passion. More recently, a significant number of churches have added the message of the prosperity gospel as the focus of their prayers and the goal of faith.[2]

My question is, "What do we need to be saved from?" First, I summarize how that question is answered in the book of Psalms, which represents well the Old Testament on this issue. Second, I look at a few New Testament examples that highlight the materiality of salvation. Third, I present a brief summary of how the question of salvation has been answered by both liberation theologians and FTL theologians.

I propose that our first response to social evils and social enemies

1. This is what Miroslav Volf called the "materiality of salvation," which is present in two movements that have been particularly strong in what is known today as the Global South. Miroslav Volf, "Materiality of Salvation: An Investigation in the Soteriologies of Liberation and Pentecostal Theologies," *Journal of Ecumenical Studies* 26, no. 3 (1989): 447–67.

2. There will of course be exceptions and the gap may not be as wide nowadays, but this brief description shows that in Latin America, as in many other contexts, the theology produced by academics travels on one road while the church runs on another one. Even though this document is not in itself a proposal to bring theology closer to the church, and vice versa, it is worth asking why theology has not influenced the church as much as it could and what can be done to remedy the situation beyond the old mutual blaming game.

should not be a prayer for the salvation of the victimizers and another for the eternal life of the victims but a rejection of these evils in the form of a prayer for salvation. Action might be required at some point, but our focus here is on prayers that result from a biblical understanding of salvation, not on the specifics of how these evils should be dealt with.[3]

The Old Testament

The biblical idea of salvation has to do largely with three things: forgiveness of sin, deliverance from danger, and the afterlife. In the Old Testament salvation alludes mostly to deliverance from individuals or situations that pose a threat to life and well-being, be it individual or collective.[4] The main issue is perhaps some form of injustice like corruption, monopoly, or oppression, among others. Forgiveness of sins may be part of salvation (e.g., Ezek. 37:23; Ps. 79:9) but not nearly as common as deliverance from real physical enemies. Eternal life is a theology still undeveloped in the Old Testament.

One obvious place in the Old Testament to see a theology of salvation at work is the book of Psalms. Prayers to God for deliverance from earthly enemies exist because of the simple yet fundamental conviction that God saves. This appears to be the case even in prayers that sound more like a complaint to a God described in some cases as absent or indifferent. This suggests that in order to be interpreted and understood, psalms have to be prayed and felt.[5]

Prayer for Salvation in the Old Testament

Regardless of the condition of the victim in the psalms, prayers asking for salvation emanate from the idea of God and his role in situations of

3. See the works by C. René Padilla on integral mission: *Global Poverty and Integral Mission* (Oxford: Church Mission Society, 2009), and *Mission between the Times* (Carlisle: Langham Monographs, 2010).

4. Church of England Doctrine Commission, *Contemporary Doctrine Classics: The Combined Reports* (Norwich: Church House, 2005), 344.

5. Luis Alonso Schökel and Cecilia Carniti, *Salmos I y II* (Estella: Verbo Divino, 1992). See also Hilario M. Raguer Suñer, *Para comprender y vivir los salmos* (Estella: Verbo Divino, 2010), 67.

human injustice and violence. Some prayers show more clearly the conviction that God will save or has saved the penitent from a specific danger. Clearly, material deliverance is understood as a form of salvation.

Psalms is the Old Testament book where the idea of salvation and prayer come together more than in any other. These prayers have at least three underlying premises: (1) God gets involved in human affairs for the sake of justice; (2) God intervenes in favor of those who believe in him; and (3) prayers of gratitude occur when the former two are true and prayers for deliverance are poured forth when God appears apathetic or unable to intervene.

God Gets Involved in Human Affairs for the Sake of Justice

The idea here is not that God gets involved in human affairs on demand. It is simply that a good number of prayers in the book of Psalms presuppose that the kingdom of God rests on justice and righteousness. Referring to Psalms 28–30, Christoph Schroeder holds that "the practice of justice and righteousness is a crucial factor for the activation of YHWH's power in favor of the petitioner. The practice of evil . . . is a perversion and a damage to creation; it will lead YHWH to respond by reverting the evil against its doers."[6]

Starting with the first two psalms, the idea of divine participation in human affairs is very clear. In Psalm 1, evil people will perish while the righteous will stand. In Psalm 2, an apparent psalm of enthronement, the enemies of God's people are threatened if they rebel against God's anointed king. We know that Israel and Judah were never a real threat to the great empires of the ancient Near East. Hymns like Psalm 2, however, were perfectly normal, just like national anthems say things that are not literally true but are culturally appropriate for the occasion.[7] Most psalms confirm that one fundamental premise for prayer is the belief that God is interested in human affairs for the sake of justice and righteousness.

There are many psalms that ask God to establish justice. In Psalm 94, for example, God is asked to shine because justice has been perverted. Social enemies are described as oppressors who abuse the poor,

---

6. Christoph O. Schroeder, *History, Justice, and the Agency of God: A Hermeneutical and Exegetical Investigation on Isaiah and Psalms* (Leiden: Brill, 2001), 221.

7. The Colombian national anthem says that all our evils are over and that the whole world understands the words of Christ.

the orphan, and the widow, the people whose voices are not heard or do not have the resources to stand up for their rights.[8] God seems to be very attentive to the situation of these people and their prayers (Ps. 18:5–7, 17). The conviction expressed in these prayers is that God will destroy individuals who use their power to subjugate and abuse others. According to Psalm 146, God executes justice for the oppressed, gives food to the hungry, sets the prisoners free, opens the eyes of the blind, lifts up those who are bowed down, loves the righteous, watches over the sojourners, upholds the widow and the fatherless, and brings to ruin the way of the wicked (vv. 7–9).

Psalms describe the enemies of justice as people who trust in their wealth and boast about it. Violence is also a common trait of these individuals (Psalm 86), whose lack of understanding makes them comparable to beasts (Psalm 49). These are social enemies who have no fear of God or civil laws, and are not likely to be persuaded by reasonable arguments. Some psalms address them just to say that God will destroy them. The predominant language is "deliver me" (*haṣṣîlēnî*), but in some cases God's actions and the victims' actions to eliminate victimizers are one and the same thing (e.g., Pss. 18:37–43; 41:10). This is the foundation of prayers that ask for justice and salvation for those who trust in the steadfast love of God (Ps. 52:8). Thus, God's justice and righteousness are objects of meditation, prayer, and discourse (Psalm 71).

We may partially conclude that (1) justice is a common concern in the psalms; (2) victims of injustice expect God to act in their favor; and (3) justice is done when social enemies are removed.

What Do We Need to Be Saved From?

People who are victims of social enemies for prolonged periods of time face the danger of despair, the sense of having been abandoned by God. Therefore, salvation from enemies is also salvation from hopelessness and unbelief:[9] "By this I know that you delight in me: my enemy will not shout in triumph over me" (Ps. 41:11; cf. 6:4). Perhaps as an encouragement in these situations there are psalms that proclaim that God is a guardian who does not fall asleep (Pss. 121:3–7; 59:5).

Justice should be promoted by legislation, upheld by all citizens, and

---

8. Even animals are saved by God! (See Ps. 36:6; cf. Ps. 147:9.)

9. In ancient times this did not lead to atheism, but to polytheism. Several gods could be better than one if the one you have appears unable to save you.

defended by judges. Since these three seem to fail rather frequently, affecting especially the weaker population, salvation from all forms of injustice becomes a permanent cry to God in the psalms. There are prayers against favoritism in the courts and a command to the contrary: "Rescue the weak and the needy; deliver them from the hand of the wicked" (Ps. 82:4). God, the "judge of the earth" (v. 8), is called on because earthly judges do not do what they are supposed to. The establishment of justice on earth is also understood as part of God's sovereignty.[10]

Along with injustice, people need salvation from physical danger. The main concerns in these prayers were not traffic or climate change, which are very important. Rather, they talk about the snare of the fowler, pestilence, the terror of the night, arrows that fly, destruction (Psalm 91), all sorts of evils like violent men, venomous tongues, wicked hands, and arrogant people (Psalm 140). Salvation in these cases is understood as having a long life well lived.

The petitioner in the psalms also needs to be saved from false hopes, like warriors and their weapons. There is a consistent warning in the Old Testament against trusting in military intelligence and power;[11] faithfulness to God is more important (Pss. 146:3; 147:10–11). This, however, does not imply the elimination of armed forces (Psalm 35).

Gratitude and Complaint

The world of the psalms appears quite dangerous. People are mistreated, abused, threatened, and persecuted. At times life feels like sleeping around lions (Ps. 57:4). This is why the cry "keep me," "hide me," and other petitions to the same effect are so common in these prayers. These are enemies of flesh and blood who pose a mortal threat to the person who prays (Ps. 17:8).

Perhaps the absence of justice on earth created the urgency in the people of God to think and produce so much literature about this issue. One common irony in prayers for justice is the need to be saved from judges, precisely the people responsible for imparting justice (Psalms

10. J. Clinton McCann, "Righteousness, Justice, and Peace: A Contemporary Theology of the Psalms," *Horizons in Biblical Theology* 23 (2001): 115.

11. For a complete study of the theme, see José Luis Sicre, *Los dioses olvidados: Poder y riqueza en los profetas preexílicos* (Madrid: Cristiandad, 1979).

58; 60; 109:30–31). Those who are meant to be protectors are the ones who "eat up my people as they eat bread" (Ps. 53:4). The identity of the enemies is not always clearly stated, but these are people who also pray to God for help but there is no response for them (Ps. 18:41).

There seem to be other grounds besides justice on which prayers for salvation are addressed to God. Some psalms state that people in vulnerable situations are saved because of God's mercy (Ps. 31:16), because "he delighted in me" (Ps. 18:19), or because "I am your servant" (Ps. 143:12). In some cases there is a clear affirmation of justice as a retribution for the believer's righteousness and cleanness. In fact, "in the Psalms it is almost always *the righteous* who are suffering, and they are generally suffering not because they have been bad, but rather because they have been faithful."[12] The reasoning of these prayers seems to be that God shows mercy to the merciful "and with the crooked you make yourself seem tortuous" (Ps. 18:20–26).

God's favorable response to a prayer for deliverance provokes, quite naturally, celebration and words of exaltation. It is one important way by which God becomes real. In some cases the issue is described using court language where evil people are judged, sentenced, and condemned to perpetual ruin. Witnessing the end to injustice is understood to be one of the ways by which God "avenges blood" and remembers those who seek him, that is, the poor.

The fact that about two-thirds of the psalms are lamentations or contain lament implies that it was not uncommon for people in ancient Israel and Judah to have their very existence threatened and, as a result, their faith challenged permanently. Can God save? Prayer, then, is often simultaneously a declaration of belief and unbelief, celebration and lament.

One expression that sums up the idea of salvation in the psalms is that God restored fortunes. The return of the exiles and the exodus are perhaps the ultimate instances of salvation in the Old Testament. In the case of the exiles who returned to Judea, salvation brought laughter, shouts of joy, and even praise to God from other nations (Ps. 126:1–4).

It is possible to speak of God in the abstract, but theology makes little sense unless there is some connection to the world as we, as human beings who live on this earth, know it. Although this sounds very obvious, perhaps it helps us understand that knowledge of God as Savior in the psalms has to do with actual acts of salvation from enemies

---

12. McCann, "Righteousness, Justice, and Peace," 122; emphasis in the original.

who can cause physical harm. It is the experience of salvation that produces descriptions of God as rest for the soul, rock, refuge, loving, powerful (Psalm 62), and many others that are used to worship God.

As indicated above, the psalms also show that salvation does not always occur in the time or in the way that it is expected, and on occasion not at all. This is also part of the picture in the prayers about salvation. The psalms that express this uncertainty about God's salvation or that complain to God for not being aware of what happens to his people are called psalms of lament. In some cases God is accused of being deaf, mute, asleep, hidden, or indifferent to the suffering of the righteous (Psalms 12; 28; 54; 83). In some psalms there is the puzzling combination of uncertainty and assurance. Social evils are denounced and the certainty of God's salvation is also affirmed.

Complaints and laments to God are expressions of faith. It is precisely because of that that the psalmists make these affirmations and questions about God's ability to save (Psalm 80). Two common questions are: "How long, O God?" and "Where are you, God?" (Psalm 89). These questions presuppose that God is absent when and where he should be present and performing some salvific act.

One of the major theological challenges expressed in the psalms is simultaneity of the prosperity of evil people and the disgrace of the righteous. In such circumstances, the righteous are tempted to follow the path of the wicked. God seems unable to save and indifferent to sin, which goes against God's expected behavior. The petitioners in these prayers need to be saved in order to believe and to avoid taking the path of corruption and injustice (Ps. 18:39–49). In at least one case (Psalm 55), in the face of unresolved violence, crime, injustice, cruelty, and deceit, the only alternative seems to be to escape.

Some psalms are perhaps comparable to videos that show a person of authority committing some kind of abuse. They are shown to stir up some sentiments of outrage and indignation in the viewers. Psalm 74 talks about the destruction of the temple, the absence of prophets, and God's indifference. Even worse, God seems to be acting against everything he believes (Psalm 79)! What could be more tragic than that? But this is done to remind God of who he is. And the reason for doing all this is that God simply cannot disappoint those who trust in him, that is, the poor and the oppressed.

Psalm 80 seems to be a national cry for salvation. God is described as pastor, Lord of hosts, and farmer who should save his people. But the pastor is asleep, the Lord of hosts is somewhere up there wrapped in clouds, and the farmer has completely abandoned his vineyard. From the perspective of this psalm, having faith means asking difficult questions to God and about God when God does not save (Psalm 102). Why is God punishing us? Shouldn't he be dealing with the pagans instead? Why are we being punished because of sins committed by our ancestors (Psalm 79)? The "how long?" and the "why?" in the Old Testament generally suggest that faith has reached a dangerous limit. These observations show that the theology of salvation in the psalms is complex. In some instances there is an acknowledgment that the people of Israel have been disobedient and their judgment is well deserved (e.g., Psalm 78). But that's not always the case. The psalms of lament seem to express an unbearable incongruity between theology and facts, between faith and experience. We might very well ask if this incongruity is caused by God's revelation itself or by expectations that all human beings would come up with given a chance to present all our petitions to an almighty God whom we believe is on our side.[13]

To summarize, this brief survey of salvation in the psalms shows:

1. Life was hard for many people.
2. God's presence and power were not always evident.
3. People protested to God and prayed to God for deliverance.
4. Salvation is a central issue in the book of Psalms.
5. Prayer makes sense because God saves.

The New Testament

Many general and specific works are available on salvation in the New Testament, some of them quite detailed.[14] Perhaps it might be safe to

---

13. For a more detailed study of this issue, see Craig C. Broyles, *The Conflict of Faith and Experience in the Psalms: A Form-Critical and Theological Study* (Sheffield: JSOT, 1989); Carleen Mandolfo, *God in the Dock: Dialogic Tension in the Psalms of Lament* (London: Sheffield, 2002).

14. For example: Charles H. Talbert, Jason A. Whitlark, and Andrew E. Arterbury, *Getting "Saved": The Whole Story of Salvation in the New Testament* (Grand Rapids: Eerdmans, 2011); Brenda B. Colijn, *Images of Salvation in the New Testament* (Downers Grove, IL: IVP Academic, 2010); J. G. Van der Watt, ed., *Salvation in the New Testament: Perspectives on Soteriology* (Leiden: Brill, 2005); Gary W. Burnett, *Paul and the Salvation of the Individual* (Leiden: Brill, 2001).

say that most works published on soteriology represent the perspective of the New Testament. This happens because of the Christ-event. Since we do not have in the New Testament anything comparable to the book of Psalms, I have selected some texts and themes in order to observe what seems to be the dominant response to injustice when it is based on the New Testament.

God's interest in human affairs is present throughout the New Testament. In fact, the incarnation is considered the climactic event in salvation history. The life, death, and resurrection of Jesus together constitute God's ultimate salvific act in favor of humanity. We must ask two questions, however: Is the presentation of salvation in the New Testament developed exponentially regarding the atonement and the afterlife, and underdeveloped in matters of life this side of the grave? Or, is our reading of the New Testament regarding these issues inadequate?

What Do We Need to Be Saved From?

According to Luke's Gospel (4:17–21), Jesus read the section in the scroll of Isaiah that talks about the liberation of the poor, the oppressed, and the marginalized and concluded that this was a description of his person and ministry. Rosinah Gabaitse has clearly shown in her chapter in this volume that this is the roadmap for Jesus's ministry, but that in the context of Botswana where she lives there is a tendency to remove the materiality of this description of salvation and to turn to spiritual poverty, oppression, and marginalization. The very fact that a chapter has to be written to warn against spiritualizing these words shows that Christians in many parts of the world do not see in the New Testament what some see in the Old Testament, that God is in the business of material salvation as well.

When Zacchaeus acknowledged that he had robbed his fellow citizens in the business of collecting taxes, he decided to give half of his wealth to the poor and to restore fourfold the money he had stolen. Jesus said in response to his decision, "salvation has come to this house" (Luke 19:8–10). In this case salvation has to do with doing justice, stopping corruption, and restoring social order. This is clearly in line with the psalms and with Luke 4 quoting Isaiah, which clearly shows the continuity between the Old Testament and the teaching of Jesus on the material aspects of salvation such as the practice of justice and care for the poor, which demonstrate what it means to love God.[15] Thus, it would be a distortion of the New Testament to limit soteriology to forgiveness of sin and the afterlife. The idea of salvation in the New Testament is rich and complex.

Suffering and Salvation

In Acts 4, Psalm 2:1–2 is applied to Jesus in order to affirm that this anointed king has been killed "according to the definite plan and foreknowledge of God." This is said by people who are being persecuted because of Christ. The disciples' request for protection seems short and mild. They pray that God would "look upon their threats" and grant them boldness to continue preaching and to perform signs and wonders by the power of God.

The way Psalm 2 is used provides a scriptural explanation for Jesus's death, but it seems to suggest that the rulers of the earth who revolt against the Lord and his anointed have succeeded. The verses quoted seem to change the tone of the psalm as a whole. The issue of God's sovereignty might be present in both texts (the whole psalm and what is quoted in Acts 4), but in its New Testament context does not seem to offer any hope of divine protection from social crimes, like the injustice of killing an innocent. We could say that this is precisely the paradox of salvation, but the point is that the issue of justice is overridden and that those who want to follow this king should be prepared to be the objects of similar injustice. This text seems to set a foundation and a pattern for other stories and future reflections in the rest of the New Testament about suffering for the sake of Jesus, especially in the writings of Paul on this issue.

We must not overlook, however, the fact that Christians are trying to survive in an antagonistic environment. Yet the political discourse of resistance is shot throughout, with Revelation being the climax of this thread that we see in Luke 4. In short, there is more oppositional discourse in the New Testament than we realize. Jesus's cross and resurrection is the center point here given the use of the cross as a tool of political repression and domination.

15. Christopher M. Hays, *Renouncing Everything: Money and Discipleship in Luke* (New York: Paulist, 2017).

The result of the prayer in Acts 4 is that the disciples got what they asked for: fear was gone, the gospel was preached, and miracles occurred. And even more, they were filled with the Holy Spirit. Justice does not seem to be a concern here, but there is resistance on the part of the apostles to the political pressure of the priests and Sanhedrin. They were jailed, but God delivered them; clearly, the powers are challenged, the authorities are dishonored, and the apostles are honored. The church does not have an army to jailbreak, but God sends his angel instead!

In his teaching about prayer, Jesus tells the story of a widow who is the victim of a corrupt justice system (Luke 18:1–8). A judge does not do his job, and nobody cares. However, the apparently helpless widow has a powerful weapon—nagging—and she knows how to use it. The conclusion is that this widow will be given justice by the unjust judge because of her persistence; he gets exasperated and she will not go away. The story seems to be in line with some prayers about justice in the psalms. For this reason some versions of the Bible reference some psalms next to it (Pss. 9:8; 58:11; 94:2).

It seems to be that on the issue of suffering, Paul and other New Testament authors are not following the theology and experiences of the psalms, but other texts, perhaps Job and Habakkuk. Paul finds strength in weakness, and sees distress, personal crises, and unanswered prayers as opportunities to trust God and his grace in those situations where justice on this earth is not done. Death is victory because it is a way to participate in the sufferings of Jesus, who died but conquered death by being resurrected. This eschatological hope means that both the faithful and the wicked will receive their recompense, a prominent theme in the Gospel of Luke.[16] So there will be justice.

This short selection of texts shows that salvation in the New Testament has to do with believing in Jesus for the forgiveness of sin and the assurance of eternal life. Salvation is also linked to protection from death in the form of healings and an unhealthy religious system.[17] And it also has to do with salvation from social evils.

16. Hays, *Renouncing Everything.*

17. These seem to be the main two foci of salvation in the New Testament observed by various authors. See Van der Watt, *Salvation in the New Testament.*

Latin American Theologies

Justice is a prominent issue in Latin American theologies, particularly because of its links to the theology of the kingdom of God and its relevance to the Latin American context. There are multiple forms of violence suffered by the poor and society as a whole. Therefore, it is only natural that Latin American theologies since their early days invite people to seek justice and to promote the values of the kingdom of God throughout the continent. Traditionally, Latin American theologies have seen government and big corporations as the main cause of poverty and oppression. Today the sources of violence have diversified and we see that the agents of violence have multiplied, in part due to the absence and weakness of the state.

What follows is not meant to be a summary of the main ideas in Latin American theologies. It is simply a small selection of how some theologians in the continent have answered the question, "What do we need to be saved from?"

Liberation Theologies

In typical liberationist terms, Brazilian theologian Leonardo Boff warns against the danger of an "antithetical dualism" where theology has to choose between "human liberation and salvation in Jesus Christ." The way out of this problem lies in the proposal of an *"integral liberation* that embraces all the dimensions of human life: corporal-spiritual, personal-collective, historical-transcendent."[18] This is evident in the Lord's Prayer: *"the essence of Jesus's message* —the Lord's Prayer— *has been formulated in a prayer, not as a dogma."*[19]

One key insight in liberation theologies is that "in order for God to liberate his creation . . . *it is necessary for human beings to participate* lest they are reduced to mere spectators; otherwise, the kingdom of God would be inhuman and an imposition. As it is, this world is not the kingdom; but with God's intervention and man's conversion acting on

18. Leonardo Boff, *El padrenuestro: la oración de la liberación integral* (Madrid: Ediciones Paulinas, 1982), 12; emphasis in the original.

19. Boff, *El padrenuestro*, 14; emphasis in the original.

this world, it is transformed into the place of God's kingdom."[20] Boff adds,

> The coming of this kingdom is not mechanical, it does not preclude human collaboration. The kingdom is *God's* kingdom, but it has to become *man's* kingdom. God does not save the world and humanity all by himself, for he has made humans partners in the messianic task until one person becomes sacrament of salvation to another. And this partnership is so decisive that its outcome impinges upon the eternal salvation of man.[21]

In brief, humans do the liberating, but this is from God because "it is God who moves and penetrates human action in such a way that liberation can be considered as God's work."[22]

Jesus's disciples' request that he teach them how to pray was like asking him for a summary of his message. Seen in this light, "prayer functioned as a type of *creed* that granted unity and identity to the group."[23] This is how Boff integrates ecclesiology, liberation, and prayer. Prayer becomes the incarnation of the kingdom of God in the church without being limited to it.

The reason why salvation has to be material is that "no matter how high the Spirit soars, no matter how deep our mystical probings, or how metaphysical our abstract thinking, the human being will always be dependent on a piece of bread, a cup of water—in short, on a handful of matter. The material infrastructure is so important that ultimately we find it the root and ground of everything we think about or plan or do."[24] The kingdom of God, which is central in the Lord's Prayer, breaks through and sprouts whenever there is reconciliation and the establishment of just structures in society. For Boff the kingdom of God is present when friendships are restored and whenever a person recovers her dignity.[25]

20. Boff, *El padrenuestro*, 25.

21. Boff, *El padrenuestro*, 91.

22. Leonardo Boff, *Gracia y liberación del hombre: experiencia y doctrina de la gracia* (Madrid: Ediciones Cristiandad, 1980), 208.

23. Boff, *El padrenuestro*, 30.

24. Leonardo Boff, *The Lord's Prayer: The Prayer of Integral Liberation* (Melbourne: Dove Communications, 1983), 75.

25. Boff, *The Lord's Prayer*, 82.

The centrality of liberation in liberation theology presupposes that the Christian response to injustice will not be a theology of suffering, but a theological formulation centered on both divine and human actions against suffering caused directly by human hands or in the form of institutions. Therefore, prayer becomes action.

In his book on Christology, Boff points out that the Latin American context is more interested in anthropology than in ecclesiology, for one simple reason: it is the human being who needs help. The materiality of salvation is not in the visible institutions of the church, but in the needs of people. Theology reflects "on reality right where it bleeds." The goal is not a permanent confrontation but a more human and fraternal world. For that theology has to identify as a fundamental problem the marginalization caused by established social structures.[26] Without this, social reconciliation is impossible.[27] In this context Boff includes loving both friends and enemies. Reconciliation can happen if there are a liberation of the human condition, a conversion of the person, and a reshaping of the world of the person.[28] In the end "what saves is love, disinterestedly accepting the other and being completely open towards God. Here there is no more friend or enemy, neighbor or not neighbor. There are only brothers and sisters."[29] No violence is needed to accomplish this.[30]

According to Boff, Jesus was not interested in understanding and explaining evil but in "assuming it and defeating it with love." It is at this point perhaps where Boff reconciles salvation and suffering:

> Jesus's behavior opened a new possibility for human existence, more precisely, an existence of faith in an absolute sense, even in the face of absurdity, such as the death caused by hatred towards the one who only just loved and sought to do good among men. For this reason Bonhoeffer says that Christians today are called to live that weakness of Christ in the world.[31]

26. Leonardo Boff, *Jesucristo el liberador: ensayo de Cristología crítica para nuestro tiempo* (Santander: Sal Terrae, 1983), 63–64.

27. Boff, *Jesucristo el liberador,* 73.

28. Boff, *Jesucristo el liberador,* 81.

29. Boff, *Jesucristo el liberador,* 91.

30. Boff, *Jesucristo el liberador,* 94, 123, 125.

31. Boff, *Jesucristo el liberador,* 130.

Where Christians have to be careful for Boff is in the timing of liberation. This is not expected to occur immediately because it could make the situation of the oppressed even worse: "For a [liberating] action to be effective, knowing how to wait is crucial. Thus, faith has to be elaborated and live a mystical dimension of liberation to the point of a general regime of oppression."[32] So for Boff liberation becomes a permanent spiral because new captivities appear constantly.[33]

In brief, liberation theology "reflects radically about the salvific mystery in its historical dimension. It is a protest against all forms of fatalism, against all paralyzing sacralization and against any theological speculation disembodied of the world." It has helped theologians all over the world to think of the material implications of salvation, or "the liberating power of the Gospel."[34]

La Fraternidad Teológica Latinoamericana

This section is mostly based on a book that C. René Padilla has described as a "mature fruit" of the theological thinking elaborated by various theologians affiliated with the Latin American Theological Fellowship: *To Be, to Do and to Say: Biblical Foundations of Integral Mission*.[35] This is not a book specifically about prayer, but through its contents we can glean some ideas about how Christians facing oppression and injustice would pray and act.

In the first essay, Old Testament scholar Edesio Sánchez states that in the book of Deuteronomy faithfulness to God has to be understood as the practice of social justice and "the pursuit of a society rooted in justice, peace and love." In other words, "the mission of God's people is founded on two inseparable components: absolute faithfulness to YHWH and social justice."[36]

---

32. Boff, *Gracia y liberación*, 117.

33. Boff, *Gracia y liberación*, 203.

34. Johannes Feiner and Magnus Löhrer, eds., *Mysterium Salutis: manual de teología como historia de salvación*, vol. 5 (Madrid: Cristiandad, n.d.), 261, 264.

35. C. René Padilla and Harold Segura, eds., *Ser, hacer y decir: bases bíblicas de la misión integral* (Buenos Aires: Ediciones Kairos, 2006).

36. Edesio Sánchez Cetina, "Misión integral en el Pentateuco," in *Ser, hacer y decir: bases bíblicas de la misión integral*, ed. C. René Padilla and Harold Segura (Buenos Aires: Ediciones Kairos, 2006), 10–11.

In this light, biblical monotheism is not just a matter of rejecting other gods, "but also the inescapable responsibility to work hard so that both in oneself and in others the image of God may be reserved without distortions or disguise [*disfraz*]."[37] The best example of this is obviously the book of Exodus, where a community of slaves is liberated from oppression in the form of slavery. "This is the heart of God's mission, and will also be the *locus* and *ethos* of the mission of the church."[38] This liberation is God's answer to the cries of the Israelites in Egypt (Exodus 3).

In an essay on the prophets, Esteban Voth holds that the prophets of Israel had a message against unjust structures and the objectification of human beings and for the "construction of theological realities that sought the complete well-being [*bien integral*] of the person."[39] This is so because God's justice "cannot be divorced from God's holiness." In biblical prophetic discourse justice is "always a theological term. The concept of justice is rooted in God's very being, who is just and also requires and demands justice from all human beings."[40] Voth also stresses that in the perspective of the prophets, not doing justice is one of the ways human beings profane God's name (Ezek. 36:20). Often when God intervenes powerfully to demand or to establish justice, this is not a pretty picture.[41]

In his application of the prophetic message to the Latin American context, Voth states that "an integral mission practiced today must take the example of Isaiah seriously. The Latin American context is plagued with situations where the foreigner, the widow, the orphan and the weakest of the population are scorned. These situations are legitimated by legislation or the interpretation of the law. The church, as a community, has the challenge not only to denounce but to transform these cruel realities." According to Voth, the church should follow the example of the prophets in so far as they saw social injustice as situations that must be confronted directly and unambiguously.[42]

37. Sánchez Cetina, "Misión integral," 14.

38. Sánchez Cetina, "Misión integral," 35.

39. Esteban Voth, "Los profetas y la misión integral," in *Ser, hacer y decir: bases bíblicas de la misión integral*, ed. C. René Padilla and Harold Segura (Buenos Aires: Ediciones Kairos, 2006), 156.

40. Voth, "Los profetas y la misión integral," 169.

41. Voth, "Los profetas y la misión integral," 170.

42. Voth, "Los profetas y la misión integral," 175.

Sánchez and Voth, two Latin American Old Testament scholars, do not see social injustice primarily as an opportunity for spiritual growth but as a form of evil that God does not tolerate and Christians should not either. Nevertheless, Voth acknowledges that since the prophets spoke out against the choking forces of the establishment, there are real dangers involved in prophetic preaching. Referring to the case of Ezekiel, Voth states that "the prophet has such passion for life that he is willing to risk his own life."[43] This means that, as for some liberation theologians, liberation and integral mission do not imply the solution to all social problems once and for all. It is a matter of faithfulness to God and to his revelation in Scripture.

A third author that we consider from this book on the biblical foundations of integral mission is Juan Carlos Cevallos, who wrote an essay on the Synoptic Gospels. As with Sánchez and Voth, Cevallos sees in the life and words of Jesus a call to seek justice on earth.[44] Since the state is not divine or the ultimate reality, Christians can never relinquish their role as critics of all acts of institutional injustice.[45]

According to Cevallos, the ideas of justice and compassion are so important in the message of Jesus about the kingdom of God that they "cannot be understood apart from a decision to serve God." In other words, since God cares especially for the victims of injustice and oppression, that is, the weak and the marginalized, indifference to their plight becomes a serious sin because it has to do with God's very being and his kingdom:[46] "Jesus was never passive when he saw the injustice of the powerful and the privileged people. Nor was he ever a promoter of the *status quo*."[47] Cevallos then sees a continuity between the teaching and preaching of the Torah, the prophets, and the psalms and the teaching and preaching of Jesus regarding justice and the kingdom of God, a continuity in the materiality of salvation.[48] The prophetic role

---

43. Voth, "Los profetas y la misión integral," 179.

44. Juan Carlos Cevallos, "La misión en los evangelios sinópticos," in *Ser, hacer y decir: bases bíblicas de la misión integral*, ed. C. René Padilla and Harold Segura (Buenos Aires: Ediciones Kairos, 2006), 183.

45. Cevallos, "La misión en los evangelios sinópticos," 187.

46. These ideas are based on Matthew's use of Isaiah 32:1–20. Cevallos, "La misión en los evangelios sinópticos," 211.

47. Cevallos, "La misión en los evangelios sinópticos," 211.

48. Cevallos, "La misión en los evangelios sinópticos," 217.

of the church means "unmasking the oppressors" within and outside the church.[49]

The emphatic call of the followers of Jesus to seek justice and to stand up for the rights of the weaker members of society implies that for FTL theologians salvation has a clear and important material component. We could even say that the materiality of salvation is central to the biblical message.

Another repeated issue in dealing with the issues of injustice is the price paid by those who speak out. The goal is not to make new enemies but reconciliation. Therefore, Cevallos insists that Christians should also follow Jesus in his commitment to the practice of nonviolence and forgiveness.[50]

The final author we consider from this book is Justo González, who focuses more on salvation in his essay on integral mission in the book of Acts. González acknowledges that "the preaching of the Gospel and the salvation of souls are both part of the church's mission, integral mission . . . has to do with human history, the nations, the freedom that people should have to 'dwell in the land.'"[51]

Acts is the New Testament book where we expect to see the practice of what the other authors have said about justice and salvation from the Old Testament and the Gospels. And we do find it but in the form of samples, not as a church-wide program for the undoing of poverty, oppression, and marginalization and the establishment of justice.

Thus, González also says that "true salvation not only has to do with eternal life but with victory over all the evils that hurt the body and the whole of life."[52] Jesus is the only source of salvation, but his field of action is not limited to the church: "wherever there is health, wellbeing, happiness, victory over the powers of evil, there is Jesus, who is the only source of all salvation. . . . The mission of Jesus is so big, so encompassing, that it reaches much further than our preaching and what it may accomplish." One example of salvation in the early church is the sharing of goods. The testimony here is of "salvation

49. Cevallos, "La misión en los evangelios sinópticos," 220–21.

50. Cevallos, "La misión en los evangelios sinópticos," 249.

51. Justo González, "La misión en Hechos," in *Ser, hacer y decir: bases bíblicas de la misión integral*, ed. C. René Padilla and Harold Segura (Buenos Aires: Ediciones Kairos, 2006), 301.

52. González, "La misión en Hechos," 309.

from greed, economic injustice, dehumanizing poverty." Wherever a person is freed from any of these evils, there is salvation.[53]

Conclusion

According to Volf, "classical (and to a large extent modern) Protestant theology since Luther has retained his radical distinction between salvation and well-being and denied that salvation can be partly experienced in the realm of bodily existence in the world."[54] Even if this thinking cannot be traced back to Luther in every work on soteriology, the truth is that the distinction does exist. This perhaps explains why in some Christian traditions salvation is mainly or merely a matter of forgiveness of sins and eternal life.

As we have seen, material salvation is a central theme in the Old Testament. Salvation is also understood in material terms in Latin American theologies under the general idea that salvation has to do with the whole person. As far as the New Testament is concerned we see that salvation also includes the body and what happens to it on the earth. Human suffering caused by social evils does play a spiritual role in both the Old and the New Testaments, but it is not an acceptance of it.

Christians who suffer from social evils will certainly have to deal with this situation, both personally and in their communities. But the Bible does not stop there. A victim may forgive a criminal, but, according to the Bible, criminals have to be held accountable for their crimes, no matter who they are. This would sound quite obvious to many people. The reason for bringing it up is that there are Christians who live in places where criminals are the law, rights are not respected, and people live in constant fear. If God does not save them, no one is going to save them. Praying psalms of deliverance from their enemies becomes normal, and their elimination a reason to praise God fervently.[55]

---

53. González, "La misión en Hechos," 310–12.

54. When soteriology deals with issues related to social evils, disease, and the economy, it is said that such theology is interested in the "materiality of salvation." Volf, "Materiality of Salvation," 453.

55. This is what a group of Christians coming from a very violent area of Colombia told me in an interview in 2012. It does not always mean their death, but the inability to carry on any criminal activity.

Volf has shown that it makes a lot of sense that theologies with a stronger emphasis on the materiality of salvation, like liberation theology and Pentecostalism (and more recently the so-called prosperity gospel) would flourish in places where socioeconomic needs are greater. As is always the case, context drives theology.

Material salvation becomes important whenever and wherever there is a need for material salvation. John Coffey describes the role of material salvation as freedom from slavery in various Western movements: Protestants from the Roman pope, Puritans who experienced an exodus and year of Jubilee, and Oliver Cromwell who was seen as the English Moses. These and other movements had to do with liberation from religious and civil slavery. Colonists in what is today the United States interpreted their emancipation from the British similarly.[56]

This confirms what has been said in various ways: "religion as a social phenomenon can function only in the context of culture, and any abstraction of a religion from the cultural context in which it is manifested will distort its essential features."[57] The other side of this is that the biblical message is appropriated through a hermeneutic that the readers of the Bible can understand in terms of both its method and the degree to which it responds to their needs.[58]

Perhaps a confirmation of Volf's affirmation about material salvation in Luther can be found in Coffey's words: "While oppression and liberation are indispensable biblical categories, they are penultimate ones. In Christianity, love is a more fundamental concept than freedom, and liberation must be crowned by reconciliation, a truth powerfully modeled by Martin Luther King and Desmond Tutu."[59]

My concern here is not that God has to eliminate all suffering and make all Christians rich. That would be nice for many, but that is a view that cannot be defended from the whole testimony of the Bible.

---

56. "Yet even as they praised God for political deliverance, white Americans held hundreds of thousands of Africans in chattel slavery, and the English had become the world's greatest slave traders." John Coffey, "'To Release the Oppressed': Reclaiming a Biblical Theology of Liberation," *Cambridge Papers* 18, no. 4 (December 2009): 1.

57. Jesse Mugambi, "Africa and the Old Testament," in *Interpreting the Old Testament in Africa: Papers from the International Symposium on Africa and the Old Testament in Nairobi, October 1999*, ed. Mary N Getui, Knut Holter, and Victor Zinkuratire (New York: P. Lang, 2001), 10.

58. Mugambi, "Africa and the Old Testament," 16.

59. Coffey, "'To Release the Oppressed,'" 3.

As D. L. Baker has said: "even in the New Testament there are unreal-ized hopes for the establishment of justice and the end of salvation his-tory."[60] The point is that soteriology has a direct bearing on Christian attitudes toward social evils, as the psalms clearly show. A more com-plete biblical view of salvation could have an impact on the prayers of Christians and in favor of Christians who are victims of serious social enemies, such as injustice, corruption, and violence.

Further Reading

Baker, D. L. *Two Testaments, One Bible: A Study of Some Modern Solutions to the Theological Problem of the Relationship between the Old and New Testaments.* Downers Grove, IL: IVP, 1976.

Boff, Leonardo. *The Lord's Prayer: The Prayer of Integral Liberation.* Melbourne: Dove Communications, 1983.

Broyles, Craig C. *The Conflict of Faith and Experience in the Psalms: A Form-Critical and Theological Study.* Sheffield: JSOT, 1989.

Burnett, Gary W. *Paul and the Salvation of the Individual.* Leiden: Brill, 2001.

Church of England Doctrine Commission. *Contemporary Doctrine Classics: The Combined Reports.* London: Church House, 2005.

Coffey, John. "'To Release the Oppressed': Reclaiming a Biblical Theology of Liberation." *Cambridge Papers* 18, no. 4 (December 2009): 1–4.

Colijn, Brenda B. *Images of Salvation in the New Testament.* Downers Grove, IL: IVP Academic, 2010.

Mandolfo, Carleen. *God in the Dock: Dialogic Tension in the Psalms of Lament.* London: Sheffield, 2002.

McCann, J. Clinton. "Righteousness, Justice, and Peace: A Contemporary Theology of the Psalms." *Horizons in Biblical Theology* 23, no. 2 (2001): 111–31.

Mugambi, Jesse. "Africa and the Old Testament." In *Interpreting the Old Testa-ment in Africa: Papers from the International Symposium on Africa and the Old Testament in Nairobi, October 1999,* edited by Mary N. Getui, Knut Holter, and Victor Zinkuratire, 7–26. New York: P. Lang, 2001.

Padilla, C. René. *Global Poverty and Integral Mission.* Oxford: Church Mission Society, 2009.

———. *Mission between the Times.* Carlisle: Langham Creative Projects, 2010.

60. Baker, *Two Testaments, One Bible,* 137.

Padilla, C. René, and Harold Segura, eds. *Ser, hacer y decir: Bases bíblicas de la misión integral*. Buenos Aires: Kairos Ediciones, 2006.

Schroeder, Christoph O. *History, Justice, and the Agency of God: A Hermeneutical and Exegetical Investigation on Isaiah and Psalms*. Leiden: Brill, 2001.

Sicre, José Luis. *Los dioses olvidados: poder y riqueza en los profetas preexílicos*. Madrid: Cristiandad, 1979.

Talbert, Charles H., Jason A. Whitlark, and Andrew E. Arterbury. *Getting "Saved": The Whole Story of Salvation in the New Testament*. Grand Rapids: Eerdmans, 2011.

Van der Watt, J. G., ed. *Salvation in the New Testament: Perspectives on Soteriology*. Leiden: Brill, 2005.

Volf, Miroslav. "Materiality of Salvation: An Investigation in the Soteriologies of Liberation and Pentecostal Theologies." *Journal of Ecumenical Studies* 26, no. 3 (1989): 447–67.

CHAPTER 6

An Indigenous Reinterpretation of Repentance:
A Step on the Journey to Reconciliation

RAY ALDRED

ABSTRACT

Under the Canadian colonial enterprise, salvation for indigenous people was defined as becoming Western and civilized. Conversion for
indigenous people meant repenting of indigenous identity, putting
it off, and becoming Western, or enfranchised into Canadian society.
Conversely, contextual Cree theology reinterprets conversion and repentance as an embracing of the Creator's fulfillment of all that our
traditional spirituality longed for. Repentance is turning to Christ by
embracing a God-given indigenous identity as a true human being. This
reinterpretation of repentance is also sufficient for non-indigenous
North Americans as they embrace their own responsibility through
repentance moving toward reconciliation.

The idea for this chapter flows out of the attempt to try to hold two
identities—Christian and *Nehiyaw* (Cree, Indian) or *Nehiyawiwin* (Cree
identity)—together within one person.[1] Indigenous people take seriously their indigenous and Christian heritage. They value the spiritual

---

1. Arok Wolvengrey and Freda Ahenakew, *Nēhiýawēwin: Itwēwina* (Regina: Canadian Plains Research Center, University of Regina, 2001).

---

legacy of their ancestors and their own indigenous experiences.[2] However, room was not always made for the indigenous experience and spirituality within North American Christian identity. This chapter is an attempt to work through some of these difficulties in hopes of promoting the possibility of a "peace treaty" between the two.

Under the Canadian colonial enterprise, salvation for indigenous people was defined as becoming Western and civilized. Conversion meant repenting of indigenous identity and becoming Western, or enfranchised into Canadian society. Conversely, contextual Cree theology would reinterpret conversion and repentance as an embracing of the Creator's fulfillment of all that our traditional spirituality longed for. Repentance is turning to Christ by embracing a God-given indigenous identity as a true human being. This reinterpretation of repentance is also sufficient for non-indigenous North Americans as they embrace their own responsibility through repentance moving toward reconciliation that could be described using the principles of restorative justice: telling the truth, or complete disclosure; listening with the heart and not just the intellect; and engaging in a shared plan built on a return to the ongoing historical indigenous treaty process.

Colonized Conversion and Repentance

The problem of reconciling indigenous and Christian identity in Canada is not just a result of the enforcement of assimilationist policies by some denominations through residential schools. These policies were made possible because in Canada there was a general consensus among Euro-Canadians that indigenous people were a problem to be solved. For example, Mohawk lawyer Patricia Monture-Angus in her book *Journeying Forward: Dreaming First Nations Independence*, observes that as recently as 1991 Judge Allan McEachern of the British Columbia court, ruling on an aboriginal land claim, described aboriginal people as a "disadvantaged" part of a "national problem."[3] The judge's words could be construed as paternalistic at best, which describes the past

2. James Treat, *Native and Christian: Indigenous Voices on Religious Identity in the United States and Canada* (New York: Routledge, 1996), 2–8.

3. Patricia A. Monture-Angus, *Journeying Forward: Dreaming First Nations' Independence* (Halifax, NS: Fernwood, 1999), 50–53.

150 years and encapsulates our current state of affairs in indigenous-Canadian relations.

The problem with the Western church was not necessarily its definition of salvation but its interpretation and application of salvation, repentance, and sin that proved problematic. Theologians such as Stanley Grenz point out that "God's activity encompasses all creation, but humankind is his focus. The Spirit applies Christ's work to humans, effecting our union with the Lord and with each other in Christ's community."[4] This definition of salvation is suitable for the purposes of the chapter. Part of the problem was the Western church's presumption that it "owned" salvation to the extent that it defined for indigenous people what salvation would look like.[5] Jesus Christ of the Nicene Creed brought salvation, but the Western church's interpretation of what that meant resulted in indigenous people being looked down on and seen as wild people that were part of a wild land. As John West, Church of England missionary to the Indians, stated, his goal was "to cultivate the heath and convert the heathen."[6]

What was necessary for indigenous people was to repent of their wild way of life and turn to the Christian way of living. Repentance was a contrite turning from sin, but for Canada, developing as a modern nation-state, aboriginal people were immoral by virtue of being indigenous. In colonial Canada, like much of the civilized world, it was necessary for all things wild to become settled. "Settlement, with its attendant emphasis on property and possession, is the bridge that links socioeconomics of colonial civilization with the Christian ideology of moral cultivation."[7] Aboriginal people had a problem fitting into Canadian society because they were immoral. The wild land needed to be cultivated and wild indigenous people needed to be converted and civilized.

This was a popular view of colonized indigenous people, as post-colonial scholar Laura Donaldson points out. Thomas Jefferson, like most Euro-Americans of his time, considered aboriginal men and women as

---

4. Stanley J. Grenz, *Theology for the Community of God* (Grand Rapids: Eerdmans, 2000), 405.

5. Paul Ricoeur, *Figuring the Sacred: Religion, Narrative, and Imagination*, ed. Mark I. Wallace, trans. David Pellauer (Minneapolis: Fortress, 1995), 148.

6. James S. Scott, "Cultivating Christians in Colonial Canadian Missions," in *Canadian Missionaries, Indigenous Peoples: Representing Religion at Home and Abroad*, ed. Alvyn Austin and James S. Scott (Toronto: University of Toronto Press, 2005), 22.

7. Scott, "Cultivating Christians," 29.

not following proper decorum.[8] A generation later, on the Canadian side of the border, John MacDonald continued this colonial way of thinking, believing the problem with Indians was a moral problem.[9] The solution then was to have proper moral training, which could be achieved through residential schools.[10] This was the view of indigenous people in Canada. As a memorandum from Catholic principles makes plain, "cardinal among these virtues was moral training . . . 'all true civilization must be based on moral law.' Christianity has to supplant children's Aboriginal spirituality, which was nothing more than 'pagan superstition'; that 'would not suffice'; to make them 'practise the virtues of our civilianization and avoid the attendant vices.'"[11] Thus, the Western conception of Christianity was aimed at making "Indians" better behaved by giving them a civilized European identity. Thus, conversion to Christianity becomes synonymous with becoming "White" civilized "Natives" while at the same time conquering and taming the wilderness to become something that could be bought and sold.[12]

Residential Schools

The goal of the residential school system was to re-socialize indigenous children.

> The residential school system was an attempt by successive governments to determine the fate of Aboriginal people in Canada by appropriating and reshaping their future in the form of thousands

8. Laura Donaldson, "The Sign of Orpah: Reading Ruth through Native Eyes," in *The Post-Colonial Biblical Reader,* ed. R. S. Sugirtharajah (Malden: Blackwell, 2006), 162.

9. J. R. Miller, "The State, the Church, and Residential Schools in Canada," in *Religion and Public Life: Historical and Comparative Themes* (Toronto: University of Toronto Press, 2001), 110.

10. The Davin Report entrenched residential schools, modeled after American industrial schools, as the way to re-socialize indigenous children. See Flood Davin, "Report on Industrial Schools for Indians and Half-Breeds, 1879," in *Reconciling Canada: Critical Perspectives on the Culture of Redress*, ed. Jennifer Henderson and Pauline Wakeham (Toronto: University of Toronto Press, 1879).

11. "Report of the Royal Commission on Aboriginal People: Looking Forward, Looking Back," ed. Government of Canada (Ottawa: Minister of Supply and Services Canada, 1996), 339.

12. Scott, "Cultivating Christians," 22–23.

of children who were removed from their homes and communities and placed in the care of strangers. Those strangers, the teachers and staff were, according to Hayter Reed, a senior member of the department in the 1890's, to employ "every effort . . . against anything calculated to keep fresh in the memories of the children habits and associations which it is one of the main objects of industrial education to obliterate." Marching out from the schools, the children, effectively re-socialized, imbued with the values of European culture, would be the vanguard of a magnificent metamorphosis: the "savage" was to be made "civilized," made fit to take up the privileges and responsibilities of citizenship.[13]

Residential schools and assimilation policies were to "obliterate" every relationship indigenous children had with their traditional way of life so that they could become civilized Christians.

Children were removed from their homes so that the relationship with the land would be severed. Terry LeBlanc, Mikmaq scholar, notes that the residential school system failed to understand the deep connectedness indigenous people had with the land.[14] The land would no longer be the mother of indigenous children; the residential school would be their "mother" and "would fit them for a life in a modernizing Canada."[15]

Not only were the residential schools to break the relationship between land and indigenous children, but they were also to destroy the children's relationship with their family. The justification for this process included co-opting aboriginal leaders' permission to remove children from homes and place them in schools.[16] Even if parents resisted sending their children to residential schools, the policy was enforced because government and church officials believed that if the children were to be "saved" they needed to be taken from the negative influence of their parents who were stuck in their "wigwam ways."[17]

Another key relationship that was targeted for "obliteration" was the

---

13. "Report of the Royal Commission on Aboriginal People," 335.

14. Terry LeBlanc, "Mission and Power—Case Studies and Theological Reflection: #1 Residential School: Policy, Power and Mission," in *Edinburgh 2010 Conference* (Edinburgh: n.p., 2010), 6.

15. "Report of the Royal Commission on Aboriginal People," 335.

16. Austin and Scott, *Canadian Missionaries, Indigenous Peoples*, 24.

17. "Report of the Royal Commission on Aboriginal People," 338.

relationship between indigenous children and their traditional culture or spirituality.[18] Therefore, traditional spirituality was to be replaced with European Christian values and morals. "A wedge had to be driven not only physically between parent and child but also culturally and spiritually."[19]

Christianity was reduced to a European Christian conception. Indigenous spirituality was seen as another religion or possibly a kind of heresy. Ephraim Radner notes that the church's slow expansion of the concept of heresy justified violence in other settings and for the church;[20] thus indigenous spirituality had to be eradicated. The church justified violence toward indigenous people by vilifying indigenous spirituality and thus making it necessary to eradicate deviant indigenous faith.

Indigenous children were subjected to institutional pressure that severely damaged all of the primary relationships of their human existence: their relationship with the land, their relationship with their parents and community, and their relationship with the Creator through their spirituality. If the effects of the cursing of creation and humanity, as seen in Genesis 3, are a warping of the relationships between humanity and creation, between man and woman or family, and between God as Creator and human beings, then residential schools entrenched the curse and followed the same pattern of cursing in its impact on indigenous peoples' lives. Salvation, or conversion, then was seen as needing to repent or turn from the sinful indigenous life and put on the "white robes"[21] of Western Christianity.

Relocation of the Sayisi Dene

Residential schools were not the only assimilationist policy of the past 150 years that "obliterated" aboriginal relationships. The relocation policies of the 1950s also took their toll on aboriginal identity. The forced relocation of the Sayisi Dene to Churchill, Manitoba, serves as

18. James William McClendon and Curtis W. Freeman, *Systematic Theology*, vol. 1, rev. ed. (Waco, TX: Baylor University Press, 2012), 66–74.

19. "Report of the Royal Commission on Aboriginal People," 340.

20. Ephraim Radner, *A Brutal Unity: The Spiritual Politics of the Christian Church* (Waco, TX: Baylor University Press, 2012), 76–109.

21. William Apess, *On Our Own Ground: The Complete Writings of William Apess, a Pequot, Native Americans of the Northeast*, ed. Barry O'Connell (Amherst: University of Massachusetts Press, 1992), lxvi–lxvii.

an example and shows the impact of relocation on the same primary relationships of indigenous people affected by residential schools.

The Sayisi Dene were nomadic hunters long before the coming of the Europeans. Europeans came to Canada and wanted land. The missionaries helped pave the way by learning the language of the people and converting people to Christianity. It was a former Methodist missionary who was the treaty commissioner in 1910, getting the reluctant Sayisi Dene to sign Treaty 5. Even though they would not be forcibly moved until 1956, this was the beginning of the move. Western people became convinced that every fur-bearing animal was endangered. To keep the caribou safe, the Dene were moved to Churchill because they were seen a threat. There more than one-third of the people died from various causes. The people were taken from the land.[22] They were given little time to pack their things. Living in Churchill without proper shelter, the ability to hunt, or a means to earn a living, they were reduced to living on "welfare vouchers and macaroni rations."[23]

Again, Western society did not take into account the relationship that indigenous people had with land. Survivor of the move Charlie Kithithee said: "The land and the people were one. That was the secret of our life . . . this is how the creator looked after us. He put animals onto our land so that we could provide for our people."[24]

As a result of the separation from the land there was a cascading effect on the other primary relationships. Relocated to Churchill, many of the people developed drinking problems. The relationships between family members eroded. "In 1968, community development worker Phil Dickman wrote: 'There is practically nothing today that binds the children to their parents and prepares them to carry adult responsibilities.'"

The relationship with land was broken, which led to a breakdown in family relationships, which resulted in such spiritual and social destruction that Ila Bussidor tells of the shame she felt over her own identity: "We lived in a slum in total darkness. As a child, I learned

22. Ila Bussidor and Üstün Bilgen-Reinart, *Night Spirits: The Story of the Relocation of the Sayisi Dene*, Manitoba Studies in Native History (Winnipeg: University of Manitoba Press, 1997), 50–55.

23. Bussidor and Bilgen-Reinart, *Night Spirits*, 4.

24. Bussidor and Bilgen-Reinart, *Night Spirits*, 37.

what it felt like to be inferior to another race, to be less than the next person because I was Dene. Because of the racism we faced every day, I was ashamed to be Dene. I wished I belonged to another race of people."[25] It is not surprising then that some indigenous people have become ambivalent about their own indigenous identity. Many have seen all of their relationships damaged through generational trauma. Therefore, repentance for Indian people has been cast as a negative thing. Just like conversion, repentance meant giving up one's identity, to turn from being First Nations and embrace the new Christian identity, an identity that just happened to look like Western European identity.[26] To be converted to Christ meant you gave up being Native. You developed hatred and regret for being made this way and you longed to be "whiter than snow."

This is the narrative of many aboriginal people in Canada. As a result of the degradation that has come about as a result of the assimilation policies such as relocation, residential schools, and underlying racism, many indigenous people are left feeling conflicted about their own identity. The gospel was used to try to annihilate aboriginal identity. Catholic and Protestant alike did this. It was systematic and pervasive. Conversion and repentance became synonymous with giving up aboriginal identity.

Repentance is seen as embracing one's own depravity and turning to God, but this translated into self-hatred by aboriginal people. I am the third generation of my family growing up not wanting to be Indian. My mother told everyone we were mostly French and Scottish. At my grandmother's funeral my brother, in true Cree fashion, made a joke to ease the pain. As all the indigenous people were arriving for the funeral, he leaned over and said, "I wonder when all the French and Scottish relatives are going to get here." I also grew up hating that I was aboriginal, wanting so much to just fit in, because in fitting in, I would escape the pain, or so I thought.

Some indigenous people suggest communal identity as nations of indigenous people is not redeemable by God. A book published by the Christian and Missionary Alliance in the United States expressed this message; it offered the theological opinion that people were redeem-

25. Bussidor and Bilgen-Reinart, *Night Spirits*, 4.

26. Marie Therese Archambault, "Native Americans and Evangelization," in *Native and Christian: Indigenous Voices on Religious Identity in the United States and Canada*, ed. James Treat (New York: Routledge, 1996), 139.

able, but not culture.[27] This could be construed as saying that in order to be Christian we must give up our indigenous culture or spirituality,[28] which amounts to our humanity. This kind of statement is a continuation of the teaching of residential schools that reduced aboriginal identity to something less than human.

As Ila Bussidor expressed shame over her own identity, many indigenous people become self-conscious about their "otherness" and feel shame. In a sense, they feel estranged from themselves. They feel shame for their own identity. They want to be something else and to solve this pain in their soul they resolve to stop being "Indian." Sadly, many have taken it further and thought that the only solution to pain is to stop feeling. They then go to any length to accomplish that, even if it means taking their own life. "Self-contempt" or "other-contempt," all flowing out of illegitimate shame, is the legacy of the assimilation policy of the Canadian government and the churches.

Thankfully we have turned a page or changed our minds, in keeping with the idea of repentance. Aboriginal people continue to struggle against institutionalized assimilationist pressures. However, a shift in the understanding of indigenous peoples' identity is occurring. An embracing of indigenous identity by aboriginal people could be described as a repenting from self-hatred to embracing a God-given indigenous identity. An identity that gives hope despite continued attempts by Western hegemony to suppress or assimilate indigenous identity. A hope that could flow out of Christianity, that does not seek to replace indigenous identity, but could be seen as trying to heal or fulfill indigenous identity.

Repentance as a Decision to Live

There are two aspects of repentance that could fit within an indigenous world that would allow repentance to be reconfigured as a decision to turn and embrace the life the Creator has provided. *Michiyu-*

27. Craig S. Smith, *Boundary Lines: The Issue of Christ, Indigenous Worship, and Native American Culture* (Glendale, AZ: Native American Association of the Christian and Missionary Alliance, 2000).

28. Among Saskatchewan First Nations the terms "spirituality" and "culture" are used interchangably. See Jacqueline Ottmann, "First Nations Leadership and Spirituality within the Royal Commission on Aboriginal Peoples: A Saskatchewan Perspective" (MEd thesis, University of Saskatchewan, 2002).

wasewin in Cree captures the idea of feeling sorry or repenting. This is an older word used in some of the teaching material of the early Methodist missions.[29] In a modern Cree dictionary the word for repentance, *kweskatisiw*, has the idea of changing one's way of life.[30] Both of these definitions would fit within a theological definition of repentance, but they must be reinterpreted within a changing context.

Repentance is a contrite turning from sin. Sin in a First Nations context refers to a "falling out of balance" into self-consciousness, which causes shame.[31] Indigenous people, whose relationships have been under attack and severely damaged, have been pushed "out of balance," resulting in illegitimate shame that can be construed as sin. Calling this illegitimate shame "sin" is not another attempt to heap guilt on abused people by telling them they are to blame for their problems. Rather, it is conceiving of sin as something that traps people, unable to effect change without grace from the Creator. This is a grace that is available if one embraces his own situation and identity that the Creator has provided. Repentance then involves sorrow for a lost identity. It is turning to embrace a Creator-given indigenous identity, and taking responsibility begins to work toward healing all relationships.

This latter version of repentance could be understood as taking responsibility. Responsibility is not primarily about guilt but about an opportunity to live in another way. As such, repentance could become an act of dreaming about what it would be like to put relationships back together, healed or made whole. The idea of taking responsibility could fit within modern indigenous thought. Monture-Angus believes taking responsibility is what is at the heart of indigenous freedom, or self-determination as she calls it: "I have realized that self-determination is both a personal issue and a collective yearning. As I have come to understand it, self-determination begins with looking at yourself and your family and deciding if and when you are

29. John Semmens, William Isbister, and John McDougall, *The Hand-Book to Scripture Truths, or, the Way of Salvation: Words of Admonition, Counsel and Comfort* (Toronto: Methodist Mission Rooms, 1893), 3; E. A. Watkins, "Repentance," in *A Dictionary of the Cree Langage*, ed. Ven. R. Faries (Toronto: Church of England in Canada, 1938).

30. Wolvengrey, "Repent," in *Nēhiýawēwin: Itwēwina*.

31. Joseph E. Couture, Virginia Margaret McGowan, and Ruth Couture, *A Metaphoric Mind: Selected Writings of Joseph Couture* (Edmonton: Athabasca University Press, 2013), 15–16.

living responsibly. Self-determination is principally, that is first and foremost, about our relationships."[32] Thus the gospel of Jesus Christ could bring hope to aboriginal people for a better day in the future. I am struck by the hope that the wounded Christ brings to aboriginal people that we will not die. Somehow, even in the midst of great pain and intensity of rage, there is one who understands. It is the abused Christ who identifies with our own abuse. It is from this place that one can then turn to this Christ and embrace life. Repentance has then ceased to be a decision to hate one's own earthly identity and has become a decision to embrace our broken identity and to live. Repentance is to change my mind about my own despised identity as something having value.

Hope is found in taking responsibility and turning to heal the relationships that have been damaged. For the Sayisi Dene it meant returning to their former territory. They are attempting to restore their relationship with the land. Returning has enabled some to begin to work on healing their wounds. The Dene understood that if we do not heal our wounds they will be passed on to our children.[33] The land is the place where this healing can occur. Again, responsibility for relationship with the land must be understood as a primary human relationship.[34] For example, Naomi Andelson writes, "A sense of health is ultimately rooted in what it means to 'be Cree,' and being Cree has everything to do with connections to the land and to a rich and complex past."[35] Repentance as turning to embrace indigenous identity then could mean to reject the teaching of residential schools that land is a commodity[36] and to remember it as part of family, as our mother.[37]

Colin Gunton reminds Christians that we share a continuity with all that is nonhuman by virtue of our being created.[38] Therefore, one

32. Monture-Angus, *Journeying Forward*, 8.

33. Bussidor and Bilgen-Reinart, *Night Spirits*, 142.

34. Sophie McCall, *First Person Plural: Aboriginal Storytelling and the Ethics of Collaborative Authorship* (Vancouver: University of British Columbia Press, 2012), 120.

35. Naomi Adelson, *'Being Alive Well': Health and the Politics of Cree Well-Being* (Toronto: University of Toronto Press, 2000), 15.

36. LeBlanc, "Mission and Power," 93.

37. Couture, McGowan, and Couture, *A Metaphoric Mind*, 4; Monture-Angus, *Journeying Forward*, 60.

38. Colin E. Gunton, *The One, the Three, and the Many: God, Creation, and the Culture of Modernity* (New York: Cambridge University Press, 1993), 3, 13.

of our primary relationships is with creation or land. Indigenous elder and Anglican priest Andrew Wesley teaches that at the heart of indigenous spirituality is understanding your creation story, a story that tells you of your connection to the land.[39] When this connection is made, you can stand on the land and feel it welcome you home.[40]

We are part of creation and as such we are responsible for living in relationship with the Creator and the created order. Karl Barth affirms that our identity as created individuals means we are responsible to God, the Creator. He maintains that in Acts 2:38, every individual is confronted with the need to repent, to give up a life apart from God, to embrace the only life possible, life with God.[41] Repentance can be seen as a return or a responding to God and entering again into this responsibility.[42] This does not mean that we are responsible for our own salvation—this is entirely the work of God—but we enter again the relationship with the Creator that brings our life into its proper frame of reference. That is, we are to live out our obedience to the Creator as a response to his grace. This idea of repentance as a return to responsibility is in keeping with the understanding of repentance as a turn to embrace indigenous identity.

When repentance is primarily characterized as the feeling of remorse over wrong, it becomes a matter of negative emotions to which we apply forgiveness to take them away. This does nothing to address the need to actually change one's conduct or way of living. Repentance is more than just a feeling of guilt that can be assuaged by talk of forgiveness. Instead of thinking in terms of repentance as primarily negative, by conceiving of repentance as a turning away from sin toward life, repentance could be interpreted as taking responsibility for one's life and working toward repairing the primary relationships of life. This includes the relationship with God the Creator, relationships with other human beings, relationships with the rest of creation, and relationship with ourselves.

39. Andrew Wesley, "Traditional Aboriginal Spirituality," paper presented at the Consultation on First Nations Theological Education, Thornloe University, Sudbury, Ontario, May 21, 2009.

40. Neal McLeod, *Cree Narrative Memory: From Treaties to Contemporary Times* (Saskatoon, SK: Purich, 2007), 61–70.

41. Karl Barth, *Church Dogmatics: The Doctrine of God*, trans. G. W. Bromiley (Edinburgh: T&T Clark, 1957), II/2, 670.

42. Barth, *Church Dogmatics*, III/2, 192.

Since God has created human beings and elected to be gracious to them, a natural response to the Creator is thankfulness.[43] Barth describes this as the returning of grace back to God. It is interesting that this circle of thanksgiving defines Cree spirituality. In the fall you pray for good hunting and in the fall you give thanks for good hunting.[44] Thanksgiving is part of indigenous spirituality in response to living in a good land.[45] Barth would affirm that thankfulness is important but it must be thankfulness directed to the Creator, not merely the characteristic of thankfulness. Thus, knowledge of the Creator is integral to fulfilling this responsibility to live in thankfulness to the Creator. Human life is to be lived in response to the word of God. God's word summons humanity into existence. This word or summons continues to call human beings to a responsible relationship with God that is new every day. As Barth defines this responsibility: "We have stated that the being of man as responsibility is response, being in the act of response to the Word of God. But if it is as it responds, then it is a being which knows, accepts and affirms the Word of God and therefore God Himself. . . . To be responsible before God is to know God."[46]

Repentance as turning to embrace indigenous identity also includes taking responsibility for healing the wounds of abuse that have separated family members and communities. Again, Barth is helpful in that he points out that repentance is more than just feelings of remorse; there is a need to come to grips with our actual situation and respond to the grace of God.[47] This might aid in healing from colonialism, though the trauma from residential schools is more complicated than just removing colonial or neo-colonial policy. Monture-Angus makes this point:

> If colonialism brought our nations to this point, then undoing colonialism must be the answer . . . [but] it is not just colonial relations that must be undone but all of the consequences (addictions, loss of language, loss of parenting skills, loss of self-respect, abuse and violence and so on). Colonialism is no longer linear, vertical relation-

---

43. Barth, *Church Dogmatics*, III/2, 174.
44. Arthur Noskey made this observation in a personal conversation in 2009.
45. Clara Sue Kidwell, Homer Noley, and George E. Tinker, *A Native American Theology* (Maryknoll, NY: Orbis, 2001), 33.
46. Barth, *Church Dogmatics*, III/2, 176.
47. Barth, *Church Dogmatics*, II/2, 768.

ships—colonizer does to colonized—it is horizontal and entangled relationships (like a spider web).[48]

Monture-Angus is not speaking from a purely Christian perspective, but her words can still be informative for a reinterpretation of repentance for Christians. Repentance can involve trying to work through the wounding by revisiting "dark stories,"[49] which can serve as tools for healing. It is reimagining the individual story by embracing the good things from our past history but also remembering the difficulties. The act of embracing one's story and continuing to share it recasts pain and difficulty as a source of hope by showing that indigenous identity remains despite facing traumatic events. Telling and listening to our stories ensures we do not forget our relatives who have passed on. It also ensures that we are not romanticizing some lost ideal, trying to engage in a kind of "primitivism" as a form of escapism to some pre-modern period.[50] Rather, it is trying to embrace identity, as it exists, by attempting to build on roots of strength that are within indigenous culture. This is accomplished by retelling difficult stories in a way that advances healing.[51]

It is not only relationships between individuals in one's own family or group that need to be healed, but there is also a responsibility to attempt to return to or heal treaty relationships between indigenous people and newcomers. This idea is part of what it means to be indigenous or connected with land. Right relationship requires a location; it must be grounded on the earth.[52] As covenant, the treaty has a spiritual and locative dimension. The relationship with the "other" is captured in the shared narrative of the treaty, particularly as the practice of treaty making in Canada developed. J. L. Miller points out that treaties evolved in Canada from "friendship compacts" eventually to covenants between newcomers, indigenous people, and the Creator.[53]

---

48. Monture-Angus, *Journeying Forward*, 11.

49. Bussidor and Bilgen-Reinart, *Night Spirits*, xix.

50. Robert J. Schreiter, *The New Catholicity: Theology between the Global and the Local*, Faith and Cultures Series (Maryknoll, NY: Orbis, 1997), 25.

51. McCall, *First Person Plural*, 120.

52. Monture-Angus, *Journeying Forward*, 36, 60.

53. J. R. Miller, "Compact, Contract, Covenant: The Evolution of Indian Treaty-Making," in *New Histories for Old: Changing Perspectives on Canada's Native Pasts*, ed. Theodore Binnema and Susan Neylan (Vancouver: University of British Columbia Press, 2007), 84.

The braid of sweetgrass illustrates this idea. One strand represents newcomers, another strand the First Nations, and the third the Creator. For the Lakota the smoke from the sweetgrass fills the whole universe and in doing the ceremony we make peace as we become like relatives.[54] Newcomers, including church officials, engaged in the indigenous ceremonies that made us like relatives or family.[55] Thus, in the healing of relationships, treaty relationships must be healed. The treaty also serves as a source of healing. As a shared narrative, it legitimates or creates shared space. The treaty holds the individuals and groups they represent together because, as covenant, the relationship is more important than the exact particulars.[56]

The healing of all relationships is premised on returning to an indigenous identity that affirms the goodness of the created world. The starting point for indigenous spirituality is the appreciation of a beautiful world. Doug Cuthand writes: "Our people believe that the earth and all the creatures that live on it are a gift from the Creator. This beautiful land of lakes, forests, rivers, plains, and mountains is a gift from the Almighty and it must be respected and treated properly."[57] In indigenous spirituality this appreciation for a beautiful world is thanksgiving. In the circle of harmony if you receive something, you give something back; in this way we live in harmony with all things.[58] Repentance is seeking to live in right relationships or in balance with Creator and creation. This is the vision and ideal that indigenous spirituality is seeking. However, it will take time to heal. Ila reminds us, "healing doesn't happen just once. We have to be healed again and again."[59] In seeking the healing of significant relationships with creation, family, clan, community, and all others, indigenous people return or reinvigorate their relationship with *kise-manitow* (Creator).

54. Black Elk, Joseph Epes Brown, and Michael F. Steltenkamp, *The Sacred Pipe: Black Elk's Account of the Seven Rites of the Oglala Sioux* (New York: MJF Books, 1996), 103; Leo J. Omani, "Perspectives of Saskatchewan Dakota/Lakota Elders on the Treaty Process within Canada" (PhD diss., University of Saskatchewan, 2010), 2, 159.

55. Jennifer S. H. Brown, "Rupert's Land, Nituskeenan, Our Land," in *New Histories for Old: Changing Perspectives on Canada's Native Pasts*, ed. Theodore Binnema and Susan Neylan (Vancouver: University of British Columbia Press, 2007), 34–35.

56. Miller, "Compact, Contract, Covenant," 83.

57. Doug Cuthand, *Askiwina: A Cree World* (Regina: Coteau Books, 2007), 1.

58. Kidwell, Noley, and Tinker, *A Native American Theology*, 33.

59. Bussidor and Bilgen-Reinart, *Night Spirits*, 132.

A reinterpreted understanding of repentance as a turning to embrace an identity given by the Creator is therefore in keeping with traditional understandings of what it means to be indigenous in Canada. Interestingly, the basic meaning of repentance as a contrite sorrow for sin and a turning to a new way of living has not needed to be altered. The context has meant repentance has to be reconfigured as hope through taking responsibility. If Christian repentance and salvation is a large enough concept to conceive of turning to Christ as being a return or embracing of a Creator-given indigenous identity, it is possible to conceive of conversion or salvation in Christ as fulfillment instead of being a replacement for indigenous spirituality.[60]

Repentance for Canada

Turning to non-indigenous or newcomers to Turtle Island (what some indigenous groups call North America), what does repentance look like for a Canada that has violated the treaty relationship and is complicit in the abuse of indigenous peoples? Would repentance as turning to embrace a God-given identity as a human being be sufficient to begin to work through the difficulties from the non-indigenous side of the relationship? The answer is positive, particularly if the treaty relationship is seen as shared narrative. It is a large enough concept to include a narrative of troubled relationships but also one of a coming back together or healing. Some of the principles from restorative justice will be put to use in this description.[61] Restorative justice is an attempt to heal the damage. In this process the affected parties must tell the truth; they must listen; they must come up with a shared plan to repair the damage. All of these steps come together as an attempt at reconciliation between indigenous peoples and the newcomers. These

60. In proposing fulfillment I am not precluding the possibility that the relationship between indigenous spirituality and Christianity could be complementary. Fulfillment might be viewed by some as placing indigenous spirituality in a lower or lesser role. It is beyond the scope of this chapter to address this question, but it is worth noting. George Lindbeck offers a brief taxonomy of possible interfaith relationships. See George A. Lindbeck, *The Nature of Doctrine: Religion and Theology in a Post-Liberal Age* (Philadelphia: Westminster, 1984), 52–53.

61. Pierre Allard, "Restorative Justice: Lost Treasure," lecture, Canadian Theological Seminary, March 11, 1999.

steps presuppose that indigenous and newcomers will both, through repentance, embrace their indigenous identity as created human beings.

Oliver O'Donovan points out that a national repentance that is rooted in Scripture must embrace a community or nation's collective history and return to its social covenant.[62] He was thinking about the atrocities committed in India by Britain. He states that repentance for the British people involves owning those things on a personal, individual level. In this way history functions as a moral mirror. He writes:

> Until we learn to root that sense of "us" in the history of a living community, it is an empty, powerless thing to speak of what "we" shall do now, what "our" good intentions are. There is an immense pathos in a community's good intentions—a point to recall at a moment when a modern democracy is heady with excitement of making new beginnings, setting its hand to do things which it is conscious of having failed to do.

By remembering past actions and owning them on an individual level, a nation may keep from making the same mistakes again. New national "blanket" policies that are applied to indigenous people would just be a continuation of colonialism. Healing will come when we base our relationships on "caring, sharing truth and strength."[63]

Canada could heed O'Donovan's observations of remembering and returning in working through its own repentance. Remembering could follow the principles of restorative justice of telling the truth and listening. Returning could embrace the historical treaties as a way forward to heal and affirm relationships in Canada. Canada needs to remember the past and confess its shortcomings—not in an apology as a one-way speech act, but in a dialogue.[64] In so doing Canada could embrace the stories of past abuse as gifts to help be a mirror for repentance.

The Canadian government has engaged in at least two national

---

62. Oliver O'Donovan, "Community Repentance?" *Transformation: An International Journal of Holistic Mission Studies*, no. 14 (1997): 13.

63. Monture-Angus, *Journeying Forward*, 12.

64. Eva Mackey, "The Apologizers' Apology," in *Reconciling Canada: Critical Perspectives on the Culture of Redress*, ed. Jennifer Henderson and Pauline Wakeham (Toronto: University of Toronto Press, 2013), 48.

attempts to effect reconciliation with aboriginal people: the Royal Commission on Aboriginal People (RCAP) and the apology to the survivors of residential schools. Sophie McCall offers the opinion that RCAP, commissioned in 1991, missed an opportunity for reconciliation because it did not lead to dialogue but reduced the response flowing out of the stories of people's trauma at the hands of the Canadian government and churches to recommendations.[65] Recommendations do not allow the reader to enter RCAP as the second-person "you." Recommendations sterilize the past and render it incapable of providing the emotive energy to dream of what repentance looks like. RCAP was limited in its ability to help individuals enter into the shared Canadian narrative to re-configure history. Instead, RCAP tended to see reconciliation as a way to forget the past.

McCall notes that "in order for reconciliation to be more than a case of amnesia, it must prioritize a politics of difference and a testimony. However, the tendency of RCAP's report is to subsume the testimony within a dominant narrative of progress—from assimilation to self-government, from loss to recovery, from mutual mistrust to reconciliation."[66] She explains that the Canadian state's conception of reconciliation saw indigenous people needing to reconcile themselves to being under the Canadian state.[67] This was not a return to the treaty relationship and a reconciliation of equals. Thus, RCAP was ineffective in allowing Canada as the offender to enter into the shared narrative of the treaty. It was limited in its ability to help individual Canadians think through what repentance looks like.

Another opportunity for reconciliation occurred with the 2008 apology by the government of Canada for residential schools. Making the apology was better than not making the apology. Indigenous people have used the prime minister's apology to embrace their wounded identity. Eva Mackey, however, points out that the apology also seems to have been used by the Canadian government not to enter into a dialogue but, as in RCAP, to forget about the past and impose new national strategies for fixing aboriginal people.[68] Mackey suggests that an apology that is not a dialogue is only a one-sided speech-act that fails to bring about a change. It fails as an act of repentance because it does

65. McCall, *First Person Plural*, 110.
66. McCall, *First Person Plural*, 113.
67. McCall, *First Person Plural*, 111–12.
68. Mackey, "The Apologizers' Apology," 50–51.

not lead to a new way of living for the abuser. A real sign of repentance would be a return to the treaty relationship and a reconceiving of repentance from institutionalized abuse. Justice Murray Sinclair, since the completion of the public Truth and Reconciliation Commission, has said that the apology and the public testimony do not amount to reconciliation. There is a need to stop racism toward aboriginal people and others, to work toward healing the relationship.[69] The Canadian people must embrace the past as their own failures. In a turn of repentance to their identity as human beings in a treaty relationship, Canadians could build on the historic treaty process, moving toward reconciliation with indigenous people.

An ideal apology must lead to dialogue, which involves listening. The Truth and Reconciliation Commission was set up as a response to the apology so that people damaged by residential schools could share their stories and perhaps heal.[70] The public testimonies given at the commission meetings were a gift. They are received as a gift if one enters into a reciprocal relationship with the speaker. If we enter into the story and embrace the pain that we have caused and use the emotional energy to help to begin to change, then we are embracing our own identity as true human beings. This is the kind of listening necessary to continue to move toward reconciliation. McCall would call it entering the story "in the second person."[71] This is not easy and the stories of the trauma cause some to disassociate. This can be mitigated if the speaker and the listeners understand the goal is healing and restored relationship.[72] Healing and restored relationship is a legitimate goal for all who call the land of Canada home.

Finally, repentance as turning to a new way of life for newcomers could mean a return for all to the treaty relationship where they are also treaty people. As treaty people, Canadians themselves are healed from being strangers in the land. The idea of treaty is the idea of making relations. Through the treaty newcomers and indigenous people were to live like family. This secures a place for the First Nations and

---

69. Justice Murray Sinclair, "Reconciliation Not Opportunity to 'Get over It': Justice Murray Sinclair," http://www.cbc.ca/news/aboriginal/reconciliation-not-opportunity-to-get-over-it-justice-murray-sinclair-1.2614352.

70. Truth and Reconciliation Commission of Canada, "Our Mandate," http://www.trc.ca/websites/trcinstitution/index.php?p=7.

71. McCall, *First Person Plural*, 111.

72. McCall, *First Person Plural*, 120–21.

it secures a place for newcomers. The following quote from the office of the treaty commissioner in Saskatchewan emphasizes this point:

> Treaties are beneficial to all people in Saskatchewan. They are considered mutually beneficial arrangements that guarantee a co-existence between the treaty parties. Newcomers and their descendants benefit from the wealth generated from the land and the foundational rights provided in the treaties. They built their society in this new land where some were looking for political and religious freedoms. Today, there are misconceptions that only First Nations peoples are part of the treaties, but in reality, both parties are part of the treaty. All people in Saskatchewan are treaty people.[73]

Repentance for Canada could mean turning and owning the mistakes of the past and embracing identity as human beings under covenant that for those in Canada includes the treaty.

Repentance then, as defined in the first section of this chapter as a contrite turning from sin and a turning to embrace an indigenous identity, is large enough to include newcomers. By entering into the shared narrative of a treaty as equals, the possibility exists for a shared identity that does not necessitate the eradication of identity. Instead, it is an opportunity to embrace the past and be open to a future of walking together in the Creator's land in a good way. Functioning as a shared narrative, a treaty allows for a re-envisioning history and becomes a tool for healing.

Conclusion

Repenting of self-hatred means indigenous people embracing their own broken identity so that they can begin to live again. The decision to repent and live is a decision to begin to put back together the relationships that have suffered so much over the years. Though these relationships have been damaged, they remain in the stories and memories of First Nations people. This repentance is not primarily about guilt, but is also about taking responsibility and seeking to rebuild

73. Office of the Treaty Commissioner, "We Are All Treaty People," http://www.otc.ca/education/we-are-all-treaty-people.

what was broken. It is a decision to embrace the hope that there is another way of life possible, one that exceeds merely surviving. The knowledge that each person and each people who share this space are also in relationship is why aboriginal people continue to advocate for a return to nation-to-nation relationships. This provides hope and resources as we continue to develop as a multicultural society.

This reinterpretation of repentance is large enough to include non-indigenous people who make up the nation of Canada. They can repent by entering the shared narrative of the treaty and embracing the stories of trauma from residential schools and relocation in an effort to own the pain and move toward healing. By becoming "second person" in the story, the listener is able to work through the pain of the past without merely wishing it away. This repentance is a turning to embrace the shared narrative of the treaty process in Canada and goes further than a one-way approach that cuts off dialogue. It is possible to see this returning to the treaty relationship as fitting within the rubric of restorative justice as telling the truth, listening with the heart, and creating a shared plan. This is an attempt at reconciliation by healing the treaty relationship or returning to the treaty relationship for healing. Repentance, as seen as a contrite sorrow for sin and a turning to a new way of life, is understandable in a Canadian context by both indigenous and Christian people. It is then possible to see Christian repentance and salvation as a fulfillment of the harmony hoped for by indigenous spirituality.

Further Reading

Apess, William. *On Our Own Ground: The Complete Writings of William Apess, a Pequot.* Edited by Barry O'Connell. Amherst: University of Massachusetts Press, 1992.

Black Elk, Joseph Epes Brown, and Michael F. Steltenkamp. *The Sacred Pipe: Black Elk's Account of the Seven Rites of the Oglala Sioux.* New York: MJF Books, 1996.

Bussidor, Ila, and Üstün Bilgen-Reinart. *Night Spirits: The Story of the Relocation of the Sayisi Dene.* Manitoba Studies in Native History. Winnipeg: University of Manitoba Press, 1997.

Cuthand, Doug. *Askiwina: A Cree World.* Regina: Coteau Books, 2007.

Mackey, Eva. "The Apologizers' Apology." In *Reconciling Canada: Critical Per-*

spectives on the Culture of Redress, edited by Jennifer Henderson and Pauline Wakeham, 47–62. Toronto: University of Toronto Press, 2013.

Miller, J. R. "Compact, Contract, Covenant: The Evolution of Indian Treaty-Making." In *New Histories for Old: Changing Perspectives on Canada's Native Pasts,* edited by Theodore Binnema and Susan Neylan, 66–91. Vancouver: University of British Columbia Press, 2007.

"Report of the Royal Commission on Aboriginal People: Looking Forward, Looking Back." Edited by Government of Canada. Ottawa: Minister of Supply and Services Canada, 1996.

CHAPTER 7

Salvation as Reconciliation: Toward a Theology of Reconciliation in the Division of the Korean Peninsula

Sung Wook Chung

ABSTRACT

Salvation has to do not only with vertical reconciliation between God and humanity but also with horizontal reconciliation between human beings. On the basis of this initial insight, this chapter explores the theme of reconciliation as the main thread that runs through the doctrine of salvation, especially in the context of the division of the Korean peninsula between South Korea and North Korea. In so doing, this chapter attempts to shed soteriological light on the current situation of the division between the two Koreas. In addition, this chapter examines the significance of a Trinitarian theology of reconciliation for mutual forgiveness, embrace, and love between the two nations.

Soteriology has been one of the major loci of Christian systematic theology or dogmatic theology in the Western tradition. Among the themes that Western Christian soteriology has traditionally discussed are conversion (faith and repentance), regeneration, redemption, forgiveness of sins, justification, adoption, union with Christ, sanctification, and perseverance of the saints. However, the idea of reconciliation in the context of soteriology did not attract much interest from Protestant Reformation theology in the sixteenth and seventeenth centuries, including its Lutheran and Reformed versions. Instead, the notion of redemption

Special thanks go to David Buschart, my colleague at Denver Seminary, who provided invaluable feedback on the first draft of this chapter.

took a more central place than the idea of reconciliation in Reformed and Lutheran dogmatics.

It was Albrecht Ritschl, a German liberal theologian, who restored the theme of reconciliation as a major soteriological issue in his magnum opus *The Christian Doctrine of Justification and Reconciliation* (*Die christliche Lehre von der Rechtfertigung und Versöhnung*) in the late nineteenth century.[1] Although Karl Barth attempted to distance himself from the presuppositions and sensibilities of German liberal theology, one of whose leading representatives was Ritschl, he entitled the second major theme of his *Church Dogmatics* "reconciliation," not "redemption."[2] He employed the word "redemption" for the title of the third main theme of the *Church Dogmatics*. Thus, for Barth, reconciliation was the notion equivalent to salvation while redemption was equivalent to the consummation or culmination of the work of salvation. This implies that Barth believed that the central dimension of salvation was reconciliation.

Nevertheless, it is still conventional and customary for many mainline evangelical theologians to use the fourfold scheme of the drama of divine engagement with human beings—creation, fall, redemption, and consummation—to delineate the progress of divine revelation and human history. In evangelical systematic theology, therefore, the theme of salvation is typically discussed under the overarching category of redemption.

Many Korean theologians have worked on soteriology in relation to reconciliation as well. We can identify three major directions and trends in Korean soteriology. First, Korean evangelical theologians have primarily focused on personal and vertical reconciliation between God and sinners. This trend is in line with the dominant tendency within the camp of Western evangelical soteriological reflection. Second, Korean *Minjung* theologians have emphasized the sociopolitical significance of liberation of the oppressed from the tyrannical rule of Korean military power,[3] although *Minjung* theology has been criti-

---

1. Ritschl, *Die christliche Lehre von der Rechtfertigung und Versöhnung*, 3 vols. (Bonn: Adolf Marcus, 1870–74).

2. See Karl Barth, *Church Dogmatics*, trans. G. W. Bromiley (London: Continnum, 2004), IV/1, 57, 58.

3. In a sense, *Minjung* theology can be viewed as a Korean version of liberation theology. See Paul S. Chung, Veli-Matti Kärkkäinen, and Kim Kyoung-Jae, eds., *Asian Contextual Theology for the Third Millennium: Theology of Minjung in Fourth-Eye Formation* (Eugene, OR: Wipf & Stock, 2007).

cized for not paying sufficient attention to the dimension of horizontal reconciliation between the oppressors and the oppressed. Third, some revisionist theologians have attempted to reinterpret the idea of salvation by incorporating Korean cultural and religious ethos, utilizing such notions as *han*, honor, and shame.[4] It is regrettable, though, that Korean theologians have not paid sufficient attention to the idea of group reconciliation or sociopolitical reconciliation in the context of the division of the Korean peninsula.

One cannot overemphasize the significance of the idea of reconciliation in relation to the Christian doctrine of salvation. The fundamental meaning of the idea of salvation in Christian theology is removing enmity and hostility between God and human sinners, which is the result of human rebellion against God. Furthermore, the central aspect of salvation consists in the idea of the restoration of a friendly and harmonious relationship because the basic character of enmity between God and human sinners is construed to be mutual: God detests the state and actions of human sinners, and human sinners hate the holy and righteous God.

Salvation involves not only vertical reconciliation between God and humanity but also horizontal reconciliation between human beings. As Genesis 3 demonstrates, the break of the vertical relationship between God and humanity had a serious impact on the horizontal relationship between the man and the woman who otherwise had been enjoying a friendly relationship. They began to blame and accuse each other, and a wall of hostility was erected between them. To be sure, horizontal reconciliation is a natural and necessary consequence of vertical reconciliation, and as the apostle Paul proclaims in Ephesians 2, horizontal reconciliation always involves a mediator and the demolition of the wall of enmity, mutual forgiveness, mutual embrace, and mutual love.[5]

On the basis of these initial insights, this chapter explores the theme of reconciliation as the main thread that runs through the doctrine of salvation, especially in the context of the division of the Korean peninsula between South Korea and North Korea. In so doing, this

---

4. See Andrew Sung Park, *The Wounded Heart of God: The Asian Concept of Han and the Christian Doctrine of Sin* (Nashville: Abingdon, 1993).

5. For an excellent discussion about the themes of reconciliation and embrace, see Miroslav Volf, *Exclusion and Embrace: A Theological Exploration of Identity, Otherness, and Reconciliation* (Nashville: Abingdon, 1996).

chapter attempts to shed soteriological light on the current division between the two Koreas. In addition, this chapter examines the significance of a Trinitarian theology of reconciliation for mutual forgiveness, embrace, and love between the two nations.

Salvation as Reconciliation: A Soteriological Sketch

When Scripture addresses the idea of salvation in its various passages, it typically highlights the theme of reconciliation. In other words, Scripture features reconciliation as the core dimension of salvation given in and through the Lord Jesus Christ. In addition, the notion of reconciliation in the Bible is construed to have three crucial aspects: Jesus the Reconciler, vertical reconciliation, and horizontal reconciliation.

Jesus Christ as the Reconciler

In the discussion of the offices of Jesus Christ in Christological discourse, the concept of mediator has played a central role.[6] In addition, the Christological concept of mediator implies that reconciliation is one of the major works that the mediator should perform as the representative of both the divine and the human. The mediator becomes absolutely necessary to bridge the gap between the holy God and sinful humanity. As the bridge builder, the mediator should remove the enmity and hostility between the King of the universe and his traitors. In this sense, Jesus Christ the mediator is ultimately the peacemaker and reconciler, as Christological tradition has unanimously affirmed.

The New Testament is not silent but explicit about the office of reconciliation that Jesus Christ voluntarily took for us. For example, the apostle Paul proclaims that believers can enjoy peace with God through the blood of Jesus Christ in Romans 5:1, 9–11:

> Therefore, since we have been justified through faith, we have peace with God through our Lord Jesus Christ. . . . Since we have now been

6. See John Calvin, *The Institutes of the Christian Religion*, trans. Ford Lewis Battles (Philadelphia: Westminster, 1960), and Barth, *Church Dogmatics*, IV/1, 122–28.

justified by his blood, how much more shall we be saved from God's wrath through him. For if, while we were God's enemies, we were reconciled to him through the death of his Son, how much more, having been reconciled, shall we be saved through his life. Not only is this so, but we also boast in God through our Lord Jesus Christ, through whom we have now received reconciliation.

Here Paul describes reconciliation as a result of justification of sinners through faith by grace in Jesus Christ. As justified and forgiven sinners, believers are now completely reconciled to God, the King of the universe. And God is pleased with those sinners forgiven, justified, and reconciled.

Furthermore, Paul stresses the reconciling work of Jesus Christ as follows:

All this is from God, who reconciled us to himself through Christ and gave us the ministry of reconciliation: That God was reconciling the world to himself in Christ, not counting people's sins against them. And he has committed to us the message of reconciliation. We are therefore Christ's ambassadors, as though God were making his appeal through us. We implore you on Christ's behalf: Be reconciled to God. God made him who had no sin to be sin for us, so that in him we might become the righteousness of God. (2 Cor. 5:18–21)

Paul presents God as the subject who reconciles his rebels to himself in and through his Son Jesus Christ.[7] God committed the work of reconciliation to Jesus Christ, the eternal mediator who is fully divine and fully human.

Vertical Reconciliation between God and Sinners

In order to restore the broken relationship between God and human sinners by reconciling them to God, Jesus Christ, the eternal Son of God and the second person of the Trinity, voluntarily emptied himself (*kenosis*), took on human nature, and became a human being through

---

7. See Barth's *Church Dogmatics*, IV/1, §57, "The Work of God the Reconciler."

the hypostatic union. So it is appropriate to observe that Christ's incarnation was geared toward reconciliation.[8] Furthermore, Christ was accused as a traitor against Caesar of the Roman Empire and a blasphemer against the God of the Jews, which means he, a sinless person, became a sinner so that he could atone for the human sin of treason and blasphemy against the God of the universe. Jesus Christ voluntarily sacrificed himself (*agapē*) for peacemaking. Paul confirms this truth by saying, "God made him who had no sin to be sin for us, so that in him we might become the righteousness of God" (2 Cor. 5:21).

Vertical reconciliation between the holy God and human sinners requires the forgiveness of sins. God forgives human sinners by "not counting people's sins against them" (2 Cor. 5:19). On the basis of Christ's atoning work on the cross and in response to sinners' faith in Christ, God forgives sinners unconditionally once and for all. God's forgiveness is complete in that it covers the sins of the past, the present, and the future. In the context of the new covenant established and endorsed by the blood of Jesus Christ, the mediator of the new covenant, God will never remember our sins. As the writer of Hebrews attests, "But when this priest had offered for all time one sacrifice for sins, he sat down at the right hand of God, and since that time he waits for his enemies to be made his footstool. For by one sacrifice he has made perfect forever those who are being made holy" (10:12–14).

Horizontal Reconciliation between Human Sinners

The second major dimension of Christ's work of reconciliation is horizontal reconciliation between sinners. Paul affirms this truth by saying, "And he has committed to us the message of reconciliation. We are therefore Christ's ambassadors, as though God were making his appeal through us" (2 Cor. 5:19–20). As justified and righteous people reconciled to God in and through Jesus Christ, we are called and appointed to be Christ's messengers of the good news of reconciliation. Just as Jesus Christ the mediator was a peacemaker, we should be like him. In the Beatitudes Jesus proclaimed, "Blessed are the peacemakers, for they will be called the children of God" (Matt. 5:9).

There are two distinct aspects of horizontal reconciliation. The

---

8. Both Calvin and Barth were correct on this point.

first is the individual aspect and the second is the communal aspect. On the one hand, the individual aspect is involved with a more private reconciliation between the two individuals estranged and alienated from each other. For instance, the biblical story of reconciliation between Esau and Jacob (Genesis 33) is an excellent example of the individual dimension of horizontal reconciliation. On the other hand, the communal aspect is related to a more public reconciliation between two communities. The biblical witness to the reconciliation between Jews and Gentiles (Ephesians 2) is a great example of the communal aspect of horizontal reconciliation.[9]

The Relationship between Vertical and Horizontal Reconciliation

What is the relationship between vertical and horizontal reconciliation? At the outset, we can affirm that salvation mediated through the gospel of reconciliation embraces both dimensions. In other words, the biblical and theological concept of salvation is comprehensive and holistic enough to include both vertical reconciliation between God and sinners and horizontal reconciliation between sinners.

However, there is a specific relationship between vertical and horizontal reconciliation: the vertical always precedes the horizontal. Vertical reconciliation gives birth to horizontal reconciliation; horizontal reconciliation is a natural and necessary fruit and evidence of vertical reconciliation.[10] In other words, the vertical is pregnant with the horizontal, and the goal of vertical reconciliation is horizontal reconciliation. Ephesians 2 demonstrates this point perfectly. In the first half of the chapter Paul addresses the vertical dimension of reconciliation, discussing the predicament of human depravity and salvation by grace through faith in Jesus Christ alone. Then, in the second half of the chapter, he deals with the reconciliation between Jews and Gentiles, which Christ's work of salvation makes possible. As Paul declares, "For he himself is our peace, who has made the two groups one and has

9. See Jarvis Williams, *One New Man: The Cross and Racial Reconciliation in Pauline Theology* (Nashville: B&H Academic, 2010).

10. Cf. Christoph Schwöbel, "Reconciliation: From Biblical Observations to Dogmatic Reconstruction," in *The Theology of Reconciliation*, ed. Colin E. Gunton (London: T&T Clark, 2003), 13–38.

destroyed the barrier, the dividing wall of hostility, by setting aside in his flesh, the law with its commands and regulations. His purpose was to create in himself one new humanity out of the two, thus making peace" (vv. 14–15).

On the basis of our discussion so far, we can conclude that the gospel of reconciliation brings us two main benefits: vertical reconciliation with God and horizontal reconciliation with others. And horizontal reconciliation is not only a natural product originating from vertical reconciliation but also our proper response to it, that is, it is both a gift (*die Gabe*) and a task (*die Aufgabe*). Furthermore, horizontal reconciliation has both individual and communal dimensions.

Reconciliation and Sanctification from a Trinitarian Perspective

Reconciliation and Sanctification

Ever since the entrance of sin into the human world, sinners' reconciliation with God has been a prerequisite for their renewed and restored life. In spite of God's forgiveness of our sins and his declaration of our justification through faith in Jesus Christ, sinful nature (*sarx*) still remains in us. Right after being pronounced right with God by grace alone, we start a lifelong struggle with indwelling sin, which we call the process of sanctification. In this progressive movement toward perfect godliness, the Christian experiences the repetition of the event of reconciliation in its vertical and horizontal aspects.

The Christian is justified once and for all through faith in Jesus Christ. At the same time, she is definitely set apart for God's possession (positional and definitive sanctification). Still, she has to go through the challenging process of practical and progressive sanctification. Sometimes she enjoys victories in the uphill struggle for the glory of God. Nevertheless, it is not always so. The Christian often fails to live up to God's expectations and this makes her estranged from intimate fellowship with God. At this point, God wants her to be reconciled to him again through confessing her sins and acknowledging the assurance of God's forgiving heart. The vertical reconciliation that the Christian has experienced once and for all becomes a repetitive event that she undergoes again and again on a daily basis. This means that her experience of reconciliation once and for all becomes the paradigm for her future experiences of reconciliation in the process of sanctification in the power of the Holy Spirit.

In addition, we tend to fail to love others as ourselves, including our neighbors and enemies. We often get involved in conflicts with others by doing harm to them or being hurt by them. We tend to exclude others rather than embrace them. This creates a "dividing wall of hostility" (Eph. 2:14) between us and others. In the context of continuous ups and downs in the Christian life, we have to go through the repetition of the event of horizontal reconciliation as well on a daily basis. Sometimes we should forgive those who hurt us and oftentimes we should ask forgiveness of those whom we hurt. "Forgive us our debts as we forgive our debtors" (Matt. 6:12). We have to repeat the Lord's Prayer and practice it continuously. Throughout the process of sanctification, we experience God's grace and others' mercy in forgiving our sins and transgressions. Furthermore, we practice God's grace and mercy in reconciling to us those who do harm to us. In this sense, we can say that the process of sanctification is the continuous journey of experiencing events of reconciliation, vertically with God and horizontally with others.

Reconciliation: Insights from Trinitarian Theology

Trinitarian theology can shed significant and further light on the doctrine of reconciliation. When the Christian is equipped with the insights of Trinitarian theology, he can lead a life of reconciliation on a deeper level with the power of the Holy Spirit.

Renaissance of Trinitarian Theology in the Twentieth Century

Christian theology experienced a renaissance and revival of the doctrine of the Trinity on a global scale in the twentieth century.[11] Karl Barth

11. For excellent introductions to this renaissance, see Stanley J. Grenz, *Rediscovering the Triune God: The Trinity in Contemporary Theology* (Minneapolis: Augsburg Fortress, 2004), and *The Social God and the Relational Self: A Trinitarian Theology of the Imago Dei* (Louisville: Westminster John Knox, 2001). See also Veli-Matti Kärkkäinen, *The Trinity: Global Perspectives* (Louisville: Westminster John Knox, 2007), and Robert Letham, *The Holy Trinity: In Scripture, History, Theology, and Worship* (Phillipsburg: P&R, 2004).

from the Reformed tradition[12] and John Zizioulas[13] from the Greek Orthodox tradition were two of the most important theologians who made indelible contributions to this revival of Trinitarian theology. Roman Catholicism also witnessed a renaissance of the doctrine of the Trinity, primarily through the contribution of major feminist theologians, including Elizabeth Johnson[14] and Catherine Mowry LaCugna.[15]

Major Theological Insights from Revived Trinitarian Theology
We can glean four major theological insights from the revival of the doctrine of the Trinity in the twentieth and early twenty-first centuries. First, God is a community or, more technically speaking, a communion of three divine persons that embodies unity in diversity and diversity in unity.[16] So diversity is not contradictory to unity, and unity is not contradictory to diversity. Unity and diversity can coexist in perfect harmony. They are not mutually exclusive. In a sense, the doctrine of the Trinity is a resolution of the perennial philosophical problem of "the one and the many." The triune God embodies both unity and plurality in absolute balance.

Second, since we are called to imitate God (Eph. 5:1), we should strive to celebrate and respect diversity and difference rather than dismissing and suppressing them. In the context of the celebration of diversity, we should pursue unity. In the context of endeavoring to materialize unity, we should respect diversity and difference.

Third, the three divine persons exist together in a perichoretic manner. The word "perichoresis" means mutual indwelling, mutual incoherence, and circumincession: the Father dwells in the Son and the Holy Spirit; the Son dwells in the Father and the Holy Spirit; the Holy Spirit dwells in the Father and the Son. Divine perichoresis en-

---

12. Among the contributors from the Reformed tradition are Thomas F. Torrance, Colin E. Gunton, and Jürgen Moltmann. Among Lutheran contributors are Robert W. Jenson, Carl Braaten, and Wolfhart Pannenberg.

13. John D. Zizioulas, *Being as Communion: Studies in Personhood and the Church* (New York: St. Vladimir's Seminary Press, 1997), and *Communion and Otherness: Further Studies in Personhood and the Church* (London: T&T Clark, 2006).

14. Elizabeth Johnson, *She Who Is: The Mystery of God in Feminist Theological Discourse* (New York: Crossroad, 2002).

15. Catherine Mowry LaCugna, *God for Us: The Trinity and Christian Life* (New York: HarperCollins, 1991).

16. This theological concern began to be described specifically as a focus on the "social Trinity." But I personally prefer the term "communal Trinity" since I believe that the triune communion is not merely a society or community.

tails further that the three divine persons penetrate into, participate in, and depend on one another. Mutual penetration, participation, and interdependence characterize the life of the triune God.

Human beings should pursue a perichoretic relationship with others characterized by mutual openness, penetration, participation, and interdependence. Therefore, extreme individualism that dismisses outright the communal dimension of human life squarely contradicts the way of being of the triune God. Furthermore, extreme collectivism that suffocates celebration of diversity and individuality is opposed to the perichoretic manner of God's existence. Rejecting both uncontrolled individualism and oppressive collectivism, we should strive to embody a communal perichoresis.

Fourth, the triune God is a communion who enjoys the *koinōnia* of mutual love (*agapē*), glorification, welcoming, embrace, respect, hospitality, service (*diakonia*), and submission (*hypotassō*). The Trinity is not an egalitarian community of entities that seek to grasp equal rights but rather a communion of submission (*hypotassō*) to one another, in which individuals set aside their rights to equality (*kenosis*) and serve one another with self-sacrificing love (*agapē*).

We should strive to embody communions like the triune communion in every area of human life, including the family, workplace, school, society, politics, nations, and international relations. The kingdom of the triune God has already come. It has already begun to impact individual human beings and their communities. Churches are communities that are called to realize a communion like the triune communion. Of course, before the eschaton, we will not be able to accomplish our task completely; but still, churches can be the signposts of the coming kingdom of the triune God who is a perfect communion.[17]

Trinitarian Theological Insights and Reconciliation

First, Trinitarian theological insights will prevent human conflicts. When we realize genuinely the truth that diversity and difference should be celebrated, respected, and welcomed, not dismissed and suf-

17. For an excellent discussion of the life application points of Trinitarian theology, see Fred Sanders, *The Deep Things of God: How the Trinity Changes Everything* (Wheaton: Crossway, 2010).

focated, many unnecessary conflicts will be prevented between human beings. For example, if we truly grasp the Trinitarian truth that racial and ethnic diversity is something to celebrate, rather than to suppress, then racial and ethnic conflicts will decrease significantly. In this context, one may ask, "Why does the Trinity then not legitimize all kinds of diversity and pluralism, including the religious sort?" This question is a legitimate and valid one. It is not difficult, however, to provide an appropriate theological response to the question. Racial, ethnic, gender, and professional differences are indifferent matters to salvation whereas religious commitments are intrinsically connected to the issue of salvation.[18] If you fall into the trap of religious pluralism, you will ultimately end up denying the absolute uniqueness and finality of Jesus Christ.

Second, Trinitarian theological insights will promote reconciliation. When we truly understand the Trinitarian truth that we are created and called to pursue and embody communions like the Trinitarian communion, promotion of reconciliation through practicing unconditional forgiveness will be a natural step to take after conflicts have occurred.[19] Enmity and vengeance against other people and communities will be condemned as totally contradictory to the calling of the Christian individual and community. In this context, one may raise two questions: (1) Isn't it difficult to see how the triune community can serve as the basis for an ethic of forgiveness and reconciliation inasmuch as the triune persons are never in need of forgiveness and reconciliation with one another? (2) Is it really true that the example of the Trinity requires full and equal fellowship among all human beings? While it may be true that human community mirrors God's own internally relational life, don't human limitations require that community be extended to only a certain few (family, friends, clan, culture, or nation), to the exclusion of others?

In relation to the first question, I would argue that the triune communion can serve as the basis for an ethic of forgiveness and reconciliation even though the triune persons are never in need of forgiveness

18. Several theologians (Mark Heim, Amos Yong, Jacques Dupuis, and Raimundo Panikkar) have recently explored theologies of religions with reference to the renaissance of the doctrine of the Trinity, most of which are sympathetic to the pluralist ideology. Keith E. Johnson has refuted those proposals successfully in his *Rethinking the Trinity and Religious Pluralism: An Augustinian Assessment* (Downers Grove, IL: IVP, 2011).

19. For a Latin American discussion of the inclusion of Trinitarian perichoresis as a factor in horizontal reconciliation, see Leonardo Boff, *Trinity and Society* (Eugene, OR: Wipf & Stock, 2005).

and reconciliation with one another. This is because both protologically (beginning) and eschatologically (ending) the triune communion should be the model of all communities. In other words, the triune communion was the model for a marriage communion between Adam and Eve in Eden before the fall, and it will be the model for the community of glorified and resurrected people of God in the new heavens and new earth. In order for communities broken by enmity and hostility to be restored to the original model of the triune communion, they should practice forgiveness and reconciliation since the processes of forgiveness and reconciliation are the means through which human beings can reach the goal of embodying the triune communion in their own context.

In terms of the second question, I would argue that in principle the example of the Trinity requires full and equal fellowship between all human beings. However, in reality, human limitations and sinfulness require that the Trinitarian communion be embodied in only a certain few communities, including marriage, family, friends, clan, culture, and nation within history. The triune communion, however, will be embodied completely and universally among all human beings who will be redeemed in Jesus Christ, the Lamb of God, at the eschaton. The glorified and resurrected people of God will be able to transcend the limitations of time and space and their sinful inclinations.

Applications to the Context of the Division of the Korean Peninsula

This section focuses on how to apply the soteriological and Trinitarian theological insights discussed above to the situation of the division of the Korean peninsula.

Analysis of the Situation of the Division of the Korean Peninsula

Korea was under Japanese colonial rule from 1910 to 1945. During this period the Korean people experienced violent atrocities committed by the Japanese colonial government and were eagerly yearning for their liberation. With the end of the World War II and the defeat of Japan, Korea was politically emancipated but divided into two areas against their will, the northern part occupied and governed by the Soviet Union and the southern part occupied and governed by the United States. In the northern area, north of the 38th parallel, Korean socialists and communists cooperated with the Soviet Union to establish their own government; in the southern area, south of the 38th parallel, Korean nationalists and democratic republicans collaborated with the United States to found their own government. With the backing of the UN and the United States, the Republic of Korea (ROK) was officially formed in the southern area in 1948, which is today called South Korea. In 1948, the General Assembly of the UN confirmed officially that South Korea was the only legitimate nation in the Korean peninsula. Regardless of this UN decision, Korean socialists and communists established the Democratic People's Republic of Korea (DPRK) in the northern area with the support of the Soviet Union and China.

National—even global, depending on one's perspective—tragedy began when the communist North Korea invaded South Korea on June 25, 1950. The Korean War continued for three years.[20] In support of South Korea, 16 UN allied forces led by the United States participated in the war. China supported North Korea militarily. The Soviet Union helped North Korea economically without sending troops. As a result of this war, about 40,000 U.S. troops, 217,000 South Korean troops, 406,000 North Korean troops, and 600,000 Chinese troops were killed. In addition, about 1 million South Korean civilians and 600,000 North Korean civilians were killed or missing. On July 27, 1953, the war ended with a ceasefire. No official truce was established between the two Koreas, which means, in fact, the two countries are still at war.

What, then, was the main cause of the war? Scholars and historians have presented various theories and analyses about the causes of the Korean War. But in a nutshell, it seems appropriate to observe that the Korean War marked the starting point of the Cold War between the communist countries, led by the Soviet Union and China, and the free countries led by the United States. This means that the Korean War was the tragic theater of global ideological conflict between communism and free market democracy.

20. Among the best sources for the history of the Korean War are Max Hastings, *The Korean War* (New York: Simon & Schuster, 1988); Bruce Cummings, *The Korean War: A History* (New York: Modern Library, 2011); and David Halberstam, *The Coldest Winter: America and the Korean War* (New York: Hyperion, 2008). A great online source is http://www.history.com/topics/korean-war.

It has already been more than sixty years since the end of the Korean War. But the communist North Korea has never given up its desire to communize South Korea and it has frequently attacked the capitalistic South Korea, although South Korea has never made a preemptive attack on North Korea. Enmity and hostility between the two Koreas have not dwindled but rather increased in spite of South Korea's numerous efforts to provide humanitarian aid for the hungry and sick in North Korea. North Korea has responded to South Korea's conciliatory gestures and endeavors with violence, cyber invasions, military attacks, and the development of nuclear bombs.[21] As a result, hostile tension between the two Koreas is still increasing on a daily basis and prospects for reconciliation seem gloomy.

Recognition of the Absolute Necessity and Urgency of Reconciliation between the Two Koreas

Many factors are causing the division of the Korean peninsula to be prolonged indefinitely: international power struggles between China, Japan, Russia, and the United States; outdated ideological conflict between communism and free market democracy; the aggressive and belligerent attitude of North Korea; and general disinterest in reconciliation among South Koreans. Whatever the causes may be, we need to recognize that reconciliation between the two Koreas is absolutely necessary and urgent.

The two Koreas share a common language, ethnicity, and historical legacy. Nevertheless, the two Koreas are getting farther and farther apart from each other in terms of values, worldviews, and lifestyles. Enmity and hostility between the two Koreas have been rapidly increasing because military conflicts continue sporadically, resulting in the deaths and injuries of many soldiers and civilians and further alienation from each other. From the perspective of South Korea, the North Korean government has been committing horrendous atrocities against the North Korean people, including serious abuse of human

21. For an excellent discussion of the character of North Korea as a state, see Victor Cha, *The Impossible State: North Korea, Past and Future* (New York: HarperCollins, 2012).

rights, suppressing and forfeiting the basic freedom of religion and press, and over-controlling citizens' daily lives.[22]

Reconciliation through Mutual Forgiveness

In this context, reconciliation between the two Koreas should be pursued through the process of mutual forgiveness. It is against human nature for the victims of violence to forgive the perpetrators. For this very reason, we need the gospel and the message of reconciliation that empowers us to forgive our enemies. God reconciled his enemies to himself by sacrificing his Son Jesus Christ. The core message of the gospel of reconciliation is that unconditional forgiveness opens the door to restoration of friendly and harmonious relationship. The two Koreas need to practice unconditional forgiveness toward each other. Without mutual and unconditional forgiveness, the two Koreas will remain divided permanently. This would be the most tragic scenario for the future of the two Koreas.

In order for mutual forgiveness between the two Koreas to occur, the issues of truth-telling and acknowledgment of guilt should be dealt with in a genuinely gracious and just manner. Both South Korea and North Korea should tell the truth about their attempts to destroy and harm each other and acknowledge their guilt to each other. And they should ask for forgiveness from each other. This is the first step toward mutual forgiveness. Without truth-telling and acknowledgment of sins and guilt, authentic forgiveness can never happen.

We have an excellent example of mutual forgiveness in a sociopolitical context in the case of South Africa. There, many theologians and Christian leaders discussed the issue of reconciliation between the white and the black communities, seeking to remove the mutual enmity and hostility brought about by the policy of apartheid. Desmond Tutu, for example, consistently promoted unconditional and mutual forgiveness between the two communities during apartheid and even after its abolition.[23] Furthermore, 152 theologians and religious lead-

22. For discussions about human rights conditions in North Korea, see Barbara Demick, *Nothing to Envy: Ordinary Lives in North Korea* (New York: Spiegel & Grau, 2010), and Jiyoung Song, *Human Rights Discourse in North Korea* (New York: Routledge, 2014).

23. See Desmond Tutu, *No Future without Forgiveness* (New York: Image, 2000).

ers signed the *Kairos Document*, which challenged the policies of apartheid and declared that the oppressors' repentance was required for genuine forgiveness to occur.[24]

Of course, we cannot forgive others on our own. We need supernatural help and empowerment from the Holy Spirit. Natural human beings tend not to forgive but to avenge. We cannot deny that. So we need to pray for the Holy Spirit to work even in unbelieving Koreans for them to open their hearts and forgive their enemies. In fact, we should pray for a miracle!

The South Korean Government's Responsibility

In the context of the division of the Korean peninsula, the South Korean government should take responsibility for reconciling the North Korean government to itself by practicing unconditional forgiveness and embrace. In spite of the irresponsibility, irresponsiveness, and unchanging hostility of the North Korean government, the South Korean government should act in a different manner. Of course, it would be too idealistic to expect a secular government to act like a religious organization or a church. However, if the South Korean government continues to act like other secular governments in the world, the division of the Korean peninsula will continue endlessly without any hope for reconciliation or reunification.

From 1998 to 2007, when the left-wing political party was in power in South Korea, the government did a good job of embracing North Korea through the so-called sunshine policy,[25] which was focused on supporting both the North Korean government and its people through unconditional economic aid. Many scholars and politicians criticized the South Korean government's sunshine policy because the North Korean government abused and misused its unconditional financial support for developing a nuclear program that threatened the security

24. Harvey J. Sindima, *The Gospel according to the Marginalized* (New York: Peter Lang, 2005), 75.

25. For an excellent discussion of the sunshine policy by one of its advocates, see Chung-In Moon, *The Sunshine Policy: In Defense of Engagement as a Path to Peace in Korea* (Seoul: Yonsei University Press, 2012). Another good reference is Key-young Son, *South Korean Engagement Policies and North Korea: Identities, Norms and the Sunshine Policy* (New York: Routledge, 2006).

of South Korea and its neighboring countries, including Japan and the United States, rather than feeding the hungry and healing the sick in North Korea.

It is undeniable that the possibility of the North Korean government's misuse of the South Korean government's economic aid is always there. Despite that, the South Korean government should not stop providing the North Korean government and people with economic support. To be sure, the South Korean government needs wisdom and discernment here. It must request transparency from the North Korean government to make sure economic aid is being distributed and delivered to the North Korean people according to the desires of the South Korean government and other donors.

Ever since the right-wing political party took power in South Korea in 2008, the sunshine policy has been officially terminated. But we should remember that apart from sacrificial giving and unconditional love and forgiveness, no flower of reconciliation can blossom. We should sow the seed of reconciliation in tears and eventually we will get a full harvest—both reconciliation and reunification between the two Koreas.

The South Korean Church's Communal Responsibility

As Murray Rae has argued, the church is the sign of reconciliation[26] because it is the community of those forgiven by and reconciled to God. As the communion of forgiveness, the South Korean church should strive to embody the spirit of reconciliation within itself (members loving and forgiving one another) and extend it to the larger society and urge the people of the two Koreas to respond to the message of reconciliation. This is how the South Korean church can fulfill its God-given mission and calling in the context of the division of the Korean peninsula.

From a Trinitarian theological perspective, the South Korean church should learn how to celebrate diversity within itself and pursue unity in the context of radical diversity in terms of theological convictions, spiritual experiences, church polities, and historical legacies. The South Ko-

26. Murray Rae, "The Remnant People: Ecclesia as Sign of Reconciliation," in *The Theology of Reconciliation*, ed. Colin E. Gunton (London: T&T Clark, 2003), 93–108.

rean church is a totality of extremely diversified organizations, denominations, and traditions. So it is very easy to fall into excessive individualism, suppressive collectivism, or irresponsible pluralism. In the past, the South Korean church failed to live up to the Trinitarian ideals of the celebration of diversity, the pursuit of unity, and the embodiment of perichoretic *koinōnia* of *agapē, diakonia,* and *hypotassō.* The South Korean church should repent of its past failures, and endeavor to become an alternative communion that can give the people of the two Koreas a new hope for the future.[27] Furthermore, it should become a paradigmatic communion that the people of the two Koreas become eager to follow and imitate in an effort to resolve their problems of mutual enmity and hostility.

The South Korean Christian's Individual Responsibility

Individual Christians in the South Korean church have responsibilities as well. First, they should recognize that God has sent them to the Korean peninsula as messengers of reconciliation. Empowered by the Holy Spirit, they should lead a life of reconciliation in their personal life, families, and churches, and in larger society. In so doing, they should sow the seeds of reconciliation in every area of human life in South Korea with the hope and prayer that their holy endeavor will eventually bear the fruit of reconciliation between the two Koreas. Second, individual Christians in the South Korean church should make every effort to embody Trinitarian spirituality, which is characterized by the celebration of diversity; the pursuit of unity in diversity; and the perichoretic life of communion of mutual love, service, and submission. Their prayer should be that their effort will have ripple effects for reconciliation among South Korean people and between the two Koreas.

Getting Down to Praxis

When it gets down to praxis, how do we lead North Korea to the table? What acts of grace would promote dialogue? These are legitimate ques-

---

27. For an excellent discussion of the church as "alternative community," see Stanley Hauerwas and William H. Willimon, *Resident Aliens: Life in the Christian Colony,* 25th anniversary ed. (Nashville: Abingdon, 2014).

tions that require appropriate responses. Considering North Korea's belligerent and warmongering attitude, it will not be easy to draw the North Korean government to the table of dialogue for reconciliation. However, given the complexities of this situation, we need to delve into how a theology of reconciliation can inform the process of reconciling with a cruel and corrupt regime rather than simply trying to conquer it. Again, my suggestion would be that the South Korean government attempt to convince the North Korean government that the South Korean government does not want to conquer it militarily or swallow it up, but rather wants to have a genuine and authentic relationship that is mutually beneficial and that will ultimately result in mutual reconciliation. In addition, the South Korean government can prepare some incentives for North Korean participation in reconciliation dialogues.

Many scholars and professional analysts of the Korean peninsula have become deeply suspicious about the possibility of reconciliation between the two Koreas, especially after North Korea's fifth nuclear detonation (since 2006) conducted on September 9, 2016. The South Korean people have recently claimed that they have been sacrificing and patient enough. Nevertheless, the South Korean government should not stop knocking on the door of North Korea, asking to open the door for a meal of dialogue together (Rev. 3:20). We should become like Jesus Christ toward North Korea, asking to return to the normal way of life and promising complete forgiveness. May God bless South Korean efforts to accomplish reconciliation with North Korea!

Conclusion

Salvation is reconciliation, and vice versa. South Korean Christians and churches have already experienced salvation as reconciliation. As a result, they are enjoying peace, friendship, and harmony with the triune God and other people. They should recognize that they are called to be the messengers and ambassadors of the gospel of reconciliation revealed in and through Jesus Christ. They should take this responsibility with full seriousness. Through the fulfillment of their God-given mission and calling in the power of the Holy Spirit, they will be able to make a great contribution to the reconciliation between the two Koreas. The reconciliation of the two Koreas is not only our task but also God's gift. For this reason, we keep on praying for the miracle of reconciliation of the two Koreas, planting the seeds of peace in tears. "There is neither Jew nor Gentile, neither slave nor free, nor is there male and female, for you are all one in Christ Jesus" (Gal. 3:28).

Further Reading

Ateek, Naim Stifan. *A Palestinian Christian Cry for Reconciliation*. Maryknoll, NY: Orbis, 2008.

Doxtader, Erik. *With Faith in the Works of Words: The Beginning of Reconciliation in South Africa, 1985–1995*. East Lansing: Michigan State University Press, 2009.

Gilbreath, Edward. *Reconciliation Blues: A Black Evangelical's Inside View of White Christianity*. Downers Grove, IL: IVP, 2008.

Lee, Jung Young. *Marginality: The Key to Multicultural Theology*. Minneapolis: Augsburg Fortress, 1995.

Yung, Hwa. *Mangoes or Bananas? The Quest for an Authentic Asian Christian Theology*. Maryknoll, NY: Orbis, 2014.

CHAPTER 8

Qohelet's Gospel in Ecclesiastes: Ecclesiastes 3:1–15, 7:15–22, and 11:1–6

ELAINE W. F. GOH

ABSTRACT

Ecclesiastes is a book that communicates hope. In 3:1–15, Qohelet conveys a realistic depiction of the concept of time. In 7:15–22, Qohelet acknowledges that a mortal, striving to be righteous, is nevertheless hampered by human limitations. In 11:1–6, Qohelet asserts that human ignorance should not deter one from carpe diem action. These passages suggest life-giving aspects to contend with the mentality of fearing death, overconfidence, and workaholic tendencies among the Chinese. Asian Chinese in general are instructed, through generations of Confucian teachings, to be pragmatic, morally guided, and diligent. Qohelet points out to Asian Chinese the reality confronting these teachings. Qohelet teaches one to live here and now, in line with Asian Chinese pragmatism. This chapter argues that the message of Ecclesiastes offers salvific hope, in line with the gospel and salvation as offered in the Christian faith.

This chapter upholds the theme of salvation history as an Old Testament theology, which accentuates the role of biblical wisdom literature to convey salvation. With this perception, I survey and evaluate the biblical passages frequently used by some Asian Chinese scholars to construct the Chinese Christian understanding of salvation. In this chapter I suggest that Ecclesiastes offers salvific hope as well. I use three passages taken from Ecclesiastes to illustrate the point. In 3:1–15, Qohelet conveys a realistic depiction of the concept of time that reduces the general fear of death. In 7:15–22, Qohelet acknowledges that humankind, striving to be righteous, nevertheless has to accept human limitations. This acceptance will guide people to be realistic and reasonable in daily living. In 11:1–6, Qohelet asserts that human ignorance should not deter one from taking action. Thus, one can be ready to act without being seen to be a workaholic. The three passages suggest life-giving aspects to contend with the mentality of fearing death, overconfidence, and workaholic tendencies among Asian Chinese. Through generations of Confucian teachings, Asian Chinese have learned to be pragmatic, morally guided, and diligent. Qohelet shows Asian Chinese the need to widen the horizons of these teachings. Nevertheless, Qohelet teaches one to live here and now in line with Asian Chinese pragmatism. As such, this chapter argues that the message of Ecclesiastes offers hope, and is consistent with the gospel and salvation proffered in the Christian belief.

Theological Construction on the Theme of Salvation: Some Asian Chinese Perspectives

Constructing a Chinese Christian theology is a task taken on by some Asian scholars in recent decades. To summarize, the basic Asian Chinese Christian understanding of salvation, or soteriology, is primarily Christ-centered.[1] Understandably, their theological construction relies heavily on the New Testament. They regard the Christ-event as the continuation of salvation history from the Old Testament, which also becomes the defining understanding of the law "before" and "after" Jesus's coming, as mentioned in Galatians 3:23–25.[2] Passages related to the Christ-event are generally quoted to articulate the theological understanding of salvation, especially the historical death of Jesus (Heb. 2:14–15), the imagery of the cross (Eph. 2:16; 1 Peter 2:24), and the blood of Christ (Acts 20:28; Rom. 3:25; Heb. 9:12).[3] These New Testament pas-

---

1. These Asian scholars and theologians are mainly from Malaysia, Hong Kong, and Taiwan, as the references suggest.

2. Kok Hon Seng, *Jialataishu Daolun* [Introduction to the Book of Galatians] (Hong Kong: Logos, 2003), 110.

3. See, for example, Dao-zong Wu, *Shenzhi Suoxin: Jidujiao Jiyao Zhenli* [Knowing What We Believe: The Fundamental Truth for Christians] (Taipei: China Evangelical Seminary, 2010), 293–96.

sages, as anticipated, have built on the idea of sacrifice in the Old Testament.

Salvation is needed because of the presence of sin. The word "sin" is a somewhat alien concept in Chinese vocabulary. Though it is commonly found in the Bible, it is often understood in light of, or is related to, the idea of "shame" among Asian Chinese. The Old Testament and the New Testament address the idea of shame in relation to sin as well because of the cultural milieu of the Israelites. In Asian Chinese culture, if a person commits murder, he has to face the law and also bear the shame of giving the family a bad name. Nevertheless, the Asian Chinese way to redeem one's shame is often through one's good works. The idea of "salvation" in this sense means bringing honor to annul shame.

In the Old Testament, a sacrifice is necessary to eliminate sin. On this founding idea, the New Testament avers that sin, regardless of its form, makes humankind fall short of God's glory (Rom. 3:23) and become alienated from God (Eph. 4:18). The death of Jesus Christ on the cross represents the sacrifice that is required to deal with sin. Redemption, therefore, takes place through the grace of God. Hence, when articulating salvation in the Bible, grace (*ḥesed* in the Old Testament, *charis* in the New Testament) is an important idea that Asian Chinese scholars deliberate. As a result of this grace of God, fallen humankind can be made "right," or "justified" (Eph. 1:4–6; Rom. 3:21–26).[4] This idea of "justification" is in relation to one's faith, and is tied closely to the interpretation of salvation based on Paul's epistle to the Romans.[5] Therefore, understandably, in the theological construction of the Christian doctrine of soteriology, the declaration of one being saved "by grace" and "through faith" (Eph. 2:8) is often purposely asserted.[6]

In a commentary on the Nicene Creed, a group of Chinese scholars

---

4. On how this "rightness," or "justification," takes place, various Asian biblical scholars differ in their interpretations depending on their perspectives on the Pauline epistles. See, for example, one that derives from the new perspective on Paul by Lo Lung-Kwong, *Baoluo Xinguan: Luomashu de Zhuti yu Mudi* [New Perspectives on Paul: The Theme and Purpose of the Book to the Romans] (Taipei: University of Donghai Press, 2007).

5. See a title by Sam Tsang, *Luomashu Jiedu: Jidu Fuyin de Zhanxin Shiye* [An Imperial-Missiological Rereading of Romans] (Taipei: Campus Evangelical Fellowship, 2009).

6. See, for example, Kok Hon Seng, *Heavenly Vision for Witness on Earth: A Commentary on Ephesians* (Kuala Lumpur: Bridge Communication, 2010), especially 180–88.

in Southeast Asia further elaborate on the creed.[7] The conviction of the salvation through Christ is partly reflected in the phrase "For us and for our salvation, He came down from heaven."[8] Citing biblical events like that of God's deliverance through Noah's ark (Genesis 6–8), the exodus (Exodus 1–14), and the deliverance from sin (Matt. 1:21), God's salvation is again affirmed. Their theological construction on salvation also relates Christian faith to the life of the church in Asia. The way of faith, according to Asian Chinese theologians, also relies on passages like Colossians 1:15–19, which declares that Christ is the head of the church, through him all things have been created, and in him all things hold together.[9]

A dual theme of creation and redemption has also shaped the Asian Chinese theological understanding of salvation.[10] The notion of creation is closely tied in with the creation account in the book of Genesis. This dual theme is reflected in the work of Yee-cheung Wong in his *Old Testament Theology—From Creation to New Creation*, which uses the terms "creation" and "restoration" to narrate the message of the Old Testament.[11] The concept of "new creation" in his work also builds on the Genesis creation account. In this dual theme, redemption refers to the restoration of the order of things that includes the human condition, lifestyle, relationships, and the cosmos.

In Chinese understanding, theology is relational. The second paragraph of the Nicene Creed spells out the relationship of the Father and the Son: Jesus Christ is the only Son of God, eternally begotten of the Father, and of one Being with the Father. This declaration is made before affirming in the creed that Jesus Christ is salvation. Salvation, therefore, is based on a relationship, and this relationship is extended "for us" in the creed, making possible reconciliation between God and

7. Yip Ching Wah and Lo Lung Kwong, *We Believe: A Commentary on the Nicene Creed*, ed. Association of Theological Schools in South East Asia (Hong Kong: Chinese Christian Literature Council, 2014).

8. Yip and Lo, *We Believe*, 109–17.

9. Andres S. K. Tang, ed., *Zai Xinyang Zhisi de Tuzhong* [On the Way of Faith Thinking] (Hong Kong: Logos, 2000), 47.

10. Watson Hua-zhong Soong, *Shengjing Shenxue* [Biblical Theology] (Taipei: Campus, 1997), 301.

11. Wong Yee-cheung, *Jiuyue Shenxue: Cong Chuangzao Dao Xinchuangzao* [Old Testament Theology—From Creation to New Creation] (Hong Kong: Tien Dao, 2003).

humankind (Rom. 5:10; Col. 1:20–22; Eph. 2:12–13).[12] The grace of reconciliation is given freely through the death and resurrection of the Lord Jesus Christ (Rom. 3:24; 5:11).[13] Based on this theological understanding of reconciliation, the identity of the Asian church is, in some way, defined by reconciling people to God. As an example in practice, such reconciliation through Christ's redemption should have an effect on human living conditions, including solving the problems of poverty in Asia.[14] Salvation, in the sense of the breaking down of oppressive and destructive cycles in that society, will then be truly experienced by all.

The understanding of relationship can be expanded into a constant dialogue between faith and context.[15] Thus, some have advocated for the task of constructing Christian theology from Chinese cultural contexts by means of native resources and terminologies. Exploring cultural connections between the Bible and Chinese literature is not new either. Archie Lee, for example, has written substantially on cross-textual hermeneutics.[16] Furthermore, the in-depth research by K. K. Yeo to pursue a Chinese Christian theology is notable.[17] Yeo asserts a Chinese Christian theology based on a study on Confucian *xin* (trustworthiness) and Pauline *pistis* (faith). He also compares Confucius

12. Zhang-lin Wang, *Shengjing Sibian Shenxue* [Speculative Theology of the Bible] (Taipei: Daosheng, 2008), 119.

13. See also Tan Kim Sai, *Fuyinlun: Fuyin de Neirong yu Benzhi* [Gospelogy: The Content and Nature of the Gospel] (Selangor, Malaysia: MBS, 2006), 30–48.

14. Kung Lap Yan, *Quanren Yushen Hehao: Jiaohui de Shenfen* [Ministry of Reconciliation: The Identity of the Church] (Hong Kong: Hong Kong Christian Institute, 2002), 127–40, points out the relatedness between Jesus Christ's redemption and the fate of the poor.

15. Benedict Hung-biu Kwok, *Chaoxiang Zhengquan Shenxue Sikao* [Toward Complete Theological Thinking] (Hong Kong: Tien Dao, 2004), 27, 33. The notion of theology being relational is inevitably informed by Karl Barth's and Dietrich Bonhoeffer's interpretation of humankind being created "in God's image." See also Tang, ed., *Zai Xinyang Zhisi de Tuzhong*, 133.

16. See his major works recently collected and published in Archie Lee, *Kuawenben Yuedu: Xibolai Shengjing Quanshi* [Cross-Textual Reading of the Hebrew Bible] (Shanghai: Shanghai Sanlian Books, 2015).

17. K. K. Yeo, *Musing with Confucius and Paul: Toward a Chinese Christian Theology* (Eugene, OR: Wipf & Stock, 2008). The Chinese version of this title is available; see Yang Keqin, *Kongzi yu Baoluo: Tiandao yu Shengyan de Xiangyu* [Confucius and Paul: An Encounter between the Heaven Path and the Holy Word] (Huadong: Normal University Press, 2009).

to Paul in their pursuit of ethics and virtues as professed in the *Analects* and the book of Galatians. By being creatively faithful to the two living texts, Yeo illustrates effectively both the ethical task and the theological task of Chinese Christians.[18]

Biblical and theological research conducted by Asian Chinese will inevitably face constant pressure. On the one hand, we are informed and nurtured by education from the West; on the other hand, we try to come to terms with the biblical and theological meanings in various Asian Chinese contexts. As Terence Fretheim correctly observes, Christians typically relate salvation to "forgiveness" granted to those who believe in Jesus Christ (Rom. 5:8–10).[19] This understanding is shared among Asian Chinese. Furthermore, Chinese Christians in Asia also largely understand the idea of salvation based on the New Testament. Nevertheless, the Christ-event and its often-quoted New Testament passages do not exhaust the experience of salvation in the Bible. The Old Testament often speaks of God as the Lord who saves God's people, for example, through acts of giving, deliverance, and guidance. The idea of God in the Old Testament is depicted through images of king, warrior, and shepherd, among many other metaphors. In the book of Isaiah, for instance, one finds a diversity of metaphors describing God—the Holy One of Israel—as a soldier at war (42:13) and a woman in childbirth (42:14). The two metaphors are rendered in both masculine and feminine understandings, and are related to God's acts of salvation in the Old Testament. In short, the Old Testament's use of salvation language differs from that of the New Testament. The Old Testament articulates different dimensions in understanding "salvation" or "soteriology."

Salvation History, Wisdom, and Old Testament Theology

In this section, I propose an Asian Chinese perspective on constructing an Old Testament theology with a dual emphasis: the theme of salvation history and the role of wisdom. The Old Testament encompasses mixed writings and is highly diverse in terms of its compositions, con-

18. See, for example, Yeo, *Musing with Confucius and Paul*, 403.

19. Terence E. Fretheim, *What Kind of God? Collected Essays of Terence E. Fretheim*, Siphrut: Literature and Theology of the Hebrew Bible 14, ed. Michael J. Chan and Brent A. Strawn (Winona Lake, IN: Eisenbrauns, 2015), 363.

tents, and themes. Due to this diversity, one is compelled to choose between constructing a coherent Old Testament theology or a combination of Old Testament theologies. The former endeavor strives to find a theological center and usually leads to a marginalization of wisdom's theological perspective.[20] The latter approach attempts to assess theological perspectives alongside Pentateuchal, historical, prophetic, and wisdom writings. Walther Eichrodt's theme of the covenant belongs to the former endeavor.[21] Gerhard von Rad's salvation history, on the other hand, represents the latter.[22] Both works have generated important contributions, but have inevitably marginalized the aspect of wisdom.[23] Brevard Childs considers theology a descriptive discipline of analyzing the Old Testament text in a canonical context, and views the final form of the Old Testament by seriously considering its various components as they stand in the canon.[24] In delivering the total message of the Old Testament, von Rad's salvation history is the most telling in my opinion. Childs's canonical approach, on the other hand,

20. Despite many attempts to find the theological center, or *Mitte*, of the Old Testament, none satisfyingly express an Old Testament theology, and none have succeeded in commanding a consensus. See Roland E. Murphy, *The Tree of Life: An Exploration of Biblical Wisdom Literature* (Grand Rapids: Eerdmans, 2002), 112.

21. Walther Eichrodt, *Theology of the Old Testament*, 2 vols. (London: SCM, 1961, 1967).

22. Gerhard von Rad, *Old Testament Theology*, 2 vols. (New York: Harper & Row, 1962, 1965).

23. Von Rad's later work, *Wisdom in Israel* (Nashville: Abingdon, 1972), which focuses solely on the aspect of wisdom, is regarded by some as his third volume on Old Testament theology as a corrective measure to his earlier endeavor (which neglected wisdom literature). Most people have a problem locating wisdom in constructing Old Testament theology. The reason is largely due to the absence of familiar themes such as election of Israelites, exodus, revelation at Sinai, and covenant. Even more unusual is the lack of well-known figures like Abraham, Moses, David, and the prophets. The absence of these common Old Testament focuses in wisdom literature, some claim, presents a universal concern and secular outlook in the wisdom corpus, hence justifying its marginality. This viewpoint demonstrates a narrow conception of Old Testament theology. The place of wisdom literature in the present form of the Old Testament can be taken more seriously.

24. Brevard S. Childs, *Old Testament Theology in a Canonical Context* (London: SCM, 1985); Childs, *Introduction to the Old Testament as Scripture* (Philadelphia: Fortress, 1979). Childs's theological reading of the final form of the Old Testament involves a process of integrating larger canonical units of Torah, Prophets, and Writings. This theological mode of study enables a Christian interpreter to apply biblical texts without marginalizing any component that comprises the Old Testament.

has the advantage of maintaining the diversity within the Old Testament. Therefore, despite striving to maintain an Asian Chinese voice, this chapter is also informed by von Rad and Childs.

Within the wisdom corpus itself, there is theological diversity. Anyone who attempts to construct wisdom's theological perspective should consider the complexity within Proverbs, Job, and Ecclesiastes. Job and Qohelet depart in form and content from Proverbs. On the other hand, all three books share a common wisdom unifying theme. In essence, wisdom is "the ability to cope," "the art of steering," and "the quest for self-understanding and for mastery of the world."[25] Therefore Job's and Qohelet's "voices of protest" should be viewed as an integral and genuine expression of faith, rather than as a rejection of traditional wisdom thought.[26]

Canonical Witnesses to Salvation History[27]

Salvation History in the Torah

Salvation history begins with God creating the world. The biblical creation narrative supplements the Chinese understanding of creation of the world in some ways. For instance, God appears in a human form (Gen. 6:1–4).[28] In the biblical account, due to humans' wrongful choices, God took steps to save his people from the consequences of

---

25. James L. Crenshaw, *Old Testament Wisdom: An Introduction* (Louisville: Westminster John Knox, 1998), 9.

26. Richard Schultz, "Unity or Diversity in Wisdom Theology? A Canonical and Covenantal Perspective," *Tyndale Bulletin* 48, no. 2 (1997): 271–306, here 279 and 290.

27. In this section of "Canonical Witnesses to Salvation History," I focus mainly on Ecclesiastes, a book of wisdom. I wish I could elaborate more on other sections of the Bible (Torah, historical and prophetic books). Alongside many others who identify a theological theme that runs through the Old Testament, I suggest "salvation history."

28. See a theological reading of the Chinese creation stories of Pan Gu and Nu Wa by Archie C. C. Lee, "Theological Reading of Chinese Creation Stories of *P'an Ku* and *Nu Kua*," in *Doing Theology with Asian Resources: Ten Years in the Formation of Living Theology in Asia*, ed. John C. England and Archie C. C. Lee (Auckland: Pace, 1993), 230–36. Lee points out how the Chinese reading of the creation of heaven and earth, and the creation of human beings, identifies with that of the Bible. Lee's work therefore has opened the door to a theological dialogue about creation narratives.

divine-human alienation. This divine initiative is also notable in Chinese understanding, wherein humans usually aspire to seek God by establishing certain connections with the heavens or by attempting to attain immortality. In the biblical account, it was God who made the connection. In seeking the return of his own people, God chose Abraham and his descendants. He established a covenantal relationship that bound his people with certain expectations and responsibilities. His people embarked on a journey of faith henceforth with notable victories and many pitfalls. Yet God delivered them from the oppressions of their enemies and from the consequences of their choices. The idea of salvation history is reflected through divine faithfulness in the midst of the struggles and rebellions of God's people. This idea of the divine *hesed* (faithfulness) is largely reassuring, especially for the Chinese who as a nation endured a long history of struggles and failures.

Salvation History in the Historical and Prophetic Books

The struggles between divine-human continuums continue in the formation of a nation and then in its fall. Leaders and kings were elected partly in the hope of carrying out the salvific task of shepherding and protecting God's people. However, God's people, including their political leaders, failed to respond according to God's salvific plan. Along with those struggles, God's message of rebuke and restoration was communicated eloquently through various prophets who were called to speak to God's people. Their message varied depending on the dispositions of the prophets and their sociopolitical contexts. Salvation history continues to mark the journey of God's people in Israel's history nonetheless.

Salvation History in the Wisdom and Poetic Books

Theology is the *logos* of *theos*. It narrates about God and the faith of God's people. In living out faith, one may either trust human ability for survival or rely totally on God's mercy. There is a tension between human confidence and human limitations within a believer. This tension is also reflected in wisdom writing, and it is often perceived as conflicts of perspectives or wisdom's self-correction. There is a theo-

167

logical reason underlying such a tension. It signifies a journey of faith by a believer alongside salvation history.

Proverbs: A Good Disciple

A disciple of God embarks on a journey of faith by learning proverbial sayings and admonitions (Proverbs 1–9). To fear God ensures deliverance from the evil path. A good disciple, therefore, may subscribe to absolute and formulaic certainty (e.g., in chapters 10–22 and 25–29). As a new beginner in faith, one exercises discernment, hoping to steer her life safely into harbor and avoid hazards that bring catastrophe to fools.[29] Misconduct like adultery brings shame to oneself, and entails abandonment by the family and the community (5:7–14; 6:32–35). Every bad consequence like suffering presumes a prior sin or wrongful behavior, and it needs divine redemption. Therefore, one holds fast to God's commandment and lives ethically in order to obtain the goodness of life, while at the same time avoiding calamity and punishment.

Job: A Questioning Devotee

The faith of a believer in God is tested in the realities of life, prompting tremendous struggles (Job 1–2). Along the journey of such struggles, the absence of God becomes offensive (chapters 3–31). The subsequent response from God also appears confrontational rather than therapeutic (chapters 38–41). Job's questioning signifies a quest to know God as a faithful follower. This quest is compounded by challenges from Job's three friends. The struggles, however, do not conceal one's hope that God will eventually come to one's assistance. In a momentous theophany, the faithful follower is confronted by God's presence. One realizes that God does not owe an answer to the human quest even though God is the one in charge of running the world (42:2–3). The faith of a questioning devotee is saved through this encounter, by journeying in faith, from "hearing about God" to "seeing God" (42:5).

29. James L. Crenshaw, "The Concept of God in Old Testament Wisdom," in *In Search of Wisdom: Essays in Memory of John G. Gammie*, ed. Leo G. Perdue, Bernard Brandon Scott, and William Johnston Wiseman (Louisville: Westminster John Knox, 1993), 1–18, here 6.

Qohelet: A Skeptical Believer

Qohelet appears to have tested the confident assertions about the way the world works, and found that they are not always valid. For instance, Qohelet questions the value of wisdom (Eccles. 2:12–17) and diligence (2:18–23) that are upheld in Proverbs. A faithful follower here faces a threatening skepticism. Ecclesiastes is Job without the theophany.[30] The rhetorical questions in 1:3, 2:15, 3:9, 4:8, and 6:8, for example, express Qohelet's observations that the truth one once learned is now in question. The realities of life become unpredictable and incomprehensible. A believer has to settle for a less structured attitude without compromising trust in God (3:14; 5:7; 7:18; 8:12–13; 12:13). A faith journey arriving at this stage has inevitably embraced a hesitant yet mature aptitude. Salvation history continues, as the tested believer does not cease to believe in God. Qohelet even challenges younger ones to be mindful of the harsh realities in life while at the same time asserting the need to fear God (12:13). This grown believer forgoes hasty judgment and refuses to absolutize any conclusion in life. Such a disciple is both a skeptic and a believer.

The fear of God in wisdom elaborated above reflects both human obedience and doubt in salvation history. Tracing wisdom from Proverbs through Job and eventually to Ecclesiastes, a believer in God embraces Torah obedience while growing in faith. Such obedience demands serious engagement with the harsh issues of life (like the suffering of the righteous, toil, and death) and with the ultimate presence or absence of God. In this journey of faith, the God-human relationship is retrospective and two-dimensional. The whole process is salvific nonetheless: a believer in God grows from a simple faith to a faith in crisis and then to a renewed faith.

The Poetic Books

The poetic books in the Old Testament represent the voices of God's people along their journey in salvation history. In the biblical poetic books, human confidence is exemplified through love songs, hymns

---

30. John Goldingay, *Theological Diversity and the Authority of the Old Testament* (Grand Rapids: Eerdmans, 1987), 209.

of praise, and psalms of trust. In the psalms of lament, however, the troubled psalmists reflect on human-God relationships, grieving for unresolved questions and pains. Outcries are heard at both individual and community levels. The psalms of lament (e.g., Psalm 13, 69, 83, and 88) resemble the Chinese poetic corpus *Shijing* (The Book of Poems), reflecting a common human experience.[31] The psalms of lament as well as the Chinese *Shijing* commonly reflect a quest for divine intervention in times of desperation. God in the Bible, explicitly depicted as an all-powerful deliverer is, at the same time the psalmists' enemy (e.g., 6:1–5; 17:3–12; 22:1–2). The deity in *Shijing, Tian*, is also perceived to be an adversary and is often questioned in human suffering.[32] While some psalmists stressed moral conduct as being an agent of change (from the reading of *Shijing*), others find comfort in piety to trust God nonetheless (from the reading of, for instance, Pss. 6:8–10; 17:13–15; 22:3–5).[33] Both of these elements of lament speak of how people in Asia would cry over poverty and injustice.

There are various perspectives on salvation history in the Old Testament. A person of faith takes on an attitude shaped by various Old Testament writings. The Bible as a whole is therefore a book of faith. It narrates the salvation that God has provided for people of faith, and the struggles and promises that come along with that faith. We now focus on the book of Ecclesiastes, which also offers hope for faithful people.

Ecclesiastes: A Book That Offers Salvific Hope

Qohelet seems to challenge the view that wisdom in the past had given enormous confidence in human intellect.[34] The literary genre of

---

31. Archie C. C. Lee, "Kuayue Bianjie: Xibolai Shipian yu Zhongguo Shijing dui Renxing de Xiangxiang" [Crossing Boundaries: A Study on Human Nature from the Readings of Hebrew *Psalms* and Chinese *Shijing*], in *YeRu Duihua Xinlicheng* [A New Turn in Confucianism-Christianity Dialogue], ed. Pin-Chao Lai and Jing-Xiong Lee (Hong Kong: Chung Chi College of Chinese University of Hong Kong, 2001), 197–221.

32. Lee, "Kuayue Bianjie," 205–6.

33. Lee, "Kuayue Bianjie," 213–14.

34. The perceived tension within wisdom thought in Ecclesiastes garners various opinions. Walther Zimmerli, for instance, suggests that Qohelet is engaged in a dialogue with the sages and their traditional wisdom, confronting wisdom's boast to

Ecclesiastes is "a vehicle of critical reflection upon traditional values and beliefs."[35] Qohelet recognizes wisdom's advantage and that folly is never better.[36] Nevertheless, wisdom has its limits and is subject to failures too.[37] At the point where such limits and failure are experienced in life, there is still hope to cope with them.

In Ecclesiastes, Qohelet launches a search for meaning amid limits and failures. The search is expressed through a compound use of verbs for seeking, finding out, and scrutinizing: *dāraš, tûr* (to seek; 1:13), *māṣā'* (to find; 7:24), *bāqāš* (to seek; 7:25), *ḥēqer* (to search; 12:9), and *'āzen* (to weigh, in piel form; 12:9).[38] In such pursuits, Qohelet is aware of the challenges in the world where humanity has to live. Qohelet avers that humankind cannot find out what God has done (3:11). Qohelet says that even the wise cannot find out what is happening under the sun (8:1–17). In short, Qohelet not only draws on the wisdom tradition, he also brings the tradition to bear on human experiences.[39] Qohelet concludes that wisdom provides no advantage in the grasping of one's

---

solve every human problem. See Walther Zimmerli, *Sprüche, Prediger Altes Testament Deutsch* 16/1 (Göttingen: Vandenhoeck & Ruprecht, 1963), quoted in Richard J. Clifford, *The Wisdom Literature* (Nashville: Abingdon, 1998), 111. K. Galling, on the other hand, has in mind that with Qohelet, wisdom has entered a crisis situation. See K. Galling, *Die Krise der Aufklärung in Israel* (Mainz: Mainzer Universitätsreden, 1952); quoted in Murphy, *Tree of Life*, 55. Elsewhere, Michael Fox maintains that Qohelet does not attack wisdom or the wise but instead favors wisdom; he nevertheless examines the contradictions observed in human life rather than explain them away. See Michael V. Fox, *Qohelet and His Contradictions*, Journal for the Study of the Old Testament Supplement Series 71, ed. David J. A. Clines and Philip R. Davies (Sheffield: Almond, 1989), 10–12.

35. Karel van der Toorn, "The Ancient Near Eastern Literary Dialogue as a Vehicle of Critical Reflection," in *Dispute Poems and Dialogues in the Ancient and Mediaeval Near East*, ed. G. J. Reinlink and H. L. J. Vanstiphout (Leuven: Peeters, 1991), 59–75, here 59. The ancient Near Eastern parallels of Job, rather than related to issues of theodicy, have been suggested by Karel van der Toorn to be "literary dialogue" as a vehicle of critical reflection on traditional values and beliefs.

36. Qohelet appears to be challenging the traditional wisdom, yet it does not mean that Qohelet dismisses wisdom. Wisdom is always better than folly in the book of Ecclesiastes.

37. Choon-Leong Seow, *Ecclesiastes*, Anchor Bible Series (New York: Doubleday, 1997), 68.

38. The rare verb *tûr* connotes an extraordinary measure of firm resolve, more appropriate to spying. The verb is used in Job 39:8 to refer to an animal's search for food, and in Proverbs 12:26 to imply examining one's friend closely. See Crenshaw, *Old Testament Wisdom*, 116 and 134.

39. Seow, *Ecclesiastes*, 69.

destiny—when it does not provide sufficient knowledge, when it is determined by chance, and when it is restrained by death.[40] Recognizing such human limitations is not depressing, but liberating.[41] For in Ecclesiastes, the scope of wisdom has extended to discern the ways to survive meaningfully regardless of circumstances. To Qohelet, life is momentary, and therefore one has to seize the moment by working diligently while at the same time observing the fear of God.

Ecclesiastes exhorts one to live pragmatically in a disorderly world. The motif of the book is often claimed to be one with a negative tone because of the recurrent *hebel* in the book, occurring thirty-eight times altogether. Yet the underlying theme of the book is constructive, and one can view Qohelet's commendation to enjoyment positively. The interplay between the commendation of enjoyment and the injunction to fear God in Ecclesiastes suggests they are positively correlated.[42] Enjoyment of life lies at the heart of Qohelet's vision of piety, which can be said to be an ethic of joy and social responsibility.[43]

There is a positive undertone in Ecclesiastes. First, the recurrent *'ĕlōhîm* (God) in Qohelet's articulation is remarkable. The verbs that have been associated with *'ĕlōhîm* in Ecclesiastes illustrate "a very active God."[44] God is the subject of two frequent verbs: *nātan* (give; 1:13; 2:26; 3:10, 11; 5:18–19; 6:2; 8:15; 9:9; 12:7) and *'āśâ* (do or make; 3:11, 14; 7:14, 29; 8:17; 11:5). God is also the one who judges (3:17), is angry (5:6), and brings all human things into judgment (11:9). Therefore, Qohelet affirms divine actions and sovereignty.

Second, *'et-hā'ĕlōhîm yĕrā'* (to fear God) is the motive behind Qohelet's quest for meaning. This phrase appears throughout the book (3:14; 5:7; 7:18; 8:12–13; 12:13). This fear of God is consistent in the wisdom tradition with aiming to promote godly behavior.[45] In 5:1–7, for

40. Michael V. Fox, "Wisdom in Qohelet," in *In Search of Wisdom*, ed. Leo G. Perdue, Bernard Brandon Scott, and William Johnson Wiseman (Louisville: Westminster John Knox, 1993), 115–31, here 123–26.

41. Von Rad, *Wisdom in Israel*, 101, states that recognizing human limitations puts a stop to the false security in human wisdom, and enables one to be open to the activity of God.

42. Eunny P. Lee, *The Vitality of Enjoyment in Qohelet's Theological Rhetoric* (Berlin: Walter de Gruyter, 2005), 32–82; see also 123–40.

43. Lee, *The Vitality of Enjoyment*, 129–34.

44. Roland E. Murphy, *Ecclesiastes*, Word Biblical Commentary 23A, ed. David A. Hubbard, Glenn W. Barker, and John D. W. Watts (Dallas: Word, 1992), lxviii.

45. Otto Kaiser, "Qohelet," in *Wisdom in Ancient Israel*, ed. John Day, Robert P. Gor-

example, Qohelet makes lengthy remarks about religion. He solicits reverence and one's faithful implementation of the covenant with God. People are advised to fear *'ĕlōhîm* in all that they do.

Finally and most significantly, Qohelet looks at human life through the lens of exception. Traditional teachings distinguish clearly between rights and wrongs, but Qohelet points out their exceptions. Such a perspective is critical and realistic, but not necessarily pessimistic.[46] The exceptions are used as contradictions, raising questions of integrity and authorship. Some have attempted to harmonize Qohelet's view of exceptions, yet have also missed his intended rhetoric.[47] The exceptions raise the possibility of the intended dialectical rhetoric of Qohelet. Leland Ryken calls this rhetoric a "dialectical structure of contrasts."[48] Craig Bartholomew opines that the exceptions are "part of the very fabric of *Ecclesiastes*."[49] Qohelet simply keeps in view two scenarios that are in tension. Through this lens of exception, Qohelet points out life's transitory nature, and advocates against life's absolute certainty. Therefore, Qohelet presents a quest for meaningful survival.[50] This quest results in Qohelet's recommendations to embrace

---

don, and H. G. Williamson (Cambridge: Cambridge University Press, 1995), 83–93, here 90–91. Kaiser distinguishes two epilogists who engage two levels of "fear of God"; the second epilogist (in Eccles. 12:13–14) appears to be more legalistic to Kaiser, with a call for obedience to God's commandment.

46. For example, like the other sages, Qohelet affirms *'ĕlōhîm* as one who is powerful in Ecclesiastes 3:14–15. But there is an exception: at times God keeps humans in ignorance (3:10–11). Similarly, God controls the details of human life, but Qohelet professes also that God is distant in human affairs (6:1–2, 11–12). In Qohelet's articulation, wisdom is asserted like the traditional teaching (2:13; 7:11–12, 19), yet the exception is that wisdom is belittled at other times (1:18; 2:15–16; 8:16–17).

47. Besides harmonizing the "contradictory views," scholars also have tried to identify one of the opinions as an unmarked quotation, or to suggest a dialectic between Qohelet with an opponent. See, for example, T. A. Perry, *Dialogues with Kohelet: The Book of Ecclesiastes: Translation and Commentary* (University Park: Pennsylvania State University Press, 1993).

48. Leland Ryken, "Ecclesiastes," in *A Complete Literary Guide to the Bible*, ed. Leland Ryken and Tremper Longman III (Grand Rapids: Zondervan, 1993), 268–80, here 271.

49. Craig G. Bartholomew, *Ecclesiastes,* Baker Commentary on the Old Testament Wisdom and Psalms, ed. Tremper Longman III (Grand Rapids: Baker Academic, 2009), 81. Bartholomew uses the idea of "gaps," which are opened up in the reading of the book when two contradictory juxtaposed perspectives are in view.

50. He communicates this quest through the recurring word *yôtēr* (6:8) and *yitrôn*, both meaning "surplus, advantage, or profit."

a certain attitude, which is a "reconstruction and recovering of meanings," according to Michael Fox.[51]

In short, a realistic attitude toward life is hopeful for God's people in salvation history. Ecclesiastes conveys honest reflections of people who search for hope and meaning in living.[52] After all, wisdom is about a way of directing life, and Ecclesiastes conveys such wisdom for living out salvific hope. As such, the book speaks powerfully to God's people who yearn for hope and meaning. It serves as a pointer to anyone who wrestles with challenges and tensions.

In the context of the marginalization of women within the church in Botswana, highlighted in the chapter by Rosinah Gabaitse in this volume, the message of Ecclesiastes offers salvific hope. The tension between the hope of salvation and the challenge of injustice against women is the very fabric of life realities. Similarly, the aspects of the "materiality of salvation" discussed by Milton Acosta in this volume convey tensions in the lives of God's people due to the presence of danger, violence, calamity, and enemies. Qohelet, too, surveys the physical (toil and death), economic (labor and gain), and sociopolitical (injustice and supreme power of the rulers) realms as well. The world does not operate according to our ideal expectations whether in fairness and justice in the experiences of men in relation to that of women or the realities of suffering from the threats of enemies. These are the exceptions that occur in the life of God's people, who are saved by God's grace yet are marked by fallen human nature. One of the similarities among the struggles of God's people in the Majority World is that we wrestle with the experiential realities of the doctrine of salvation. For God's people, issues of injustice, violence, and social enemies are real. One is nevertheless instructed to seize the opportunity to live right, and to be diligently working for better days. Also, embracing certain attitudes in life, such as fearing God amid injustice, unfairness, and danger, can guide one to reconstruct meaning toward authentic witnessing to the gospel. Specifically, what constitutes certain attitudes in life, and how one reconstructs meaning to authentic witnessing, are largely interpretive and are bound by contextual considerations.

---

51. Michael V. Fox, "The Innerstructure of Qoheleth's Thought," in *Qoheleth in the Context of Wisdom*, ed. A. Schoors (Leuven: Leuven University Press, 1998), 225.

52. See another similar view by Costa Rican scholar Elsa Tamez, *When the Horizons Close: Reading Ecclesiastes* (Eugene, OR: Wipf & Stock, 2006), especially 1–10.

Readings in the Asian Chinese Context

Qohelet's Concept of Time in Ecclesiastes 3:1–15[53]

The catalogue of seasons and times in Ecclesiastes 3:1–8 is the most illustrative of Qohelet's insistence that God makes everything "beautiful in its time" (3:11). In upholding God's "making" (*'āśâ*) in 3:11, the list of human events is then depicted in fourteen sets of antithetical parallelisms. The antithetical pairs point out a certain tension. The tension reflects favorable actions (e.g., to live, to laugh, or to dance) or unfavorable ones (e.g., to die, to cry, or to grieve). It does not show any order or pattern, but represents life occurrences in a spontaneous manner. Qohelet asserts that there is a time for these human circumstances, but he rules out human determination for the outcome of these circumstances.

Even if humankind does not determine life occurrences, people can still respond to them and discern the appropriate moment for any human activity.[54] Life occurrences are not just out of human control, they are also beyond human comprehension (3:11). Yet in the same verse, Qohelet affirms clearly that for God, the scenario is otherwise: God is the one who determines life occurrences for humans. The concept of *'ôlām* (eternity) can be understood as the time-transcending nature of God's activity, which is not bound by time.[55] God puts "eternity" in human hearts, so that people can cope with various situations, one at a time. Therefore, for a human, one can still do well in one's lifetime (3:12), as well as eat, drink and see *ṭôb* (good) in one's toil (3:13). The idea of *'ôlām* returns in 3:14, describing what God has done, with an added concept of fearing God as one's purpose. This concept of fearing God first appears here and elsewhere in 5:7 (Hebrew 5:6), 7:18; 8:12–13, and 12:13. It is a theological marker for Qohelet's articulation of life elusiveness. In light of 3:15, it is also an affirmation of God's activity in the human realm (3:10, 11, 13–14).

---

53. Ecclesiastes 3:1–15 is a logical unit by itself, though the thought on timing can be detected again in 3:17: God "has appointed a time for every matter and for every work." This thought echoes what Qohelet has declared in 3:1, that for everything there is a season, and for every matter a time. Still, Ecclesiastes 3:16 suggests a new turn with the phrase "and again I saw" and new subjects (justice and righteousness).

54. Seow, *Ecclesiastes*, 171.

55. Seow, *Ecclesiastes*, 174.

On Fearing Death: Time Is in God's Hand

Among the taboos in Chinese thought, the idea of death generates a sense of fear. People are fearful of losing everything that has been accumulated in their lifetime. Ecclesiastes 3:1–15 affirms that there is a time for everything in life, including living and dying. The Chinese in general work hard to make life better, more so in Asia where living is competitive due to rapid social and economic developments. Losing everything at the point of one's death can be frightening because all the hard work that one has done would become void. Nevertheless, Ecclesiastes 3:1–15 avers that even death is beautiful in its time because God is in the picture. The passage, too, is a reminder of the differences between God's actions and human activities. Knowing these differences, one is reminded of the affirmation of eternity when human works are done in full awareness of God's presence. Furthermore, reading Ecclesiastes 3:1–15 prompts one to fear God yet while at the same time endeavoring to live meaningfully in the present. One can still see the good in life and live it out abundantly while one is able to. Death, in this sense, does not cancel out one's possessions, accomplishments, and wealth. For these things have their meaning under God's time-transcending activities. Death also testifies that one has eventually lived to the depth and height of life. At one's death, therefore, one's total achievement in life is being witnessed and celebrated. Death can be called "beautiful" when it comes.

Qohelet's View of Righteousness in Ecclesiastes 7:15–22

Qohelet's articulations on the topic of righteousness occur in Ecclesiastes 7 three times (vv. 15–16, 20), and in 3:17; 8:14; 9:1–2. Most of these articulations appear to question the common pursuit of righteousness. In 7:15–22, Qohelet questions the absolute value of being righteous. Verse 15 states that righteous people do perish in their righteousness, and wicked people have their lives prolonged despite their evildoings. Once again looking through Qohelet's "lens of exceptions," righteous people do not necessarily have better lives as the wise had commonly thought.

Though this view on exceptions does have canonical witnesses from other parts of the Bible (for instance, the psalms of lament and the prophetic books), Qohelet goes further, advising people "do not be overly righteous" and suggesting that "to be overly righteous could be destructive" (v. 16). Verses 17–18 are even more perplexing because wickedness and folly "should not be let go." One assumes here that Qohelet does not engage righteousness as affirmatively as the sages do but appears to commend half-hearted righteousness. This leaves him open to the allegation of negotiating immorality. Schooled by Confucian teachings, the Chinese in general believe that righteousness is needed to alleviate social injustice. Therefore, scholars of Chinese descent may find it disturbing and uncomfortable to accept Qohelet's idea of half-hearted righteousness here. Some may even choose to interpret the passage from the lens of the Confucian golden mean to secure the idea of morality, so that *yi* (righteousness) is still necessary. This reflects Confucian confidence in upholding righteousness to reorder individual and communal life. Righteousness is seen as an initiative to guide human behavior, unlike Qohelet who stresses human limitation in living out righteousness.

In addition, the passage is understood by some as a warning against self-righteousness, as the adverb *harbēh*, from the word *rābâ*, means "much, many, great" or "numerous" but not "too" or "over."[56] In light of this, it is not an aspect of moral agency that is absent in Ecclesiastes. There is yet another view suggesting that Qohelet's dissent is aimed at overconfidence in righteousness.[57] This warning is directed against the person who lays claim to righteousness as absolutely attainable. This view is consistent with Qohelet's thought against the certainty of wisdom (7:23–29; 9:13–16) and of advantage (1:3; 3:9; 6:8) elsewhere in the book. In this light, the passage does not advocate unrighteousness. Rather, Qohelet perceives an actual human limitation in trying to live out righteousness. Therefore, "the one who fears God" (7:18) finds a balance between being righteous and acknowledging human limitation. The idea of this limitation continues in verses 19–22, including the idea of wisdom as well. It is no surprise that Qohelet's address in

56. For example, R. N. Whybray, "Qoheleth the Immoralist? (Qoh 7:16–17)," in *Israelite Wisdom: Theological and Literary Essays in Honor of Samuel Terrien*, ed. John G. Gammie et al. (New York: Union Theological Seminary, 1978), 191–204, here 191. The adverb *harbēh*, according to Whybray, does not express any value judgment such as "too righteous" in Ecclesiastes 7:16, but an ironical sense, that is, a "self-styled *ṣaddîq*"; see 195–96.

57. Seow, *Ecclesiastes*, 267.

7:15–22 regarding righteousness appears to be half-hearted. Qohelet is less convinced of the human success in living out righteousness. Regardless of striving to be righteous and wise, one cannot just deny the realities of wickedness and folly in life.

Be Confident but Not Overconfident

Hardworking and diligent, the Chinese are generally confident of what can be done and achieved. Such confidence may mistakenly sneak into our understanding of faith experience, that as long as one attends church worship, tithes, and serves well, one attains the "righteousness" required by the Bible. Being righteous becomes attainable as long as one obeys what the Bible tells us. Righteousness has also become something that can be attained and worked for, such as having a good reputation, holding an important position in Christian ministry, serving many years in Christian ministry, and so forth. One therefore becomes overconfident about living "right," as if that were easy and natural. As a result, some may not be able to cope when fellow Christians fail in witnessing and are involved in scandals and lawsuits. Qohelet advises us to be cautious about such certainty. Overconfidence can be destructive, as Ecclesiastes 7:15–22 suggests. There is an actual human limitation on practicing righteousness in life and we must simply acknowledge our humanness. A righteous and wise person does not necessarily rule out the chances of being wicked and foolish.

Qohelet's Idea of Human Ignorance in Ecclesiastes 11:1–6[58]

There is an observable double theme of "what a human does not know" and "what a human does know" in Ecclesiastes 11:1–6.[59] In this

---

58. Ecclesiastes 11:1–6 is an independent unit for several reasons. First, the change in subject matter is discernable from the political rhetoric in 10:16–20 to the economical concern in 11:1–6. Second, the verbs in 11:1, 2, and 6 are found in the imperative mood, unlike the ones from the preceding chapter, and the one after in 11:7–8. Third, the passage is framed by a purpose clause that is introduced with *kî* (twice in 11:1–2, once in 11:6). Fourth, there is a fourfold expression of "you do not know" in 11:2, 5 (twice), and 6, which comprise its theme. See also the observations by Graham S. Ogden, "Qohelet 11:1–6," *Vetus Testamentum* 33 (1983): 223.

59. Graham S. Ogden and Lynell Zogbo, *A Handbook on Ecclesiastes* (New York: Uni-

passage, although human knowledge is limited, the author advises readers "to embark upon life." The idea of action frames the theme of human ignorance. This means that one can be doing something without knowing exactly why or how, yet at the same time be preparing for multiple contingencies. Thus verses 1 and 6 present the chances for spontaneous actions despite uncertain outcomes.

In verses 1–2, Qohelet quotes a popular proverb in the ancient Near East to commend liberality and its proliferation.[60] Some interpret these verses as an investment, whereby *leḥem* (bread) is a metaphor for merchandise. According to this interpretation, one can avoid losing everything in a business venture by dividing one's risks in the investment. However, the idea of *leḥem* as "goods" is unattested elsewhere in the Bible. Besides, one should *māṣā'* (find) more than what is invested from any venture. Yet the idea of profit is not found in verse 2 but rather the "getting back" of what is originally sent.[61] Qohelet argues that the *unknown* future may bring forth

---

ted Bible Societies, 1997), 391. See also T. Francis Glasson, "'You Never Know': The Message of Ecclesiastes 11:1–6," *Evangelical Quarterly* 55 (1983): 43–48, who singles out "you do not know" as the theme in Ecclesiastes 11:1–6.

60. The proverb resembles the Egyptian *Ancksheshonq*, which says, "Do a good deed and throw it in the water; when it dries up you will find it." See Miriam Lichtheim, ed., *Ancient Egyptian Literature*, vol. 3 (Berkeley: University of California Press, 1980), 174. The interpretation of liberality is evident in Proverbs 19:17, and in the Targum and Midrash, and in the understandings of Rashi, Ibn Ezra, and Rashbam; see Michael V. Fox, *Ecclesiastes*, JPS Bible Commentary (Philadelphia: The Jewish Publication Society, 2004), 72, and Thomas Krüger, *Qoheleth: A Commentary*, Hermeneia, trans. O. C. Dean Jr. and ed. Klaus Baltzer (Minneapolis: Fortress, 2004), 192.

61. Seow, *Ecclesiastes*, 335. There is yet another interpretation taking in the sense of beer production; see Michael M. Homan, "Beer Production by Throwing Bread into Water: A New Interpretation of Qoh. XI 1–2," *Vetus Testamentum* 52 (2002): 275–78. According to this interpretation, Qohelet recommends beer production and consumption in risky times similar to the advice in Ecclesiastes 9:7. Isaiah 22:13 is quoted, "eat and drink for tomorrow we die," to support his thesis. However, Homan might be informed by a pessimistic understanding of Ecclesiastes. Qohelet is recommending a proactive attitude of seizing opportunity amid life's uncertainty, rather than the escapism of drinking, being merry, and dying. His interpretation needs to establish links to the previous and subsequent passages concerning beer production. It appears unlikely too that Qohelet would contradict the warning given in 10:16, and his criticism rendered in 10:19, by suggesting beer production and consumption here. Ecclesiastes 11:6 appropriately closes the passage in a proactive outlook that advocates human's endeavor. In sum, Ecclesiastes 11:1–2 most likely refers to good deeds given freely and plentifully.

desirable results or undesirable misfortunes, yet one can *know* that charitable giving at present is the recommended thing to do. The appropriate action is thus doing something useful, and it is better than doing nothing at all.

In verses 3–5, knowing the uncertainties of life, some people refuse to take certain risks to act and consequently end up being unproductive.[62] The double theme of "one does know" and "one does not know" persists. In human ignorance, some people resort to obsessive weather-watching, thus halting agricultural efforts and missing the proper time for action.[63] There is an opportunity for sowing and reaping despite not knowing the right time. The danger remains that one who is always watching for the perfect moment will never act.[64] While one cannot ascertain the result, it does not mean one should do nothing at all. The motif "one does not know" reappears twice in verse 5, conveying that no one knows how new life begins in a mother's womb, much less the work of God. In short, the action of God is beyond human calculation.

Therefore, in verse 6, one should act according to what one knows, without being bothered by what is unknown.[65] There is an imperative followed by a motive clause here. This idea recalls verses 1–2, and hence is an *inclusio* of Qohelet's rhetoric. Qohelet advises that one should live and work according to what one has been taught. Being diligent by sowing seeds in the morning and keeping active in the evening may secure some relative advantages. Taken as a whole, Qohelet is realistic about how much a human does not know, yet how much one can do based on understandable facts. Qohelet's thesis, namely, the twin themes of what humans can and cannot know, is specified clearly in verses 1–2, the illustrative materials for these themes are set forth in verses 3–5, and concluding advice is offered in verse 6.[66]

---

62. Qohelet uses the aphorism of a farmer who awaits perfect conditions to sow and harvest, criticizing the idling state of people who should have done something constructive. There is some predictability from nature; for example, one knows that strong wind and a storm would uproot a tree, but one does not know in which direction it will fall.

63. William P. Brown, *Ecclesiastes,* Interpretation, ed. James Luther Mays and Patrick D. Miller (Louisville: John Knox, 2000), 103.

64. Murphy, *Ecclesiastes,* 109.

65. Crenshaw, *Ecclesiastes,* 181; see also Ogden, "Qohelet 11:1–6," 223.

66. Ogden, "Qohelet 11:1–6," 227.

Carpe Diem but Not Workaholic and Kiasu[67]

The Chinese are generally hardworking. Having vast opportunities for social and economic growth in Asia, many pragmatic Chinese toil diligently to acquire more opportunities and greater advantages. Yet, people at the same time are fearful of failing to secure these opportunities and advantages, especially when they are confronted by factors beyond their comprehension and control. People do not know when it is the best time to act or when a financial crisis will occur. The calculations of uncertainties in life may paralyze some observant and careful people. This is true in business ventures, career planning, and investments. Yet, there is always a place for human efforts. One cannot remain inactive under the pretext of waiting for the best time. Ecclesiastes 11:1–6 conveys that instead of pondering life's obscurities, one should act promptly based on what one is able to comprehend in order to seize the opportunity. So, on the one hand, this passage informs Asian Chinese of the importance of timely hard work. It is carpe diem advice, directing people to seize the day despite life's uncertainties. It is about human effort, not about blind chance.

Yet, on the other hand, some people may have worked too hard to secure maximum results. Many Asian Chinese have become too busy and are workaholics. To them, profiting the most during their youth will make life comfortable later. Under such circumstances, one may also resort to a *kiasu* mentality. It is a mentality that generally reflects the way some Asian Chinese think: they aspire to have something greater, bigger, or more valuable as compared to others. Yet, there are exceptions to one's experiences in life and one cannot be sure of everything. There is always the chance that one may face limitations amid many possibilities. It often happens that one may gain this time but lose the next. Again, as Ecclesiastes 11:1–6 suggests, one does not know the certainty of the outcome of one's over-diligence. Therefore, one should just work sensibly and be productive, without compromising the good things in life. Asian Chinese in general, through generations of Confucian teachings, are pragmatic and diligent. Qohelet attunes us to the realistic sides of being so.

67. *Kiasu* is taken from the Hokkien language, which is a division among Chinese languages, and means an "afraid to lose" mentality.

Conclusion

Qohelet teaches one to live here and now in line with Chinese pragmatism. This chapter argues for the message of Ecclesiastes that offers hope, in line with the message of salvation as outlined in Christian belief. Wisdom represents one of the three ways in which God's salvation history is being communicated: through the priestly laws, the sages' worldviews, and the prophetic utterances. Within the wisdom corpus, Proverbs, Job, and Ecclesiastes demonstrate the progress of salvific faith grounded in the fear of God. The book of Ecclesiastes conveys hope between the two extremes of human potential and limitation, its ideal and its realities. The emphasis on human potential harmonizes with the emphasis on covenantal revelation. The two different points of departure should prompt biblical interpreters to defend wisdom heritage in the proclamation of salvation. It is enriching to know that human limitation is acknowledged, not judged, and that human potential is affirmed, not dismissed. The affinity between wisdom literature and other canonical witnesses is important as we articulate salvation history in biblical theology.

Further Reading

Fox, Michael V. *A Time to Tear Down and a Time to Build Up: A Rereading of Ecclesiastes*. Grand Rapids: Eerdmans, 1999.

Kok, Hon Seng. *Heavenly Vision for Witness on Earth: A Commentary on Ephesians*. Kuala Lumpur: Bridge Communication, 2010.

Lee, Archie C. C. "Cross-Textural Hermeneutics and Identity in Multi-Scriptural Asia." In *Christian Theology in Asia*, edited by Sebastian C. H. Kim. New York: Cambridge University Press, 2008.

Lo, Lung-Kwong. *Baoluo Xinguan: Luomashu de Zhuti yu Mudi* [New Perspectives on Paul: The Theme and Purpose of the Book to the Romans]. Taipei: University of Donghai Press, 2007.

Longman, Tremper, III. *The Book of Ecclesiastes*. The New International Commentary on the Old Testament. Grand Rapids: Eerdmans, 1998.

Seow, Choon-Leong. *Ecclesiastes*. The Anchor Bible. New York: Doubleday, 1997.

Wong, Yee-cheung. *Jiuyue Shenxue: Cong Chuangzao Dao Xinchuangzao* [Old Testament Theology—From Creation to New Creation]. Hong Kong: Tien Dao, 2003.

Yeo, K. K. *Musing with Confucius and Paul: Toward a Chinese Christian Theology.* Cambridge: James Clarke & Co., 2008.

Yip, Ching Wah, and Lo Lung Kwong. *We Believe: A Commentary on the Nicene Creed*, edited by the Association of Theological Schools in South East Asia. Hong Kong: Chinese Christian Literature Council, 2014.

Contributors

Milton **Acosta** (PhD, Trinity Evangelical Divinity School) is an Old Testament professor at the Seminario Bíblico de Colombia in Medellín. He is the author of *El humor en el Antiguo Testamento* (Puma, 2009) and Old Testament editor of the forthcoming *Comentario Bíblico Contemporáneo*. His areas of research include rhetorical patterns in the Hebrew Bible, forced migration, and violence in the Bible. He also leads a small group of pastors and academics in Medellín who explore the issue of worship and liturgy in evangelical churches.

Ray **Aldred** (ThD Candidate, Wycliffe College) is the director of the Indigenous Studies Program at the Vancouver School of Theology. He is a Cree from Northern Alberta, Canada. He has written chapters in *Prophetic Evangelicals* (Eerdmans, 2012), *Evangelical Postcolonial Conversations* (IVP Academic, 2014), and *Strangers in This World* (Fortress, 2015). He is also a storyteller and grandfather.

Emily J. **Choge Kerama** (PhD, Fuller Theological Seminary) is an associate professor at Moi University, Eldoret, Kenya. She has written many essays, among which are "Social Ethics" in *The Global Dictionary of Theology* and "Hospitality in Africa" in the *Africa Bible Commentary*.

Sung Wook **Chung** (DPhil, Oxford University) is a professor of Christian theology at Denver Seminary in Littleton, Colorado. He is a native Korean and the author and editor of twenty-five books published in English and Korean. Among them are *Admiration and Challenge: Karl*

Barth's Theological Relationship with John Calvin (Peter Lang, 2002), *Christ the One and Only: A Global Affirmation of the Uniqueness of Jesus Christ* (Baker Academic, 2003), and *Diverse and Creative Voices: Theological Essays from the Majority World* (Wipf & Stock, 2015). His current research focuses on Trinitarian theology, eschatology, and Christian systematic theology in conversation with other religions.

Rosinah Mmannana **Gabaitse** (PhD, University of Kwa-Zulu Natal) is a lecturer in biblical studies at the University of Botswana within the Department of Theology and Religious Studies. She is also a post-doctoral fellow in Germany sponsored by the Humboldt Foundation. She researches and publishes in the field of feminist biblical hermeneutics, Luke-Acts, and Pentecostalism. Her research focuses on establishing a link between teaching and researching in a university and grassroots communities, hence some of her publications on the spread of HIV and AIDS, gender-based violence, and masculinities.

Elaine W. F. **Goh** (ThD, South East Asia Graduate School of Theology) is currently a lecturer in Old Testament studies at Seminari Theoloji Malaysia (Malaysia Theological Seminary). She has published a book on Ecclesiastes entitled *Wisdom of Living in a Changing World: Readings from Ecclesiastes* (Genesis, 2013). Her areas of research are in Old Testament studies and biblical wisdom literature. In her dissertation research, she worked on cross-textual hermeneutics between Ecclesiastes and the *Analects*. Her published essays include one on intertextual reading in *Reading Ruth in Asia* (Society of Biblical Literature, 2015).

Jules A. **Martínez-Olivieri** (PhD, Trinity Evangelical Divinity School) is an adjunct professor of theology at the Seminario Teológico de Puerto Rico and an adjunct professor of theology and philosophy at Universidad Interamericana de Puerto Rico. He is the author of *A Visible Witness: Christology, Liberation, and Participation* (Fortress, 2016).

Daniel J. **Treier** (PhD, Trinity Evangelical Divinity School) is Blanchard Professor of Theology at Wheaton College Graduate School. He is an author of four books and an editor of several others. Among his most recent books are *Theology and the Mirror of Scripture: A Mere Evangelical Account* (IVP Academic, 2015) and *Introducing Theological Interpretation of Scripture: Recovering a Christian Practice* (Baker Academic, 2008).

K. K. **Yeo** (PhD, Northwestern University) is Harry R. Kendall Professor of New Testament at Garrett-Evangelical Theological Seminary (Evanston, Illinois) and an affiliate professor in the Department of Asian Languages and Cultures, Northwestern University. He is a visiting professor at Peking University, Zhejiang University, and Fudan University, and co-director of the Center for Classical Greco-Roman Philosophy and Religious Studies at Tsinghua University, China. He has authored and edited twenty-five Chinese books and twelve English books on cross-cultural biblical interpretation, including *Musing with Confucius and Paul* (Wipf & Stock, 2008) and *Zhuangzi and James* (Shanghai VI Horae, 2012).

Index of Names

Index of Subjects

Index of Scripture References